GIOVANNA SILVA

444 DAYS
IRAN HOSTAGE CRISIS

NARRATIVES – RELAZIONI N.7

Documents From The U.S. Espionage Den (60)

U.S. INTERVENTIONS IN IRAN (9)

Muslim Students Following the Line of the Imam

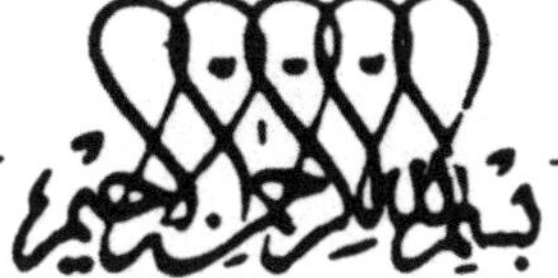

In the name of Allah
the most
Compassionate and Mercifull

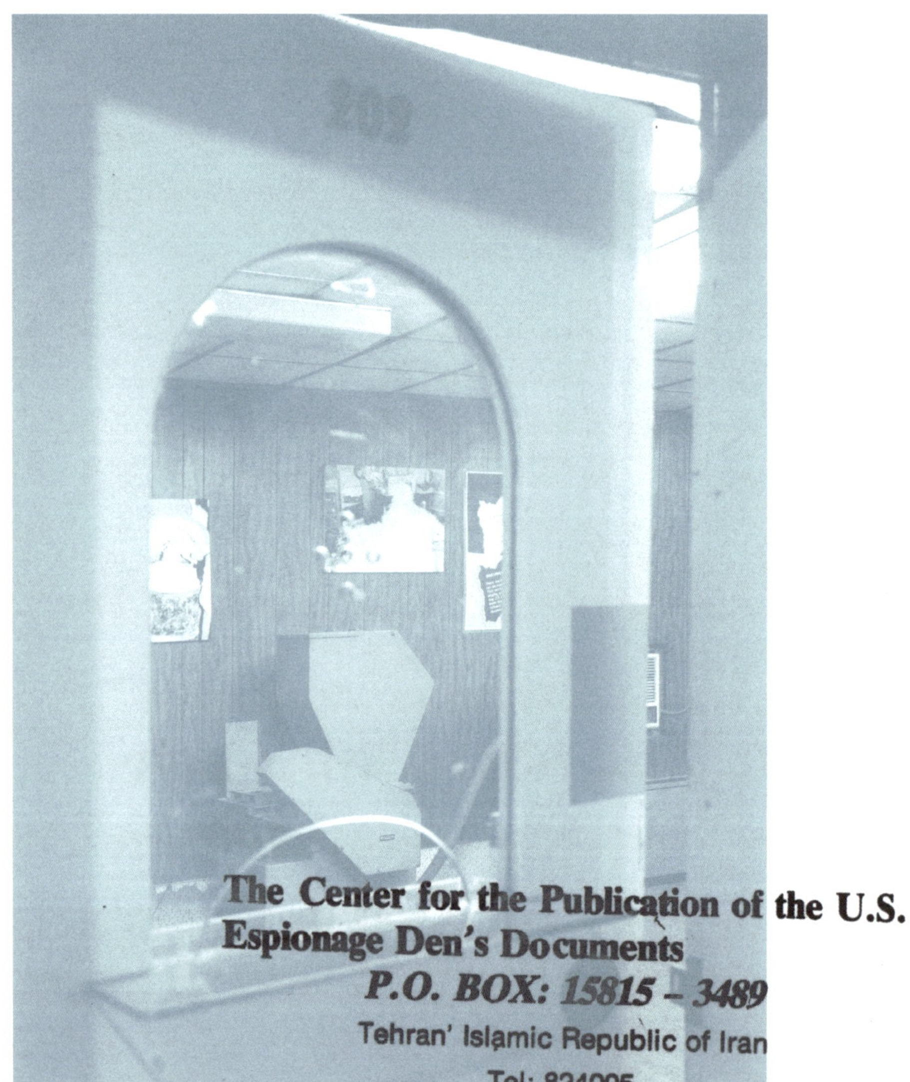

The Center for the Publication of the U.S. Espionage Den's Documents

P.O. BOX: 15815 – 3489

Tehran' Islamic Republic of Iran

Tel: 824005

THE MOST COMMPASSIONATE AND MERCIFUL

TABLE OF CONTENTS

ONE-SECURITY IN THE GOVERNMENT OF IRAN 1

A REVIEW OF THE SECURITY SYSTEM OF IRAN 2

I- INTRODUCTION 2

II- BASIC SECURITY LEGISLATION 3

III- PUBLIC ATTITUDE TOWARD SECURITY 5

IV- NATIONAL ORGANIZATION FOR SECURITY 6

1- NATIONAL SECURITY COUNCIL 7

2- NATIONAL ORGANIZATION FOR INTELLIGENCE & SECURITY ... 8

3- J-2 SECTION SUPREME COMMANDER'S STAFF 10

4- G-2 SECTION OF GENERAL STAFF 11

5- COUNTERINTELLIGENCE CORP (CIC) 12

6- IRANIAN NATIONAL POLICE 13

7- IMPERIAL IRANIAN GENDARMERIE 14

8- SPECIAL INTELLIGENCE OFFICE 15

V- INTERAGENCY RELATIONSHIPS AND COORDINATION 17

VI- SECURITY IN GOVERNMENT DEPARTMENT 19

VII- PHYSICAL SECURITY 20

1- CIVILIAN MINISTERIES 20

2- ARMED FORCES 20

VIII- CONTROL OF CLASSIFIED MATTERS 21

IX- PERSONNEL SECURITY 23

X- INDUSTRIAL SECURITY 26

XI- FINDINGS 27

XII- RECOMMENDATION 29

XIII- CONCLUSION 30

ANNEX A

ANNEX B

ANNEX C

ANNEX D

TWO- MEMORANDUM OF CONVERSATION WITH FRENCH COUNSUL, KHORRAMSHAHR 36

KHUZESTAN 36

DOMESTIC POLETICS 36

PERSIAN GULF 36

FRENCH OIL COMPANIES AND EQBAL 37

TREE- SEMI ANNUAL ASSESSMENT OF THE POLITICAL SITUATION IN IRAN 38

1- SUMMARY 39

2- THE SHAH 40

3- THE ECONOMIC SITUATION 41

4- IRAN-U.S. RELATIONS 43

5- IRAN AND THE PERSIAN GULF 45

6- IRAN AND IRAQ: THE SHATT CONFORNTATION 46

7- IRAN AND OTHER COUNTRIES 48

8- IRAN-COMMUNIST RELATIONS 50

9- THE GOVERNMENT, PARLIAMENT AND THE PARTIES 53

10- DISSENT AND INTERNAL SECURITY 55

FOUR- REFORM IN IRAN 58

SUMMARY AND INTRODUCTION 59

1- LAND REFORM 61

3- STATE OF GOVERNMENT FACTORIES 62
4- WORKER PROFIT SHARING 62
5- ELECTION LAW REFORM 63
6- LITERACY CORPS 63
7- HEALTH CORPS 64
8- EXTENSION AND DEVELOPMENT CORPS 65
9- HOUSE OF JUSTICE AND ARBITRATION COUNCIL 66
10- NATIONALIZATION OF WATER RESOURCES 67
11- RECONSTRUCTION OF THE COUNTRY 67
12- ADMINISTRATIVE AND EDUCATIONAL REVOLUTION 68
13- OTHER MEASURES 69
COMMENT 70
FIVE- YOUTH 72
SIX- REFORM PROGRAM 75
SEVEN- IRAN NATIONAL INTELLIGENCE SURVEY 78
GENERAL SURVEY CHAPTERS 81
CHANGE FROM THE TOP 84
OBSTACLE TO CHANGE 86
THE STRONG MAN TRADITION 88
MONOPOLIZING POLITICAL POWER 90
THE WHITE REVOLUTION 91
OIL AND WHAT ELSE? 91
LOOKING WEST, EAST AND TO THE MIDDLE EAST 93
AS THE SHAH GOES, SO GOES IRAN 94
CHRONOLOGY 96
AREA BRIEF 98
EIGHT- BRIEFING FOR TDY PERSONNEL 100
INTRODUCTION 100
U.S. INTERESTS 101
PHYSICAL CHARACTERISTICS 104
PEOPLE, RELIGION, CULTURE 107
SOCIAL AND INDUSTRIAL DEVELOPMENT 114
INDUSTRIAL DEVELOPMENT 118
EXTERNAL THREAT 120
IRAQ IS IRAN'S MOST ACTIVE ANTAGONIST 121
STRATEGY 124
DEFENSE ORGANIZATION 125
FORCE DISPOSITION/DEVELOPMENT 126
GROUND FORCE 126
AIR FORCE 128
ORGANIZATION OF THE IMPERIAL IRANIAN NAVY 129
DISPOSITION OF FORCES 131
HISTORY OF MILITARY ASSISTANCE AND ARMISH-MAAG 131
ORGANIZATION OF ARMISH-MAAG 132
ARSEC 132
AFSEC 133
NAVSEC 133
EUCOM SUPPORT ACTIVITIY 133
TECHNICAL ASSISTANCE FIELD TEAMS 134
FOREIGN MILITARY SALES 135
CONUS TRAINING ..... [illegible]

MIC 206/171

February 7, 1966

This document consists of 37 pages,
No. 46 of 49 copies, Series A.

UNITED STATES

MILITARY INFORMATION CONTROL COMMITTEE

SECURITY IN THE GOVERNMENT OF IRAN

Note by the Secretary

1. The attached report was prepared to record the observations of the United States Military Information Control Committee Team which examined the security program in the Government of Iran during the period October 25 - November 3, 1965.

2. The United States Military Information Control Committee approved the report at its meeting on December 15, 1965.

3. This document requires "Special Handling." It is "Not Releasable to Foreign Nationals."

4. Distribution of this document is limited to those having an official need-to-know.

Donald S. Harris

Donald S. Harris
Secretary

SPECIAL HANDLING REQUIRED
NOT RELEASABLE TO FOREIGN
NATIONALS

GROUP 1
EXCLUDED FROM AUTOMATIC DOWN-
GRADING AND DECLASSIFICATION.

SECRET

SECRET

A REVIEW OF THE SECURITY SYSTEM OF IRAN

I INTRODUCTION

In view of proposals by the U.S. Department of Defense that t HAWK and BULLPUP missile systems be supplied to Iran and because the security system of Iran had last been evaluated officially by a State Defense Military Information Control Committee Team which visited Ira in August - September 1960, the United States Military Information Co Committee (USMICC) decided to dispatch a Security Survey Team to Iran to review that country's security system. The Team conducted its surv in Iran from October 23 to November 4, 1965. Discussions were held by it with key Iranian officials and with representatives of the American Embassy, ARMISH-MAAG and GENMISH.

The security evaluation referred to above was documented in MIC 206/129, dated February 8, 1961. This current report is intended primarily to bring up to date the information contained in MIC 206/129 Statements made in it are based primarily on observations of the Team and on information supplied to it by Iranian and American officials.

Annex A contains a list of Team members; Annex B a list of the principal Iranian officials with whom the Team conferred; Annex C a list of the principal American Officials with whom the Team held discussions; and Annex D a schedule of the Team's meetings.

SECRET

II BASIC SECURITY LEGISLATION

There have been no changes in the basic security legislation of Iran as recorded in MIC 206/129. The constitutional laws of 1906, 1907 and 1925 still form the legal base for the Iranian Government and its division into separate executive, legislative and judicial branches. Despite the nominally democratic form of government, the Shah appears to be more than ever an autocratic ruler in the long tradition of absolute monarchy which has usually prevailed in Iran down through much of its recorded history. Thus the attitude of the Shah toward security and the firmness of his position remain essential aspects to be considered in any survey of Iran's security system.

Civilian security laws also remain unchanged; these being still based on Articles 60-79 of the 1925 Iranian Public Penal Code with revisions of 1945, and the 1931 Law of Opponents to the Country's Independence and Security. Military activities continue to be governed by the 1936 Army Laws of Procedure and Penal Code (also known as The Military Justice and Penal Law of Iran). It may be noted that under the 1925 Penal Code referred to above provisions are made for civilians and members of the armed forces to be tried by military courts in cases of espionage. Various sections of the Military Justice and Penal Law of Iran also provide for trial of civilians by military courts; e.g., for attempts on the life of the Shah or the Crown Prince. While the Team was in Iran a military court concluded the trial of a number of civilians involved in the April 1965 Marble

Palace attempt on the life of the Shah. Among the sentences passed out, two were for death, one for life imprisonment, and nine were for imprisonment from 3 to 8 years. (Note: The actual attempt on the Shah's life was made by a conscript member of the Imperial Guard who did not survive his unsuccessful attempt at assassination.)

Attempts on the life of the Shah or the Crown Prince are not the only crimes punishable by the death sentence under the provisions of the several laws referred to above. There are numerous other crimes for which the perpetrators may receive the death sentence and among these is espionage. Evidence that this penalty is applied for espionage was given in early 1965 when three Iranian Officers were executed after conviction by a military court on charges of spying for the Soviets. (Note: The espionage for which the officers were convicted was not recent. The case was broken by the Imperial Iranian Counter Intelligence Corps — IICIC.)

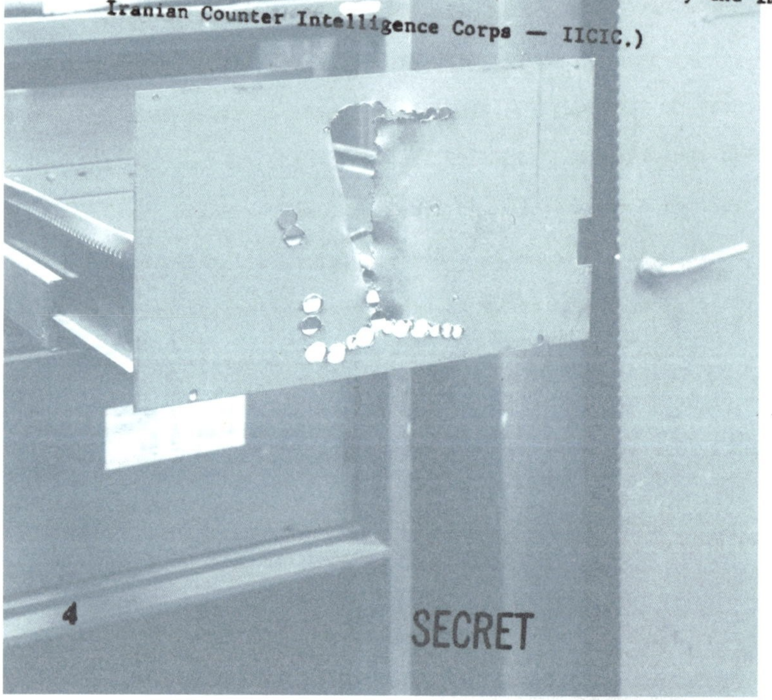

III PUBLIC ATTITUDE TOWARD SECURITY

There is no reason to believe that the Iranian public is any more aware of the need for protective security now than was the case when the previous security survey was made in 1960. While changes in society are under way; e.g., in the slow growth of a middle class and a small decline in the percentage of illiteracy, these are not sufficient to overcome the lack of a national concsiousness as known by Western nations, the very low standard of living of the average Iranian, the lack of formal education (over 80 per cent of Iranians are still illiterate), and the generally backward conditions prevailing throughout much of the country. However, assuming that the Shah will be successful in his efforts to raise the standard of living, to make drastic inroads into the level of illiteracy, to improve communications and to develop a national consciousness, one may expect this situation to improve in the next generation.

IV NATIONAL ORGANIZATION FOR SECURITY

Since this subject was discussed in considerable detail in MIC 206/129 and most of the material therein is still essentially correct, this section of this report will concern itself primarily with updating and revising the previous report where necessary or desirable. The dominant factor to be taken into consideration in any evaluation of security in Iran is the position of the Shah, whose role in the government of Iran has grown no less central and autocratic than was the case at the time of the previous security survey in 1960, and whose interest in and control of security has increased. The various security organizations in effect function as appendages to his one-man government. Since resuming power after the fall of Mossadeq in 1953, the Shah has taken a deep and personal interest in the day to day operations of the various intelligence and security organizations. All major, and many minor, decisions in this field are made by the Shah. After the nearly successful Marble Palace attempt on his life in April 1965, the Shah's interest in security became even more intense. The primary objective of security in Iran is preservation of the monarchy. Other main objectives are to counter the Soviet threat and to counter the threat from other countries in the area; i.e., Iraq and the UAR. It is from the latter country, as personified by Nasser, that the Shah sees the biggest threat to Iran in this decade. By contrast, the Iranian attitude toward the Soviets is more relaxed than it was in 1960.

So far as can be determined, the Shah's influence on security in Iran is, at least from the United States point of view, a positive one. However, the unique role which he plays necessarily raises the question of what would happen in the event of his sudden demise. There does not appear at this time to be any likelihood of the Shah being deposed through organized opposition to him, since no such effective organization appears to exist. The possibility of assassination always exists and thus the situation, in the words of former Ambassador Holmes remains "stable but brittle." In such an event, and in view of the lack of any organized opposition to the present regime, it is likely that the military could insure the continuance of some form of stable government whose policy objectives would continue to run parallel to those of the United States in the area.

1. National Security Council

The National Security Council (NSC) remains, at least in theory, the top policy formulating body for the intelligence community. So far as is known there have been no changes in its organization. The subcommittees created at the same time as the NSC (1956), the Internal Protection Coordinating Committee (IPCC) and the Intelligence Coordinating Committee (ICC) continue to function adjunctively with the NSC.

During the Team's meeting with SAVAK representatives, it was informed by Brig. Gen. Mahootian (Chief of Security for SAVAK) that the two subcommittees meet each month, with the IPCC sometimes meeting twice a month. According to Gen. Mahootian, the ICC members consist primarily of the Security Officers of the various Ministries. These Officers rank as senior officers of the Ministries and are appointed by their Ministers in consultation with SAVAK. ICC meetings are normally presided over by Gen. Mahootian.

Gen. Mahootian made it clear that the IPCC, which is presided over by the Chief of SAVAK, is the more important of the two subcommittees. He said that all Ministries are represented on it, and in addition the National Iranian Oil Co., the National Planning Organization and the Tehran Municipality. An interesting security aspect of this Committee is that each of its members is required once a year to submit a report listing security problems in his organization and any relevant ideas which he may have. This report is submitted to the Chairman, i.e., the Chief of SAVAK. It should be noted that both the ICC and the IPCC regularly discuss security problems of the various Ministries, the latter Committee taking up those problems which the ICC has not been able to resolve.

2. National Organization for Intelligence and Security (SAVAK)

At the time of the previous survey SAVAK was headed by the competent and powerful Maj. Gen. Teimur Bakhtiar, who was removed from office in early 1961 by the Shah, presumably because he had grown too powerful. Gen. Bakhtiar was succeeded by Gen. Pakravan, who in turn was removed from his post shortly after the assassination of Prime Minister Hasan Ali Mansur on January 21, 1965. Unfortunately for Pakravan, his organization had no advance knowledge of the conspiracy to assassinate the Prime Minister. The present Chief of SAVAK, Lt. Gen. Nematollah Nasiri, enjoys the reputation of being a ruthless and efficient officer who is loyal and devoted to the Shah. The Chief of SAVAK also serves as an Adviser to the NSC and as a Deputy Prime Minister.

SAVAK continues to be a powerful organization with overall security responsibility for the country. Its responsibilities include monitoring of political activities of Iranian students abroad, the investigation of espionage, sabotage, treason, insurrection and other subversive activities; the collection of intelligence information on political opposition; surveillance of foreign embassies, official delegations from abroad and resident aliens; foreign operations connected with intelligence and counterintelligence; official liaison with friendly foreign intelligence services (especially with the Israelis); and security in the civilian Ministries. According to Ransom Haig, Attache, American Embassy, the Shah had said, sometime during the last six months, that he wants SAVAK to get out of police type work and to concentrate on espionage and counterespionage. However, he added that not much change has been noticed so far.

The Team was particularly interested in SAVAK's responsibility for security in the civilian Ministries. SAVAK exercises control over this in a number of ways. In the first place, each Ministry has a Security Officer as one of its senior officers. He is appointed by the Minister in consultation with SAVAK, which approves him and makes sure that he is a competent person. SAVAK emphasizes that these Security Officers should not be changed lightly. Their basic instruction is given by SAVAK. (Mr. Haig told the Team that these Officers are generally considered by the personnel of the various Ministries to be mere stooges of SAVAK, and that for this reason they are generally avoided.) In any case, the Security Officers are obligated to report any security problems within their Ministries to SAVAK. In addition these Officers sit in on the regular meetings of the ICC, where there is a regular airing of security problems. For these reasons, SAVAK does not feel it necessary to have any regularly scheduled security inspections of Ministries; however, SAVAK has the right to investigate any of the Ministries anytime it thinks it necessary or desirable to do so.

Mr. Haig judged that SAVAK has made considerable progress but that by American standards it has a long way to go. He felt that plus points for SAVAK are its keen awareness of the Soviet threat and its competence in the political field.

3. J-2 Section, Supreme Commander's Staff

J-2 in 1958, by order of the Shah, absorbed many of the functions previously carried out by G-2. It now directs and coordinates Iran's military intelligence effort and collects, collates and disseminates military intelligence. It also has overall responsibility for the security of military personnel and installations; military counter-espionage operations; supervision of Iranian military attaches abroad;

and the activities of the National Resistance Organization (which organization, so far as the team was able to ascertain, appears never to have gotten off the ground). The head of J-2 since the Spring of 1961 has been Lt. Gen. Azizollah Kamal. His immediate predecessor, Lt. Gen. Haj Ali Kia, was removed by the Shah because he appeared to be growing too powerful, a not uncommon cause for dismissal from power in Iran. Lt. Gen. Kamal's technical competence does not seem to be very highly regarded; however, there is general agreement that he is a wily old fox who always seems to manage to come out on top. There seems, however, to also be a wide measure of agreement in the view, among Americans who have official contact with J-2, that security consciousness and practices within J-2 (and hence within the Armed Forces) have improved greatly within the last year -- and especially within the last six months. This seems to be traceable to a number of reasons, the most important being the possibility of Iran getting sensitive equipment (such as the HAWK and the BULLPUP), the desire of the Shah that security practices be improved, and the psychological effect (related to the two preceding points) of the visit of the USMICC Team. The ARMISH-MAAG has worked closely with J-2 to improve security and intelligence. In the respect particular credit is due to Maj. Robert Hand, U.S. Army, whose helpful collaboration with the J-2 appears to have been a major factor in improving its security consciousness and procedures.

4. <u>G-2 Section of the General Staff</u>

G-2 today plays only a minor role in security matters and was therefore of no special interest to the Team. It is concerned primarily with collecting combat intelligence and order of battle information.

ANNEX B

PRINCIPAL IRANIAN OFFICIALS WITH WHOM USMICC TEAM CONFERRED

Berendjian, Col. H., IIAF CIC Commander and IIAF A-2

Haskem, Mr., Dept. 4, SAVAK

Kamal, Lt. Gen. Azizollah, Chief, J-2

Mahootian, Brig. Gen., Chief, Security (Dept. 4), SAVAK

Moghadam, Col., Dept. 3, SAVAK

Mobasser, Maj. Gen. Mohsen, Chief, National Police

Motahari, Col. M., Deputy Base Commander, Mehrabad Air Base

Motazed, Maj. Gen., Chief, Foreign Intelligence, SAVAK

Samadianpur, Brig. Gen. Samad, Chief of Information Bureau, National Police

Tadjbakhsh, Brig. Gen. Ardeshir, Chief, CIC

ANNEX C

PRINCIPAL AMERICAN OFFICIALS WITH WHOM USMICC TEAM CONFERRED

Meyer, The Honorable Armin, American Ambassador

Ash, Brig. Gen. Hughes L., Chief, Army Section, MAAG

Cannady, Col. Preston B., Chief, GENMISH

Cavness, Col. William D., Defense Attache and Army Attache

Conway, Alan C., Attache

Dunn, Leland M., Economic Officer

Haig, Ransom S., Attache

Hand, Maj. Robert D., J-2, ARMISH-MAAG

Harlan, Robert, Counselor for Economic Affairs

Helseth, William A., Political Officer

Herz, Martin F., Counselor for Political Affairs

Jablonsky, Maj. Gen. Harvey A., Chief, ARMISH-MAAG

Locke, Brig. Gen., Chief, Air Force Advisory Section, MAAG

Mudd, R. Clayton, Special Assistant to the Ambassador

Olson, Richard L., Regional Security Officer

Prim, Maj. Billy R., Assistant Air Attache

Wallis, Capt. F. H., Chief, Navy Section, MAAG

York, Lt. Col. B. M., Air Attache

ANNEX D

SCHEDULE USMICC VISIT

IRAN — 1965

Monday, October 25, 1965

1000 - 1100	Meeting with Ambassador Meyer
1300 - 1330	Meeting with Maj. Gen. Jablonsky, Chief ARMISH-MAAG
1330 - 1515	Meeting with Maj. Hand, ARMISH-MAAG
1530 - 1700	Meeting with Mr. Alan Conway, Attache

Tuesday, October 26, 1965

1000	Meeting with Mr. Ransom S. Haig, Attache
1100	Meeting with Mr. William A. Helseth, Political Section

Wednesday, October 27, 1965

0930 - 1230	Meeting with Maj. Gen. Kamal, J-2, SCS, and Brig. Gen. Tajbakhsh, Chief, IICIC
1245 - 1630	Lunch and Meeting with Chief IICIC

Thursday, October 28, 1965

0930 - 1230	Col. Berendjian, Chief, IIAF CIC, IIAF Headquarters
1415 - 1530	Col. Cannady, USA, Chief GENMISH
1530 - 1630	Col. York, Maj. Prim, Air Attache and Assistant Air Attache
1630 - 1730	Mr. Herz, Counselor for Political Affairs

Friday, October 29, 1965

0900 - 1000	Mr. Olson, Regional Security Officer, Iran
1000 - 1100	Col. Cavness, USA, Defense Attache
1100 - 1200	Mr. Harlan, Counselor for Economic Affairs, and Mr. Dunn, Economic Officer

ANNEX C (cont'd.)

Saturday, October 30, 1965

0930 - 1230 Meeting with SAVAK officials

1415 - 1630 Visit to 101st Fighter Wing, Mehrabad Air Base, Tehran, talks with Col. M. Motahari, Deputy Base Commander.

1700 - 1830 Talks with Maj. Gen. Mobasser, Chief of National Police, and Brig. Gen. Samadianpur, Chief of Information Bureau of National Police

Monday, November 1, 1965

0800 Travel to Mehrabad AB in connection with planned two-day trip to Dezful, Abadan and Khorramshahr.

1630 - 1730 Mr. Ransom Haig, Attache

Tuesday, November 2, 1965

0930 - 1130 Maj. Hand, ARMISH-MAAG

Wednesday, November 3, 1965

1000 Brig. Gen. Ash, Chief, Army Section, MAAG

1400 Farewell call on Gen. Kamal, J-2

1530 Exit Briefing, Maj. Gen. Jablonsky

1800 Exit Briefing, Ambassador Meyer

Thursday, November 4

0830 Depart for Rome

A-384

SECRET

Department of State

INFO : ANKARA, BEIRUT, BUCHAREST, JIDDA, KUWAIT, KABUL, LONDON, MOSCOW, NEW DELHI, PRAGUE, RAWALPINDI, USCINCSTRIKE/USCINCMEAFSA

POL-6

CHARGE
A/DCM
ECON-3
SA
CR-2
USIS
DAO
MAAG
CONS
CRU-2

POUCH:
KHOR
TABR
ANKARA
BEIRUT
BUCHAREST
JIDDA
KUWAIT
KABUL
LONDON
MOSCOW
NEW DELHI
PRAGUE
RAWALPINDI
CINCSTRIKE

34/lhr

Amembassy TEHRAN DATE: SEPTEMBER 04, 1969

Semi-Annual Assessment of the Political Situation in I

Tehran A-068 of February 20, 1969

Table of Contents

1. Summary
2. The Shah
3. The Economic Situation
4. Iran-U.S. Relations
5. Iran and the Persian Gulf
6. Iran and Iraq: The Shatt Confrontation
7. Iran and Other Countries
8. Iran-Communist Relations
9. The Government, Parliament and the Parties
10. Dissent and Internal Security

GROUP 3
Downgraded at 12-year intervals, not automatically declassified.

SECRET

POL:JHRouse/CMcCaskill/JArmitage:gh 8/30/69 CHARGE:MGThacher
Contributor:ECON:EPrince

SECRET

1. Summary

This six months was a period of even greater than usual calm. The dominant position of the Shah remained unchanged and unchallenged. Rapid economic growth and spreading prosperity continued to underpin stability at home. There were financial strains but the highly competent team of government planners seemed to have the situation in hand. Changes in the Cabinet of Prime Minister Hoveyda appeared to strengthen his position vis-a-vis other members of his government, though he and the rest of the Cabinet remained at the disposition of the Shah. The Parliamentary pantomime played-on with no sign of change in the Majlis role of lawmaking largely by rote. Following the ouster of Secretary General Khosrovani, an Iran Novin Party Congress was called for September with indications there might be changes in the structure as well as the personnel of the lassitudinous party. Any latent opposition elements remained demoralized and disorganized by penetration by the state security apparatus and by the pace of economic and social change. Recruitment efforts of government-sponsored Iraqi Kurds continued to require substantial Iranian security force commitments in Iranian Kurdistan but the Government clearly controlled the situation. Students and workers kept quiet except for an occasional brief, localized strike.

In its foreign policy, Iran continued to chart a forceful and independent course. Relations with the United States remained excellent, reinforced by early personal contact between the Shah and the President and by the fantastic local impact of Apollo 11. The annual negotiations on military sales and oil company revenue payments had their difficult moments but brought satisfactory agreements. The Shah's continued policy of rapprochement with the Soviet Union and Eastern Europe produced some expansion of trade and cooperation particularly with Romania and Czechoslovakia. Iran renounced its Shatt-al-Arab boundary treaty of 1937 with Iraq but Iraq showed no inclination to bargain on Iran's terms, and after somewhere rattling the situation stagnated into a protracted war of words. The prime focus of Iranian interests remained the Persian Gulf. The Shah made clear that after British withdrawal in 1971, no foreign presence would be welcome in the Gulf, and he expressed the view that the U.S. should give up its port facilities in Bahrain. Continuing efforts to harmonize relations with Saudi Arabia and to woo the Gulf sheikhdoms went on quietly, although the Shah reiterated his renunciation of force regarding Bahrain, and appeared willing to accept formation of an FAA which excluded Bahrain. Elsewhere, Iran obdurately broke diplomatic

SECRET

relations with Lebanon over its failure to extradite former SAVAK chief Bakhtiar, but showed moderation in its (as yet unanswered) overture to the UAR removing its previous demand for a UAR apology before relations might be resumed. Iran paid particular attention to Pakistan where, concerned at the prospect of insecurity on its eastern frontiers, it was quick to lend recognition to the Government of Yahya Khan and has cultivated close relations since.

As the reporting period ended, there were no signs that the months to come would bring any weakening in Iran's political stability, although there was some room for worry over the expected slowdown in economic expansion. There were hopeful indications that continued restraint and quiet diplomacy might produce a solution to the Bahrain problem and ease the way to better relations across the Gulf. In U.S.-Iran relations, those hardy annuals, the military credit sales and oil revenue negotiations, were again expected to pose difficult problems. But the official visit of the Shah to the U.S. scheduled for October offered the opportunity to reinforce our relations at a time free of pressing issues while our continuing mutuality of interest and will to cooperate inspired confidence that these problems could again be resolved to our common benefit.

2. The Shah

The Shah remained the undisputed master of his house during the past [illegible] months untroubled by any significant threat to the country's almost monotonous domestic political stability or by any serious set-backs in economic growth, in the White Revolution, or in Iran's foreign policy of independent self-interest. Feeling, as he said, like "an older statesman" on the world scene in his 28th year as Monarch, the Shah conducted Iran's foreign policy with accustomed confidence. He continued to profess privately the preferred position of the U.S. among Iran's friends, but played a balanced public role largely directed at furthering Iran's ambitions in the Gulf and cultivating relations with Western, third world and bloc countries alike. The Shah's usual sensible statesmanship was marred somewhat by his rancor and rigidity in the oil negotiations, his uncompromising insistence on a diplomatic break with Lebanon over Bakhtiar, and his aggressive stance against Iraq over the Shatt-al-Arab boundary.

At home, the Shah maintained his impatient and persistent pressure for accelerated economic development despite signs of strain in the economy. With the British departure from the Gulf ever approaching and the Shatt-al-Arab confrontation with Iraq, much of the Shah's attention concerned Iran's military preparedness, and his constant interest in obtaining new defensive weapons quickened. In a major military overhaul, more than 50 field-grade officers, including the Chief of the Supreme Commander's Staff, the Commander of the Ground Forces and seven of the eight Navy admirals were retired and large numbers of senior officers reassigned. The new Chief of SCS, General Feridoun Djam, was given an unprecedented, clear mandate as the Shah's top aide but Air Force General Khatami's position remained strong. The installation for the first time in recent memory of an SCS Chief with well-regarded professional qualifications seemed a measure of the Shah's confidence in the security of his own position.

The Shah's personal stock remained high as increasing numbers of the elite seemed to be finding in their roles in economic modernization an acceptable substitute for political participation, as prosperity continued to spread its benefits, and as the rural-oriented White Revolution carried to the villages a picture of the Shah identified with positive and benevolent government action. A continuing effort was made to humanize the image of the monarchy through publicity of the Royal Family together and individually in homey undertakings and charitable activities. The Empress remained widely popular for her unpretentious warmth, and it looked as if she were being given a somewhat broader exposure for her possible role as regent when she initiated a campaign against royal flattery and spoke with new authority on such questions as preserving the country's cultural heritage. But the Royal Family's popularity still seemed manifestly inadequate as a substitute for the Shah's actual authority in maintaining the monarchy, and the problem of its preservation should the Shah pass from the scene was still far from resolution.

3. The Economic Situation

Iran's booming economic growth continued unabated, but the heat and stress being generated indicate that a modest deceleration may be in the offing. The economic planners have already moved to meet immediate pressures and expectations are for continuing economic progress to remain the foundation of Iran's political stability.

During the Iranian year ending March 31, the first year of the Fourth Development Plan, GNP rose at a rate of 10.3% in real prices to more than $300 per capita for Iran's 28 million people. For the first six months of 1969, oil exports, construction, domestic production, level of employment, and rate of investment remained high. Crop expectations generally were good though down in most major cash crops--excepting cotton--from 1968

SECRET

record levels. Progress, though more costly than expected in some instances, continued on the major industrial undertakings--the petrochemical complex now getting into production, gas line, steel mill, and tractor and machine tool plants. Plans were laid which could lead to major increases in agro-industry.

On the worrisome side was the realization that the monetary controls of late '68 had not stemmed inflationary pressures. When the cost of living index, itself old and oddly weighted for a general index, showed an increase in prices of 3.2% for the period March 21 - June 21, 1969, over the same period of the previous year, the Central Bank acted again for monetary restraint raising the rediscount rate, the reserve requirements of the commercial banks, and their maximum interest rates for term and saving deposits.

Of concern too, were dwindling foreign exchange reserves which by March 1969 had left only $15 million in free foreign exchange. With these reserves up to $45 million by the end of June the situation was on the mend, and it was clear that there was a new appreciation in the Plan Organization of Iran's growing foreign debt burden and of the need for more selective foreign borrowing. Shortage of money domestically was also a problem with the Government not always able to meet current bills despite high levels of inflationary domestic borrowing. Current account spending remained hard to curb as budgetary estimates for the present Iranian year rose by 10.5% over the previous.

Faced with these problems, with substantial overruns on such major industrial undertakings as the pipeline and the Shahpour Petrochemical plant and with the real possibility that oil revenues next year may not meet Development Plan targets, the Plan Organization is reviewing priorities in recognition of the insufficiency of available resources to finance all projects within the framework of the Fourth Plan. Thus some major Plan projects appear to be in for delay.

But if Iran in its short term development goals has bitten off more than it can comfortably chew, there appears to be little danger that it will choke. While maintaining balance in the economy will continue to be difficult in face of Imperial pressures for rapid development and military purchases, even at the top there is growing awareness of the limits of possible progress. Steps seem to be underway to tailor the economy closer to the possibilities. Though this may result in a reduction in the present unusually high growth rates, the outcome could be a more orderly and healthy development.

SECRET

SECRET

4. Iran - U.S. Relations

The character and content of U.S. - Iran relations remained essentially unchanged during the past six months and the rapport and understanding underlying these ties survived intact despite some minor strains along the way. Particularly important was the occasion afforded the Shah by his attendance at the Eisenhower funeral for the early renewal of old acquaintance with President Nixon and for personal contact with other leaders of the new Administration. The participation of Secretary Rogers in the CENTO Ministerial Conference in Tehran in May reinforced this atmosphere of personal rapport between leaders of the two governments. The outstanding success at the end of the period of the Apollo 11 moon walk received unprecedented attention in Iran and elicited the emotional involvement of Iranians of all walks of life. It gave an enormous boost to U.S. prestige and renewed luster to the image of U.S. technical and managerial superiority. The official visit to Washington of the Shah scheduled for October should reinforce further the important personal element in our relations.

The relationship of the U.S. to Iran even in the context of Iran's expanding "independent nationalism" remained that of primus inter pares with much of our retained special status deriving from the key military cooperation which the Shah values so highly. Negotiations on the Military Sales Program (7th tranche) came around again, and agreement was reached with dispatch despite the fact that the Shah's professed requirements particularly for F-4 aircraft far exceeded tranche fund limitations. Appreciation on both sides of each other's problems helped reach a satisfactory solution whereby the majority of F-4's could be ordered on a "dependable undertaking" against future payment perhaps with U.S. Government credit. One area of potential difference arose which was not entirely resolved--the question of employing U.S. Air Force technicians to service jet aircraft that might be used if differences with Iraq were to turn into hostilities. The question of redeployment of U.S. personnel to the south with the aircraft came up informally, and was withdrawn when we informed the Iranians that such a request might raise serious problems in Washington. The incident probably reminded the Shah of the U.S. posture toward Pakistan during the Indo-Pak fighting, and the question may be raised again when the Shah goes to Washington.

The annual oil negotiations between the GOI and the Consortium were even stickier than usual. At times they threatened to lead to an impasse,

SECRET

A-376

CONFIDENTIAL

TO: Department of State

INFO: ANKARA, DHAHRAN, JIDDA, KABUL, KUWAIT, LONDON, RAWALPINDI

POL-4

CHARGE
A/DCM
ECON-3
SA
CR-2
USIS
DAO
MAAG
CONS
CRU-2

POUCH:
KHOR
TABR
ANKARA
DHAHRAN
JIDDA
KABUL
KUWAIT
LONDON
RAWALPINDI

27/1hr

Amembassy TEHRAN AUG 28,69

Reform in Iran

Tehran A-630, May 22, 1967

TABLE OF CONTENTS

Page

SUMMARY AND INTRODUCTION 2
1. Land Reform 2
2. Nationalization of Forests 4
3. Sale of Government Factories 5
4. Workers Profit Sharing 5
5. Election Law Reform 6
6. Literacy Corps 6
7. Health Corps 7
8. Extension and Development Corps 8
9. Houses of Justice and Arbitration Councils 9
10. Nationalization of Water Resources 10
11. Reconstruction of the Country 10
12. Administrative and Educational Revolution 11
13. Other Measures 12
COMMENT 13

Group 3
Downgraded at 12-year intervals,
not automatically declassified.
CONFIDENTIAL

POL:CWMcCaskill:psk POL:JAArmitage

(Contributors: EPPrince, ALRaphel, LWSemakis)

SUMMARY AND INTRODUCTION

As the economy of Iran has moved ahead and the country has enjoyed unprecedented stability, the Shah has continued his efforts to maintain his image as a modernizer and reformer. He continues very much the man in a hurry, anxious to accelerate Iran's development. A large part of his public image is based on his desire to solidify the concept of modern monarch, interested in the welfare of his people, pulling his nation forward.

Since the announcement of the original six-point White Revolution in 1963, enunciation of reform has become the order of the day in Iran. The original program was expanded to nine points in 1965 and later increased to twelve. Other reform measures have been identified with the White Revolution piecemeal to reinforce the identification of the Shah personally with change and progress in Iran.

Some of the programs are meaningful, some are not. Most do make some contribution, however, to the overall impression of reform. From the average Iranian's point of view, half a loaf is probably better than none, and he is willing to tolerate the large doses of Government propaganda which accompany most new programs for the measure of real economic and social progress he sees in the country. His share in the increased average per capita income may be modest, but he now has the hope that things can be better for his children and grandchildren. There is, of course, the inherent danger in this process that additional expectations will be awakened. Need for reform will continue on the agenda, if the Shah is to sustain the impression of a reforming as well as a developing Iran.
END SUMMARY AND INTRODUCTION

1. Land Reform

Land Reform, the heart of the Shah's White Revolution, has gone through a number of phases. The first phase required large landowners to sell all of their holdings except one village to the Government to be distributed among the peasants working the land. Under the second phase, owners of one village were given the option of selling all their remaining lands to the farmers, dividing their holdings among the farmers while retaining a portion for themselves, or leasing their land for thirty years. By spring of 1969, 209,708 landowners had leased their lands, making a total of 54,183 (of the approximately 62,000) villages, 19,020 farms and 2,414,447 farmers directly affected by the provisions of the Land Reform.

Concurrent with the first two phases of Land Reform, Rural Cooperatives have been established to supply cooperative members with credit, inexpensive seed and fuel, and the services of extension agents from the Ministries of Land Reform and Agriculture. So far, 8,600 Cooperatives have been established with a total membership of 1,278,389 in 23,697 villages and total capital of

YOUTH

Summary

The urban, educated activist youth of Iran comprises only a segment of the total youth population. However, it is believed that the future managers of Iranian society will be drawn from this group. More immediately, as 54% of all Iranians are under the age of 24, the views of this group are important. A constant target of SAVAK, urban activists have muted their dissidence and confined themselves recently to mild protests and sympathy strikes.

Embassy contacts with and knowledge of Iranian youth are restricted to the urban, educated and activist group. This group constitutes only a relatively small segment of the youth population of Iran -- a country in which 54% of the total population is under 24 years if age -- but the views of young farmers and young workers are not well known and even less well articulated. There is general agreement, however, that these youths hew more closely to the line followed by their elders, and they do not, therefore, constitute a notable group in themselves.

Much can be said of the urban activist minority, however. The campus demonstrations of several years ago -- which usually provoked a brutal response by the police and resulted in some bloodletting -- have given way in the 70's to mild demonstrations and sympathy strikes. Some of the vigor seems to have gone out of student protests. The 25th Centenary Celebrations in late 1971, provoked a certain amount of student opposition; however, arrests were few and violence minimal. The more recent trials of subversives and terrorists also caused some student anxiety. but the response was mild compared to that of the past.

Iran's educated youth -- the young technocrats, bureaucrats and academicians -- generally view the White Revolution's Educational Reform as a stillborn failure. Outside inter-

Group 3
Downgraded at 12-year intervals
not automatically declassified

ference, jurisdictional disputes, substandard equipment and instruction continue as before. While from time to time dynamic, generally western-educated professors and administrators appear on the scene, their effectiveness, the students feel, is vitiated by the presence of SAVAK. At a time when protest has become more restrained, the activities of SAVAK have reportedly become less so. Students and young people are less willing to voice their opinions today than they were some years ago (when SAVAK seemed to them more capricious), and the efficient and methodical penetration of any opposition group has served to still much of the dissent. Students seem to have learned that protest that goes beyond academic dissent on specific issues is usually met with a crushing response. This response is bolstered by the enlistment of the media and the organization of the Government's supporters into nation-wide protests against the students. Greater control and improved technology therefore, have helped to stifle dissent.

Young Iranians, not unlike older ones, are capable of submerging rebellious attitudes to work within the system. That more than 15,000 Iranians each year wish to enter universities but are unable to for reasons of finances and lack of space is testimony of the attractiveness of higher education in Iran. For many, university and the diploma are passports to a good life in Iran. However, the constraints placed on higher education may take a toll as young Iranian students learn that the Iranian Establishment requires even greater conformity than most and that meaningful discussions -- the kind students all over the world engage in -- are closed to them. Sports and student union buildings are substituted to an increasing degree for student participation in an effort to keep student minds occupied. This substitution of other things for student participation has been relatively successful in keeping the lid on the campuses the past few years, but it might well have the unhappy by-product of producing intellectually sterile young people.

Among young Iranians, the Shah and the Government are viewed with feelings ranging from awe and respect to outright distaste. Without question the young military officers are devoted to the Shah and Iran, a feeling which may be shared in part by the thousands of young Literacy, Health and Development Corps members. These groups seem to have a sense of dedication and elitism that does not extend to Iranian youth as a whole. For reasons not entirely clear -- but perhaps associated with both the Iranian sense of individualism and the Iranian feeling that nothing is really worth fighting for -- there seems to be no real sense of purpose, no notion of "common good" among Iranian youth.

Rightly or wrongly, young Iranians believe that the State apparatus has never been more tight and restrictive than at present. After the celebrations the security precautions which had been taken throughout the country continued as the Government's efforts to crush the guerilla/terrorist groups continued. As a consequence, student/youth groups seem more inhibited than ever, and political discussion among students even more rare.

For the urban, educated activist, neither the much-publicized reforms nor the improving job market hold much interest or attractiveness. The universities have been significantly democratized by the admission of large numbers of economically disadvantaged youngsters, but for some, the course of study is a farce, the university a circus. The economy is dynamic but real unemployment and marginal employment is high among recent graduates who have nothing more to offer than an Iranian university degree.

Educated young people are disillusioned and unhappy. They want the benefits of the affluent, but resent the total prohibition on their participation in Iran's national political life.

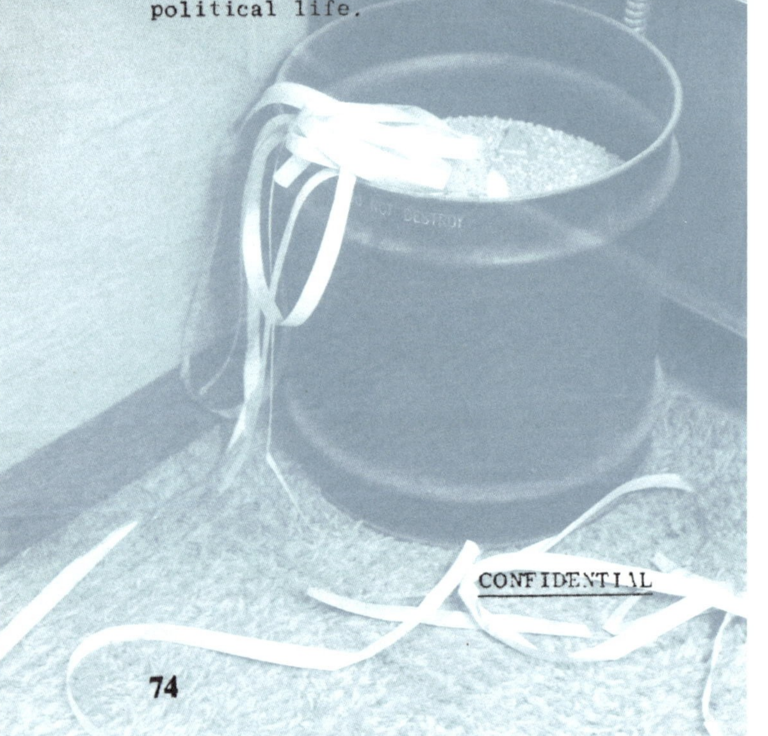

REFORM PROGRAM

Summary

Launched in 1962 with great fanfare, Iran's White Revolution has lost some of its momentum in recent years. The 13-point reform program, designed to bring the nation into the 20th century, has had great success in some areas such as land reform and adult literacy but in others, such as administrative reform and the educational revolution, have accomplished little or nothing. The overall impact of the reform program has helped to change the image of the Shah from that of a dilletante to a concerned and capable ruler but the lack of adequate political reforms may pose problems for the future.

Under the momentum of the Shah's personal prestige and implemented by Iran's increasingly competent technocrats, the reform program has become very much a part of Iranian life. Since the announcement of the original six-point program in 1962, reform has become a byword and efforts are made to associate almost every piece of legislation -- no matter how remotely -- with the reform program. The reform concept appears to have lost some of its momentum in the last two years but will probably come very much alive again in the next year or so. In truth some of the bold imaginative programs of the White Revolution have contributed significantly to Iran's progress of recent years and the Shah can, and often does, point with pride to his accomplishments. In fact, some of Iran's reform programs have become models for other underdeveloped countries.

The White Revolution includes the following individual programs:

1. Land Reform
2. Nationalization of Forests
3. Sale of Government Factories

4. Workers Profit Sharing
5. Election Law Reform
6. Literacy Corps
7. Health Corps
8. Extension and Development Corps
9. Houses of Equity and Arbitration Councils
10. Nationalization of Water Resources
11. Reconstruction of the Country
12. Administative and Educational Revolution
13. Religious Corps

Of these, about half have helped to open the way to progress in Iran. Land Reform, the cornerstone of the whole reform program and by far the most successful, has freed the peasants from the almost feudal absentee landlord system and has opened the way for them to become landholders. As a result of the work of young conscripts in provincial areas with the Literacy Corps, the literacy rate has almost doubled since 1956 and the UNDP, which is involved in the literacy program in certain areas of Iran, has reported that the country is on the verge of a breakthrough in the field of adult literacy. The Health Corps, which provides medical facilities in remote areas, and the Development Corps, which provides extension-type services in distant provinces, have both had good results and continue to grow. Houses of Equity have taken justice to the village level for the first time.

Other aspects of the White Revolution do not stand up so well under scrutiny. Nationalization of Forests and Nationalization of Water Resources have been implemented slowly and have contributed little to Iran's forward movement though they are expected to have long-term benefits for the country. The sale of Government Factories has generated little enthusiasm and is recognized as a government effort to unload unprofitable enterprises. The Workers' Profit Sharing Program has hardly gotten off the ground and the Election Law reform has done little to lead to the development of real political contests (indeed, under the present political system it could hardly do so and thus was probably intended by the Shah more as window dressing than as a true reform). The Reconstruction of the Country has produced almost nothing and the Administrative Reform, still viewed with considerable scepticism, has been criticized for failure to make any meaningful contribution to decentralization or overhaul of the massive Iranian bureaucracy. The Educational Reform, inaugurated with considerable fanfare in the summer of 1968 (in part, we thought, to give some semblance of movement to the reform movement), has failed to come to grips with the problems of Iran's universities and students and professors alike tend to look upon the Educational Reform indifferently. The Religious Corps has been virtually stillborn due to pressure from the mullas who regard the program (probably correctly) as a government plan to reduce their influence among the people.

The White Revolution has had its greatest impact so far in the rural sector: the peasants now own their land and their lives and villages are being noticeably improved. They are enjoying other derivative benefits and the way is now opening for them to participate to a greater degree in the nation's progress. The urban population shares in the prosperity generated by the reforms but students and intellectuals have not participated or shared in the reform program, refusing, they say, to accept the substitution of economic development for real social and political reform.

Partly as a result of his reforms, the Shah's image has undergone a major change in the past few years. Peasant awe of former years is being replaced by a new respect. With the help of Empress Farah's humanitarian activities, the Shah now appears less the playboy king and far more the serious ruler of men, concerned with the welfare of his land and people. While this enthusiasm is not shared by all, Iranians in general recognize and admit that only the Shah could have pushed the reform program through in such a short time and, because of his performance, respect for him has increased.

The Shah's commitment to reform and the indications that reform is here to stay may have pitfalls however, since the promise of continued reform inevitably raises expectations. Pressures for additional reform, expecially political reform may be expected to increase as the Shah's political honeymoon comes to a natural end. He himself admits that his people should be prepared for the day when they will have to participate to a greater degree in their Government, but he has, on the other hand, seemed reluctant to allow them to participate. How he reconciles these two positions and accomodates himself to the new and changing situations may well hold the key to Iran's political future since it now seems likely that the question of reform will have to be faced again and again in the coming years.

SECRET
33/GS/CP

Iran

May 1973

NATIONAL INTELLIGENCE SURVEY

SECRET

NATIONAL INTELLIGENCE SURVEY PUBLICATIONS

The basic unit of the NIS is the *General Survey,* which is now published in a bound-by-chapter format so that topics of greater perishability can be updated on an individual basis. These chapters—Country Profile, The Society, Government and Politics, The Economy, Military Geography, Transportation and Telecommunications, Armed Forces, Science, and Intelligence and Security, provide the primary NIS coverage. Some chapters, particularly Science and Intelligence and Security, that are not pertinent to all countries, are produced selectively. For small countries requiring only minimal NIS treatment, the *General Survey* coverage may be bound into one volume.

Supplementing the *General Survey* is the NIS *Basic Intelligence Factbook,* a ready reference publication that semiannually updates key statistical data found in the Survey. An unclassified edition of the factbook omits some details on the economy, the defense forces, and the intelligence and security organizations.

Although detailed sections on many topics were part of the NIS Program, production of these sections has been phased out. Those previously produced will continue to be available as long as the major portion of the study is considered valid.

A quarterly listing of all active NIS units is published in the *Inventory of Available NIS Publications,* which is also bound into the concurrent classified Factbook. The Inventory lists all NIS units by area name and number and includes classification and date of issue; it thus facilitates the ordering of NIS units as well as their filing, cataloging, and utilization.

Initial dissemination, additional copies of NIS units, or separate chapters of the *General Surveys* can be obtained directly or through liaison channels from the Central Intelligence Agency.

The *General Survey* is prepared for the NIS by the Central Intelligence Agency and the Defense Intelligence Agency under the general direction of the NIS Committee. It is coordinated, edited, published, and disseminated by the Central Intelligence Agency.

WARNING

The NIS is National Intelligence and may not be released or shown to representatives of any foreign government or international body except by specific authorization of the Director of Central Intelligence in accordance with the provisions of National Security Council Intelligence Directive No. 1.

For NIS containing unclassified material, however, the portions so marked may be made available for official purposes to foreign nationals and nongovernment personnel provided no attribution is made to National Intelligence or the National Intelligence Survey.

Subsections and graphics are individually classified according to content. Classification/control designations are:

(U/OU)	Unclassified/For Official Use Only
(C)	Confidential
(S)	Secret

GENERAL SURVEY CHAPTERS

COUNTRY PROFILE Integrated perspective of the subject country • Chronology • Area Brief •Summary Map

THE SOCIETY Social structure • Population • Health • Living conditions • Social problems • Religion • Education • Artistic expression • Public information

GOVERNMENT AND POLITICS Political evolution of the state • Governmental strength and stability • Structure and function • Political dynamics • National policies • Threats to stability •Subversion and insurgency •Police forces

THE ECONOMY Appraisal of the economy • Its structure—agriculture, fisheries, forestry, fuels and power, metals and minerals, manufacturing and construction • Domestic trade • Economic policy and development • Manpower • International economic relations

TRANSPORTATION AND TELECOMMUNICATIONS Appraisal of systems • Strategic mobility • Railroads • Highways • Inland waterways • Pipelines • Ports • Merchant marine • Civil air • Airfields • The telecom system

MILITARY GEOGRAPHY Topography and climate • Military geographic regions • Strategic areas • Internal routes • Approaches: land, sea, air

ARMED FORCES The defense establishment • Joint activities • Ground forces • Naval forces • Air forces • Paramilitary

INTELLIGENCE AND SECURITY Structure of organizations concerned with internal security and foreign intelligence, their responsibilities, professional standards, and interrelationships • Mission, organization, functions, effectiveness and methods of operation of each service • Biographies of key officials

This General Survey supersedes the one dated November 1969, copies of which should be destroyed.

Country Profile:

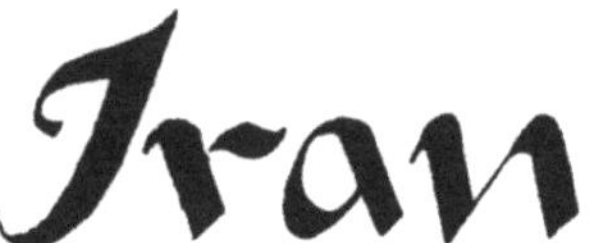

Change from the Top 1

Obstacles to Change • The Strong-Man Tradition • Monopolizing Political Power • The White Revolution • Oil and What Else? • Looking West, East, and to the Middle East • As the Shah Goes, So Goes Iran

Chronology 11

Area Brief 16

Summary Map . . . . *follows* 17

This Country Profile was prepared for the NIS by the Central Intelligence Agency. Research was substantially completed by January 1973.

SECRET

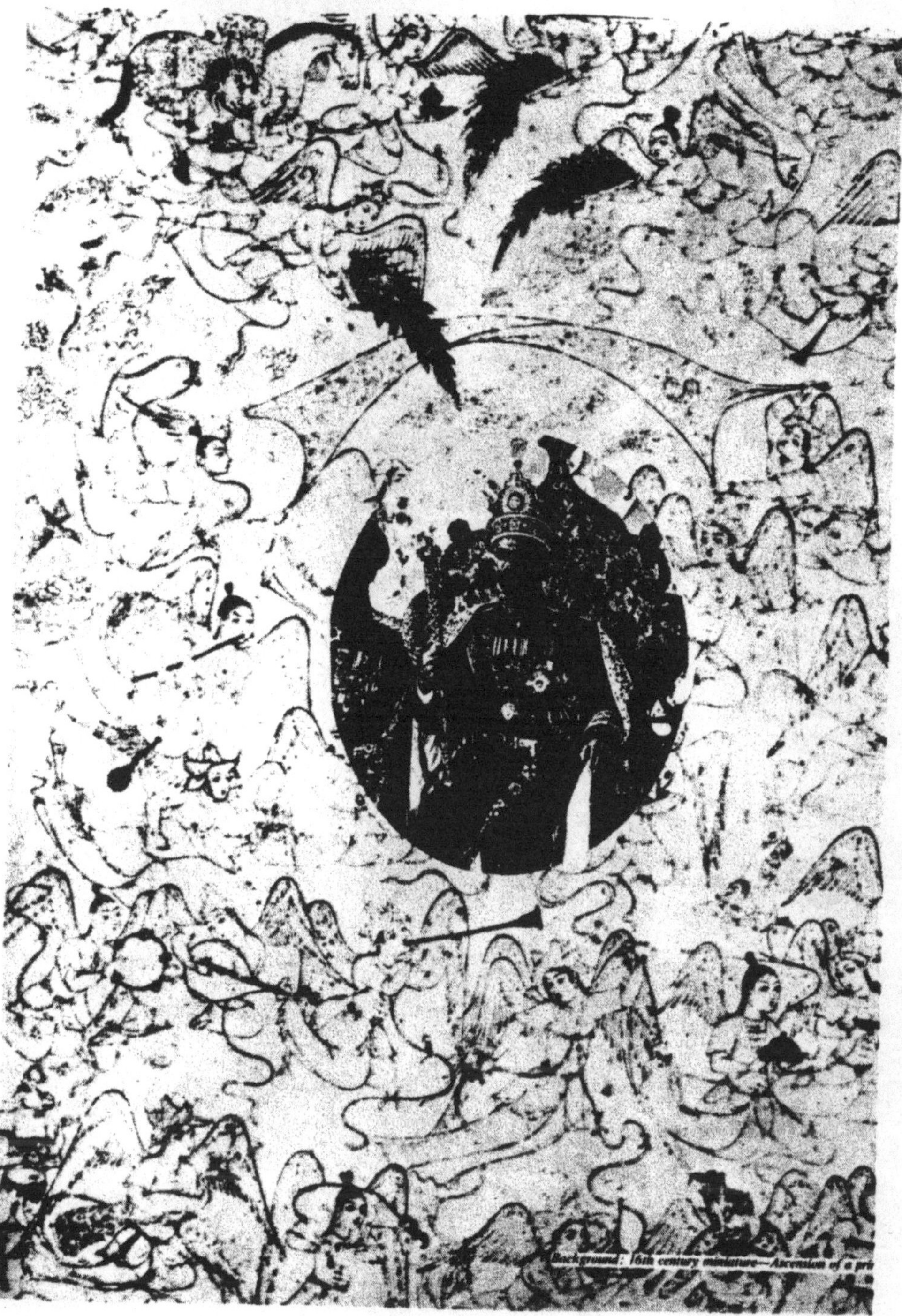
Background: 16th century miniature—Ascension of a pr

CHANGE FROM THE TOP

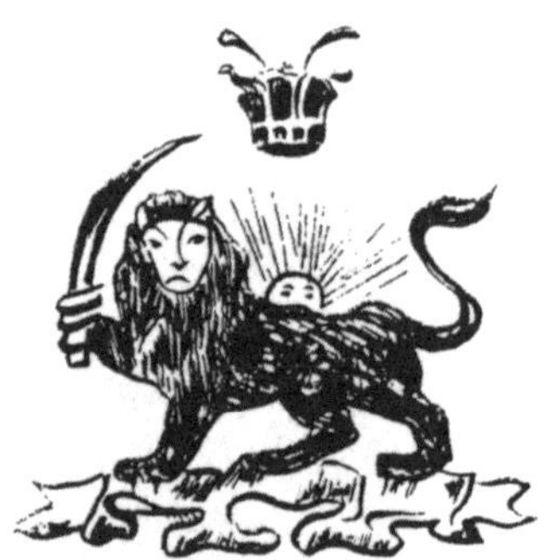

Iranian national emblem

One of the most dramatic efforts at modernization among the less developed nations is taking place in Iran. Unlike most countries in Asia and Africa, and especially the Middle East, Iran has taken steps toward modernization not as a result of revolution or the violent overthrow of the social order but rather because of the initiative of the country's ruler, Shah Mohammad Reza Pahlavi. (U OU)

Mohammad Reza has not always been the prime mover of modernization. He assumed the throne in 1941 when his father, suspected of collaborating with the Nazis, was forced to abdicate by the Soviet Union and the United Kingdom, who occupied Iran to halt the growing influence there of the Axis powers. The young Shah, only 22 years old when he suddenly succeeded to the throne, for a time lived in the shadow of his forceful and talented father, the founder of the dynasty and a dominating figure. Moreover, in the first 10 years of his reign, Mohammad Reza seemed uncertain about the role he should play in the administration of his country. Schooled in Switzerland and influenced by Western democratic traditions, the Shah tended to view his role as that of a constitutional monarch on the European model, allowing an elected government to set national goals and determine national policies. (U OU)

The turning point in the political development of the Shah toward his present style of rule and involvement came during the turbulent prime ministership of Mohammad Mosadeq, from 1951 to 1953. Mosadeq had risen to power when a simmering dispute between the Iranian Government and the British-owned oil company over increased royalties resulted in the nationalization of the company. In the face of British economic countermeasures and with the shutdown of production at the company, Iran experienced growing financial difficulties. (U OU)

Unable to check the deterioration of the economic situation, Mosadeq resorted to repressive, strong-arm tactics to silence his critics. In so doing he alienated most of his conservative supporters and, when they abandoned him, the Communist-led Tudeh Party was left as his main support. Mosadeq then sought to prop up his position by dismissing parliament. When the Shah tried to remove him, he called crowds into the street to demonstrate in his favor, deposed the Shah, and established a regency council. The Shah fled to Baghdad and later to Rome before Iranian army troops, backed by the United States, led a countercoup against Mosadeq in August 1953 and reinstated the Shah.

Apparently aware that he must assume a more forceful role in government or again risk losing his throne, the Shah began to strengthen his position. After resolving the oil dispute with Britain, he devoted the rest of the 1950's to consolidating his authority throughout the country, but especially in the military and the government bureaucracy. Having done this, he turned his efforts to the modernization of his country, proposing and initiating a wide-ranging program of social and economic reform. (LOC)

One feature of the Shah's effort to modernize Iran carries on a goal his father had: the creation of an army strong enough to maintain internal control, in a land of ancient rivalries and animosities, and to win for the country a position of influence in the Middle East. Modernization of the armed forces, however, could not be accomplished in a vacuum. A whole range of changes in the country's social and economic structure had to occur also. Providing manpower for an armed force to be trained and equipped with the weapons of modern technology would require better educated and healthier soldiers, available only if the general populace were better educated and healthier. The operation of a military system would require a sophisticated administrative apparatus. (LOC)

The Shah has also sought to consolidate his position through a program of land reform. Great wealth had enabled a number of families in Iran (probably fewer than the 1,000 usually cited) to encroach steadily upon the power of the monarchy and at times to challenge it. Wealth in Iran has traditionally been based on the ownership of land. In making land redistribution an integral part of his new program the Shah had two aims: to break the political power of the landowning elite by dividing the holdings that were their source of wealth and, at the same time, to win the gratitude of the peasants. The Shah hoped to use this gratitude to forge a political alliance with the peasants that would counter the remaining political muscle of the landed elite who, in the mid-1950's, were still in control of parliament. (LOC)

Altruism and nationalism have also had important parts in the Shah's effort to modernize his country. He has professed and evidently has a personal commitment to reform. In his coronation speech he pledged his devotion to "the constant improvement of the Iranian nation . . . to bring [it] up to the level of the most progressive and prosperous societies of the world." He has stressed the importance of changing the essentially feudal social system. Thus in *Philosophy of the Revolution*, his 1967 book on the reform program, he declared that:

> The old social order, which prevailed for centuries and in which class privileges and class distinctions are more or less considered in the nature of things, is no longer acceptable. Consequently if our nation wishes to remain in the circle of dynamic, progressive, and free nations of the world, it has no alternative but to alter the old and archaic order of society completely, and to build its future on a new order compatible with the vision and needs of the day. (LOC)

In keeping with his words, the Shah in 1952 began to sell the vast lands that he himself held as personal property. He sold them on long-term credit to the peasants working them, and the final distribution was achieved in January 1963. The Shah also pushed for the popular distribution of all public domain land in excess of that needed by government institutions, a process begun in 1958. In 1961 the Shah formed the Pahlavi Foundation, which takes revenue from business enterprises owned by the Shah and contributes it to support various social services. The Shah postponed his own coronation until 1967, 26 years after coming to the throne, maintaining that though the crown was his by inheritance, he could not wear it until he had earned the right to do so. (LOC)

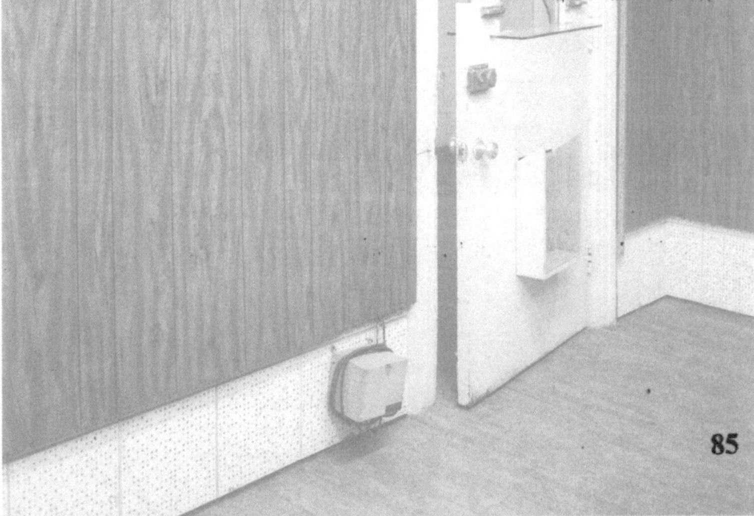

Obstacles to Change (c)

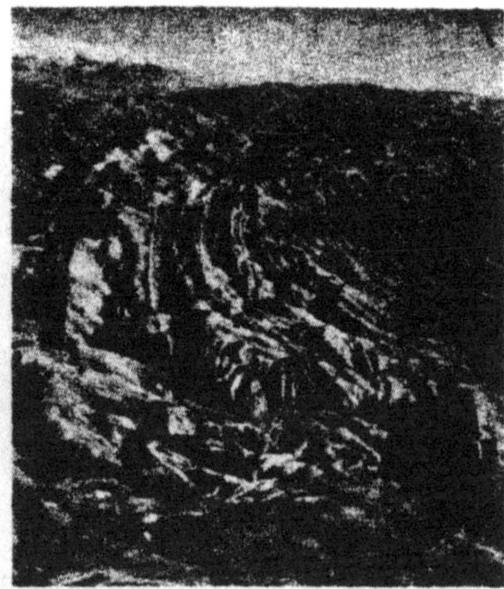

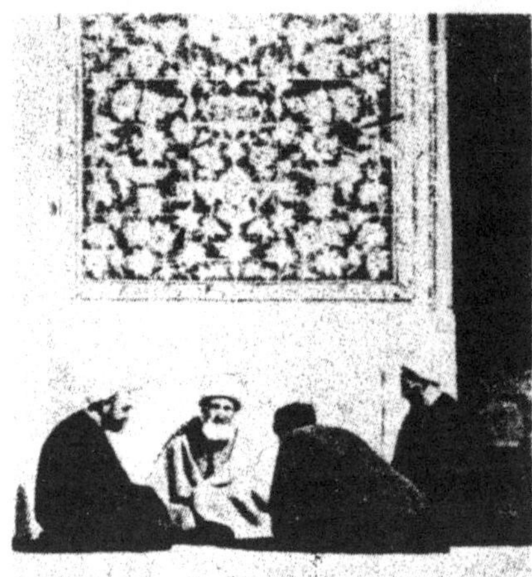

Change has not been easy to accomplish in Iran, and the Shah has had to contend with many difficulties which directly affect both the rate and the direction of modernization. Because a modern army must have mobility and a modern industrial economy must have ready access to raw materials and markets, the physical environment has provided a challenge.

Iran is a harsh land, located on a high triangular plateau surrounded on all sides by mountains. The variegated territory breaks up physically into four regions: the western and southern mountains, the northern chain and the lowlands around the Caspian Sea, the arid central plateau, and the eastern highlands. The nature of the country results in a wide range of climates. Rainfall in the area just below the Caspian Sea averages 50 inches per year, with slightly less in the western and northern mountains and the amount decreasing in areas toward the southeast and central area. The mountains cut off moisture into the central area, which is a large desert constituting nearly half the country.

The availability of water has been a major factor determining the size, location, and pattern of human settlement in Iran. Outside the northern and western areas, where most of Iran's 30.8 million people live, villages are centered around the water supply. In some places the supply is so small that people survive only by adopting nomadic habits, migrating from near desert lowlands to grasslands in the higher areas.

The roads which connect the various parts of the country must skirt the desert, wind through mountain passes, and follow valleys. In the central portion of the country there is one road that traverses the area from north to south, and only two go from east to west. The country's rail system is poorly developed, consisting only of about 3,000 miles of track which connect the Persian Gulf with the Caspian Sea and the major agricultural centers of the northeast and northwest with Tehran.[1] Air transportation is available to the larger towns, but for the average traveler the journey from the capital to provincial areas must be made by other, more difficult means.

The resulting physical isolation of various portions of the country has kept the people divided. Many of them are descendants of the invaders who swept through the land centuries ago, and they remain separated into minorities, of which the largest are the Turkic peoples, the Kurds, and the Arabs. Only about 50% of the population speaks Persian as a native

[1] For diacritics on place names see the list of names on the apron of the Summary Map and the map itself

tongue, although many more learn the language in school. The language barriers are weakening, and integration is being hastened by the increasing urbanization, but strong provincialism still characterizes the society.

Little thought was given historically to the concept of the nation-state and programs that affect the whole country. Even today only the small urban segment of Iran's people identifies to any significant degree with the nation. Most people live in villages, and their first allegiance is to their families and then to the village. They do not aid the next village, let alone the rest of the nation. The nomadic tribes have been even further removed from participation in national life. Government efforts to settle the nomads have been successful, and the 1966 census enumerated only about 500,000, probably undercounting them to some extent. Many of the settled nomads, however, retain tribal affiliation, and they see the state and government as nothing more than a central authority attempting to change their way of life.

Even without the problems of provincialism, the Shah and his government would have difficulty in garnering the support of the peasant masses for most reform programs. Conditioned by their way of life, the typically conservative farmers are prepared to accept changes that allow them to own or add to their own land, but are not willing to accept those that affect their personal affairs, such as raising the status of women. They are, for the most part, impoverished and illiterate; they are resigned to their condition, expect little from life, and are concerned primarily with survival.

In the upper levels of Iranian society, most individuals seek above all else to enhance their personal position and wealth. Self-seeking individuals are not novel, of course, but Iranian society has traditionally viewed self-aggrandizement as a singular virtue. The person who rises to the top by whatever means he can use is looked upon with admiration. Thus, when the Englishman James Morier wrote the satire *Hajji Baba of Isfahan*, in which just such an unscrupulous and ambitious schemer is the central character, the book won instant popularity with Iranians as the tale of a folk hero, rather than the intended indictment of a disagreeable personality trait. As a result of this prevailing attitude, it is hard to find individuals who are willing to join in national programs, either as administrators or as participants, unless they see personal reward in the undertaking.

In a sense, there is an aura of history that hinders acceptance of the Shah's forward-looking programs. The mere fact that Iran has existed as an entity for over 2,500 years has fostered a general resistance to rapid change unless it is forcibly imposed. For most of Iran's history this tendency has been a virtue because there was real danger that the society would lose its cultural identity as the country was successively invaded and occupied by Arabs, Turks, Mongols, Tatars, and Afghans. Now the Shah is criticized by some segments of the population for his alleged disruption of cultural continuity and for the challenges to religion that they perceive in his policies.

Particularly strong objections to the Shah's reform program have come from the religious establishment, traditionally one of the most powerful groups in the country. The importance of religious leaders and scholars in Iranian society can be understood only by realizing that Islam is not merely a religion. It is an all-encompassing religious, economic, legal, social, and intellectual system that controls all aspects of life, ranging from worship to inheritance laws to the relationship between individuals. Because of their knowledge and professed ability to interpret Islamic law, members of the religious establishment have traditionally demanded veto power over any government action they consider a contradiction of Islamic law.

For over a century the religious establishment, taking this tack, has objected to the government's entry into such areas as education, landownership patterns, and the status of women. The religious leaders fully realized that the end result of the government's course, if not checked, would be secularization—i.e., that personal affairs would be regulated by government laws and courts rather than by religious ones. Thus when the Shah's reform program was transformed into law in January 1963, the reactionary members of the religious establishment were the first publicly to oppose it. They also led the rioting that erupted in a number of urban centers in June of 1963. Although the government has subsequently restricted the influence of the establishment in Iran's cities, religious leaders in the rural areas continue to exert an important influence over the deeply religious peasants. To assuage religious opposition, the Shah stresses the close identification of the nation with Islam and is punctilious in the public performance of his religious duties.

The Strong-Man Tradition (u/ou)

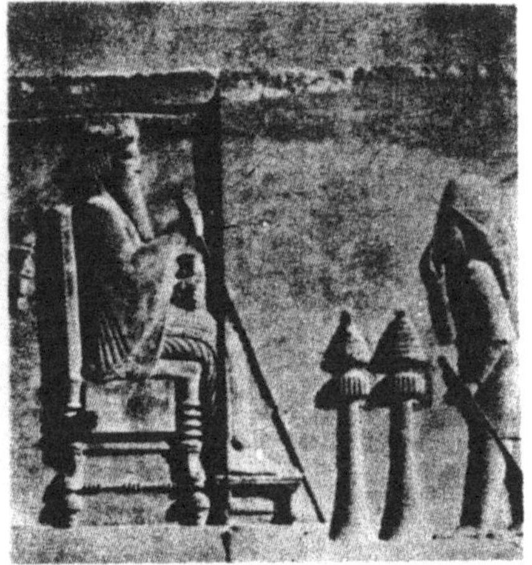

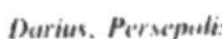

Darius, Persepolis

Carpet depicting Nadir Shah

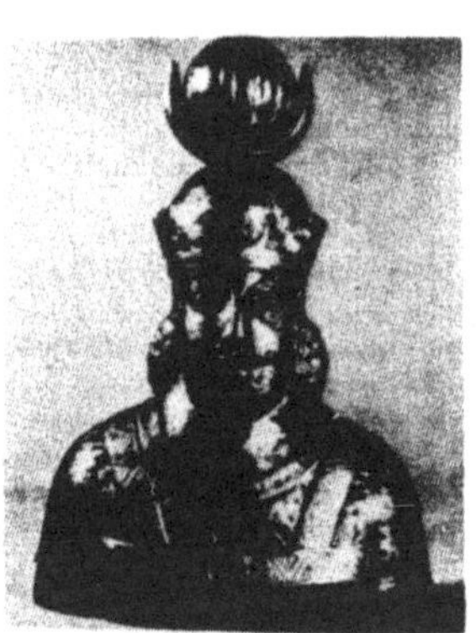

A Sassanian king

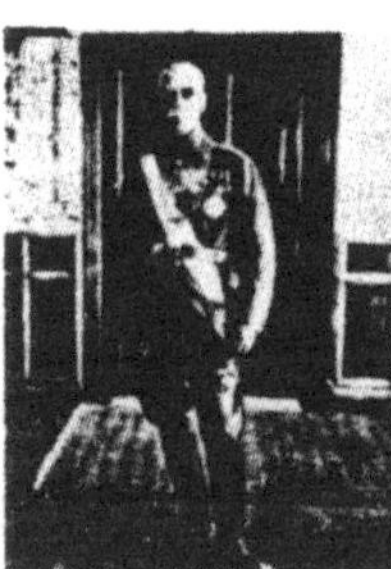

Reza Shah

Shahs crown themselves

The centrifugal nature of the forces at work in Iran is offset to a degree by another aspect of Iranian history: the tradition of a strong ruler at the head of an authoritarian government imposed on the nation by fiat. Throughout the invasions and conquests of history, the emergence of the strong leader has been a recurrent feature and probably an important factor in the preservation of the culture of the land. Iran was under foreign domination at times for centuries, but it never completely adopted the ways of its conquerors; instead, sometimes the descendants of the conquerors became themselves strong Persian rulers. The monarchy—the shah of shahs—has proved an enduring institution, an apparent embodiment for the people of a beneficent power far away and far above them. While the peasants may not be conscious of the nation-state, they are familiar with its rulers, for they know about the glorious history of their land, largely through oral or written acquaintance with the great poets of the past.

Cyrus the Great founded the first Persian[2] empire, that of the Achaemenid dynasty, in the sixth century B.C. by conquering the Medes and other kingdoms between the Mediterranean coast of Syria and the Oxus River in central Asia. His grandson Darius developed the system of dividing the empire into 20 satraps or provinces connected by an excellent network of imperial roads. After conquest by Alexander and centuries of Greek rule came the Parthian dynasty, followed by the Sassanian empire, which modern Iranians revere as second only to the Achaemenids. The Sassanids strengthened the power of the central government during their 400-year reign from the beginning of the third to the middle of the seventh century A.D. They carried out administrative reforms and surveyed the area that is now Iran. With the overthrow of the last Sassanid Shah by Arab invaders in 651, Iran entered a period of nine centuries during which it was ruled by a succession of foreign conquerors. With the rise to power of the Safavids in 1501, however, a native Iranian dynasty again held sway. Shah Abbas, the greatest of the Safavids, was an excellent administrator, and by the time of his death in 1629 the empire was again under the control of a strong central authority.

After two centuries, the Safavids were overthrown by the king of neighboring Afghanistan. The Afghans in turn were driven out by Nadir Shah, a Turkic-speaking tribesman, who has been called the last of the great Asian conquerors. A tyrannical monarch, he led a brilliantly successful invasion of India and brought back a vast treasure including the famous Peacock Throne and the Koh-i-noor diamond. The next dynasty of note was that of the Turkic Qajars, whose long period of rule was characterized by the intrusion of foreign political and economic interest, notably British and Russian.

The overthrow of the Qajars in 1921 by Reza Shah, the present monarch's father, restored a forceful ruler to the throne. Until he was forced to abdicate in 1941 by the Soviet Union and the United Kingdom, Reza Shah was able to reverse the decline that had marked the reign of the Qajars. Governing Iran with a strong hand, Reza Shah centralized the government, molded the heterogeneous military bodies in Iran into a unified army, and made the first moves to crush the power of the religious establishment.

The present Shah has endeavored to underscore his ties with his historical predecessors by stimulating his countrymen's pride in Iran's past imperial greatness—and doubtless, in the process, their acceptance of the legitimacy of the historic institution of a strong sovereign. The latest and most famous of his efforts to glamorize this tradition came in 1971 with the extravaganza at Persepolis, which celebrated the 25th centenary of the Persian monarchy and was attended by kings, presidents, and statesmen from more than 60 countries.

[2] The inscriptions left by the Achaemenid rulers refer to their clan as the Achaemenid, their tribe as the Parsa, and their nation as Arya. Iran as a geographic term derives from Arya, and it was formally declared the legal name of the country in 1935. From Parsa came the Greek word Persis, which became Persia in other European languages. The word went into Arabic, which lacks the letter *p*, as *fars*, and that is the term the Persians themselves use for their language and a province of the country.

Monopolizing Political Power (s)

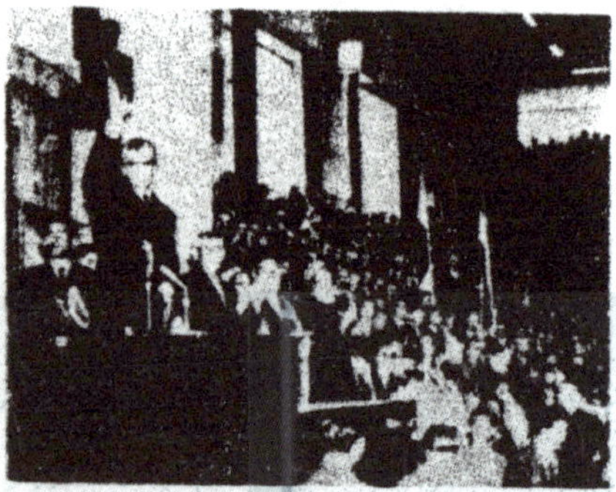

Parliamentary opposition to his program has been one problem the Shah has not had to face, for controlling the parliament as he does, he has had little difficulty in obtaining the necessary approval and funding from it. Although Iran is a constitutional monarchy with a popularly elected representative body, the Shah has been able by bribery, cajolery, and threats to make parliament little more than window dressing for his regime, giving the appearance of a democratic system. To insure that he encounters no opposition, candidates for offices in the legal political parties or for seats in the lower house of parliament, the Majlis, are carefully screened and personally approved by the Shah. That relatively small segment of society which is politically aware is perturbed by the Shah's interference in the political process, but they realize there is little they can do about the situation other than to draw public attention to it when they can. The Shah, for his part, allows a measure of freedom for them to vent their vexation verbally in order to underscore the fact that he is in complete control of the political scene. Thus a few years ago the following tongue-in-cheek interview with an imaginary parliamentary deputy appeared in a Tehran daily:

Q. What is the population of your constituency?
A. 10,000.

Q. How many votes did you get?
A. 150,000.

Q. Don't you think there is some discrepancy here?
A. I do but I was told to shut up.

Q. How many rival candidates were there? Did any of them get more votes than you?

A. There were many. All of them got more votes.

Q. Then how did you manage to get elected?
A. That is the miracle of the ballot box.

Q. What were the three most important events of your parliamentary term?

A. The first occurred when I was sitting at home wondering what kind of job to find and the radio announced that I had been elected to parliament. The second was the day that parliament raised our salaries to $1,000 a month and the third was when we were given a big housing allowance.

By monopolizing political power the Shah is, in fact, the government, and he alone determines the direction and content of national policies. To help in the actual process of governing he has surrounded himself with a coterie of cabinet officials, high-level civil servants, senior military officials, parliamentary leaders, professional men and businessmen, members of the royal family, courtiers and confidants. To serve as his political agents in the provinces there is a second level of middle and lower grade civil servants and local officials. To make certain that he continues to control the reins of power and that no one rises to challenge him, the Shah gives no individual or group the opportunity to build up an independent power base. Usually anyone suspected of harboring such ambitions is transferred from his position to an unrelated field.

Although Iranian security has suppressed opposition to the Shah's monopolization of power, there have been eruptions of violence to indicate to the world that the country indeed has dissident elements capable of rash actions. One such incident occurred in May 1972 when several bombs were set off in Tehran during a state visit by President Nixon. During the course of the year Iranian officials announced that 28 people had been executed and 109 others imprisoned for offenses ranging from attacks on police and security forces to assassinations and kidnapings.

Most of the political extremists, numbering at a minimum several hundred, are young, educated middle-class Iranians. There is no serious threat that they will take over the government. It can be said, however, that to a degree they pose a danger to the current political and economic course charted in Iran by the Shah, inasmuch as one or more of their number might mount a suicidal attempt on the Shah's life. As the Shah is architect and prime mover of the country's reforms and economic development policies, his assassination would place their continued implementation in question. The pervasive security apparatus commanded by the Shah is capable of minimizing this danger, however, as well as keeping the lid on any potential for organizing larger scale threats to public order.

7

The White Revolution (c)

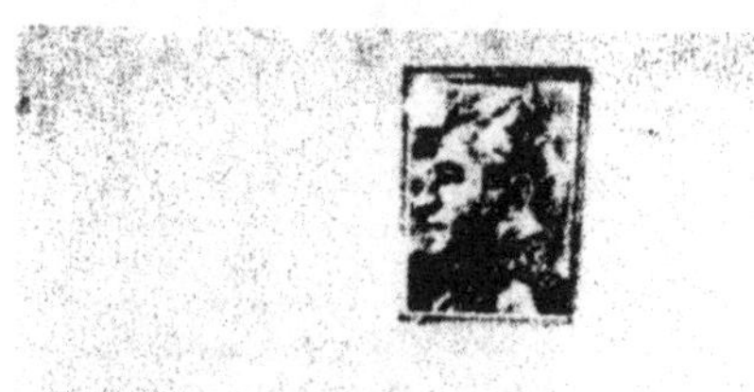

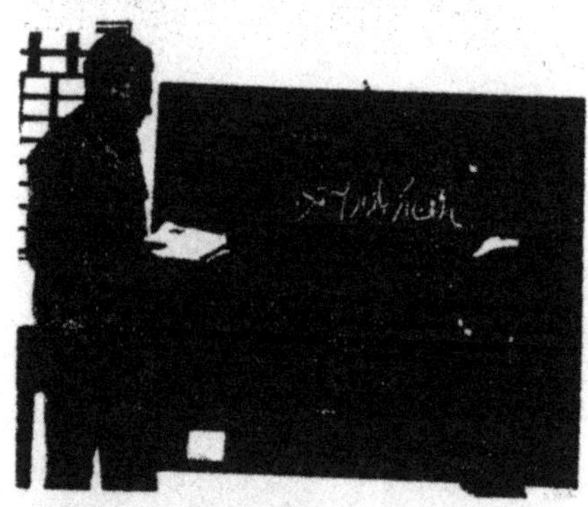

To signify that the change he would bring to Iran would be accomplished without bloodshed, the Shah has called it the White Revolution. He has also said that land reform is its core. When the revolution was formally launched in 1963, Iran's economy was primarily agrarian in nature. Although agriculture now accounts for only about 16% of the gross national product (GNP), it continues to be vital in providing the necessary food for the country's growing population and furnishing raw materials for the expanding industry. The plans of the Shah have thus called for a rise in farm productivity. Under the traditional system of land tenure, this had been given little thought. The landowning class sought profits only to invest in quick turnover areas such as urban real estate, not in new techniques for modernized farming. The peasants had no stake in the land and were in fact ready to leave their rented farms to migrate to urban centers in search of better paying jobs. By giving peasants a share of the land, it was hoped that a desire for more productive farming could be instilled in them.

Before the Land Reform Law, only 1% of the people—many of them absentee landowners—owned over half the agricultural land. The law forced them to sell all their holdings over a fixed amount and provided for the peasants to pay for the land over a 15-year period. Religious endowments, which held another 15% to 25%, were required to give their tenants 99-year leases. In 1971, the government proclaimed that the physical task of redistributing the land had been completed. Although there are no detailed statistics on the number of landowners affected by the reform, the government claims that all 52,818 villages in Iran have been involved and that there are now 1,850,000 new landowners.

The economic benefits have not, however, been as great as expected. The peasants, who under the traditional tenure system had had a bare subsistence level of existence, still need money to buy seeds and other supplies and now have the added financial burden of paying for their new land. For the government, agricultural output has not risen at the rate it had sought. The peasants also have not had the necessary capital to invest in mechanized equipment and chemical fertilizers, moves that would increase productivity. The government believes mechanized farming is feasible only if the small farmers band together in cooperatives, and it is trying to foster the formation of such cooperatives in the current phase of the land reform program. Iran does not have enough trained manpower, however, to manage the cooperatives that have already been formed. Those that have put together a staff have been plagued by administrative inefficiency and lack of capital.

The peasant's problems are not due just to a lack of money. He also is hampered by ignorance, ill health, and simply unawareness that there are different and more efficient ways of farming. Each weakness seems to reinforce the other in preventing the farmer from getting out of the rut he finds himself in. Thus the White Revolution seeks to improve literacy, health care, and community development. The government's approach has been to form task force groups known as corps, organized along military lines. The corps concept offers secondary school and university graduates an opportunity to serve rural areas and villages in their field of special training, in lieu of military service. The most successful of the various task groups has been the Literacy Corps, which operates in those villages in which no formal school has been established. Government statistics indicate that by 1971 the Literacy Corps had trained 1.1 million people to do some rudimentary reading and writing.

Soon after the Literacy Corps showed signs of being a success, the Health Corps was organized and by 1972 it was providing a large part of the health care. In the course of the program, some 6,600 corpsmen, including doctors and medical aide personnel, have been assigned to clinics and dispensaries and to some 500 mobile units throughout the countryside. According to the Shah, the number of citizens who have access to the facilities of the corps rose from 1 million in 1962 to 8 million in 1971—almost 50% of the rural population.

Plagued by the lack of qualified personnel in the fields of agronomy, veterinary medicine and civil engineering, the Development Corps has thus far been the least successful of these ventures. Other obstacles that have hampered its work include a shortage of funds and a lack of resources in the villages that are supposed to be aided. Some corpsmen have been able to fill the void in the cooperative phase of the land reform program, however, and are advising some farmers in the use of modern agricultural techniques.

A good start has been made in achieving the goals of the White Revolution. Nevertheless, some persistent problems have affected all aspects of the program. The most obvious and immediate has been the shortage of skilled personnel. Closely tied to this has been a lack of capital to finance the various projects once they have been initiated. To a degree the government, bent on pressing for more progress, has brought these problems upon itself. Rather than consolidating what has been achieved, projects often have been hastily expanded.

Oil and What Else? (s)

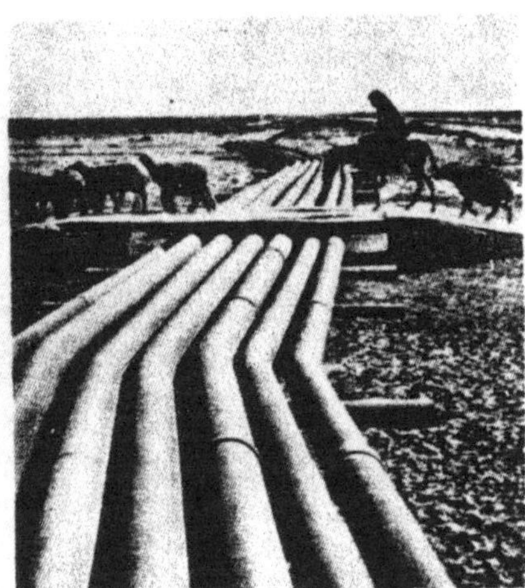

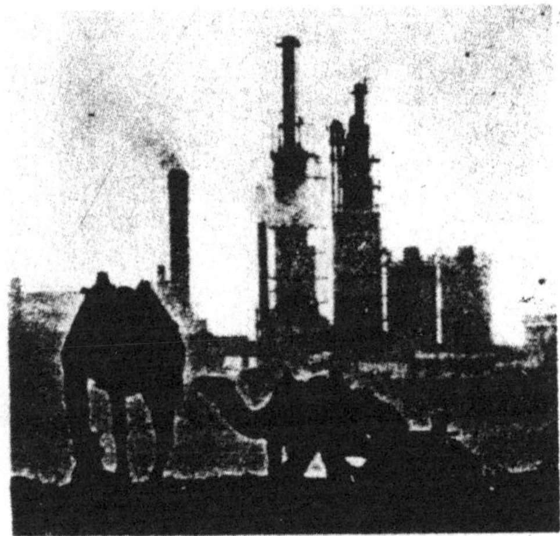

To move as rapidly as possible to industrialize Iran, the Shah has relied heavily upon petroleum. In the long run, however, he wants to build up manufacturing as a hedge against dependence on oil, for the estimated reserves will last only another 42 years even at the present rate of extraction. Because of the large sums of money needed in the initial stages of establishing a variety of modern industries, the government has had to shoulder the major burden of providing the investments needed.

The private sector of the economy consists mainly of assembly type operations that have quick, high profits. Most of these companies are not very large; according to Iranian Government statistics, 91% of Iranian plants employ 9 or fewer workers. While the government would like to see privately operated satellite industries grow up around such basic ones as steel and petrochemicals, the private sector is held back by many of the same handicaps that affect the whole modernization and reform program the government has undertaken. There is a shortage of development capital, and there simply is not enough technical and managerial personnel available to satisfy the needs of both sectors. The government has attempted to solve the first problem by making more funds available to investment banks, and has attempted to relieve the shortage of skilled personnel by setting up on-the-job training programs. The larger firms, at least, are benefiting from these moves.

Despite the fact that private manufacturing has not developed as rapidly as the government hoped, the rest of the industrial sector is burgeoning and is the fastest growing part of the economy. New developments, such as the government's plans to exploit large-scale copper deposits and newly discovered iron ore fields, are likely to fuel the continued expansion of industry in Iran.

To date, however, the Shah has been able to carry out his social and economic modernization, in addition to creating a modern army, largely because of his nation's oil boom. Iran's GNP is currently the largest in the Middle East and more than double that of either Israel or Egypt. For the past 7 years it has been growing at an average annual rate of 11%. The largest contributor to the GNP and the one thing most responsible for its continued growth is the oil industry. For the fiscal year ending in March 1972, Iran earned from oil $2.2 billion in foreign currencies; the estimate for the current fiscal year is $2.7 billion.

In the decade from 1961 to 1971, Iran's oil production rose at an average annual rate of 14.5% compared with 8% worldwide and 10% for the rest of the Middle East. Today Iran has become the world's fourth largest supplier of oil, following the United States, the U.S.S.R., and Saudi Arabia. Its output in 1971 was 1.7 billion barrels, one-tenth of the world's total. With estimated reserves of some 70 billion barrels—about 10% of the world's total—Iran's importance as an international supplier of oil is assured.

Iran's oil revenues have not risen solely because of increased output. For some time the Shah and his representatives have negotiated astutely with foreign oil companies for an increased share of the profits that the companies derive from their export and sale of Iranian petroleum. The actual amount of the profit is determined by establishing an artificial fixed price that Iran receives for the oil. Since the initial agreement was signed in 1954, both the percentage of profit and the fixed price have been raised in Iran's favor. Under the terms of new agreements that have been signed, Iran can expect to receive some $14 billion in revenue during the period 1971-72 to 1975-76. Moreover, in mid-1972 Iran entered negotiations for still further arrangements which would give Iran's national oil company increased amounts of oil for unrestricted sale in international markets. Tehran has also demanded operational control of refining facilities and increased investments from the foreign companies in refining and other operations. In a move to pressure the oil companies to agree to his proposals, the Shah on 23 January 1973 threatened to abrogate current agreements; discussions with the consortium were underway at that time. In any case, Iran stands to gain even greater amounts of oil revenue with which to finance the Shah's programs.

Iran is also developing other sources of revenue. It has the world's third largest reserve of natural gas, the volume of which is conservatively estimated to be over 200 trillion cubic feet. Its largest customer at present is the Soviet Union, which purchased nearly 200 billion cubic feet of gas valued at $37 million in 1971. Iran has a contract with Moscow to sell, in time, some 5,000 billion cubic feet. Production of liquefied gas is also undergoing negotiations; as 1973 began, new plants involving a total investment of $3 billion were under consideration with Japanese and other foreign firms.

Oil revenues alone, of course, have not been enough to pay the way for all of the Shah's ambitious reform, modernization, and industrialization programs. Foreign credits, however, will finance nearly one-fourth of Iran's projects during the current 5-year plan. The United States has been a major source of this assistance, having provided since 1946 about $1.1 billion in grants and credits for the economy and about $1.7 billion for the military. Other large developmental credits have come from West Germany, France, the United Kingdom, Italy, and Japan; and the Communist countries since 1958 have extended over $1 billion in economic credits, more than half of it from the Soviet Union, which between 1967 and 1971 also gave about $325 million in credits for military use.

population is growing at more than a million a year; from a total of 31 million in 1973, it is estimated that there will be 50 million Iranians by 1989. Much of this population will be economically unproductive. Nearly 57% of Iran's people are now under the age of 20, and the median age will fall as the population increases.

As the young are entering the labor force faster than the economy can absorb them, Iran is paradoxically confronted with the problem of growing unemployment at the time of its greatest economic surge. In the cities, where people from the countryside continue to come in search of jobs, unemployment has been estimated as high as 12% of the labor force. For some, the opportunities for social mobility are increasing as a result of the economic development, but there is no evidence that the gap between the rich and the poor has been substantially narrowed. Essentially, Iran must still be considered underdeveloped because of the low per capita GNP (about $400 a year) of its inhabitants.

Nevertheless, the country's stability and economic outlook make its overall prospects good and its future promising. Its ties with the West are strong ones. Moreover, Iran has managed to remain relatively unembroiled in the highly charged Arab-Israeli quarrels on its one side, while nurturing a rapprochement with the Soviet Union on the other.

There is no effective challenge to the Shah's position. It is secure. He dominates Iran. He has wrought dramatic and peaceful change from the top. The major weakness of what remains very much the Shah's system—political, social, and economic—is that it has not been institutionalized. It seems to depend for its essential impetus, inspiration, and direction upon him alone. Although an administrative apparatus has been erected and is engaged in the daily operation of the various projects he has launched, few decisions are made by anyone but the Shah.

His decade of modernization may have built loyalties and momentum of its own. And the Shah's age (he will turn 54 in October 1973) and good health augur well for him to have a number of years in which to further his policies and give them deeper roots. But, as is the case with systems molded so single-handedly by one who has monopolized the instruments of policy, the full test of Iran's viability must await his passing.

Chronology (u/ou)

c. 559-330 B.C.
The first Persian empire, founded by Cyrus the Great of the Achaemenid dynasty, eventually extends from what is now Afghanistan in the east to the Mediterranean and Aegean seas in the west.

c. 330 B.C.
Alexander the Great is crowned king of Persia after defeating Persian forces, marking beginning of Greek rule, which lasted until c. 250 B.C.

c. 250 B.C.
Revolt against Greek rule leads to establishment of the generally undistinguished Parthian dynasty, which lasts for almost five centuries.

226-651
The Sassanian rulers restore the Persian empire to greatness.

651
All Sassanian domains come under Arab Muslim control, marking an almost 900-year period of political decline, disunity, and disorder under the Arabs, Turks, and Mongols.

1501-1736
Under the Safavid dynasty internal order and unity are restored and Shia Islam is established as the state religion.

1795
Long dynasty of the Turkic Qajars begins.

1906
December
Fundamental Laws (i.e., national constitution) adopted by Iranian Parliament under Qajar dynasty monarch.

1907
October
Supplementary Fundamental Laws passed, also part of the constitution.

1921
February
Successful coup led against Qajar regime by Reza Khan, leader of an Iranian army Cossack brigade, and Sayyid Zia ed-Din Tabatabai, who later became Prime Minister. Treaty of Friendship signed with the Russian Soviet Federal Socialist Republic.

1925
December
Coronation of Reza Khan, henceforth known as Reza Shah Pahlavi.

1941
August
United Kingdom and the USSR invade Iran to counter threat of expanding German influence.

September
Reza Shah abdicates in favor of his son, Mohammad Reza Shah.

1946
May
USSR withdraws its troops from Iran after Iranian complaints to the UN Security Council regarding Soviet failure to withdraw occupying troops after end of World War II.

1949
February
Tudeh (Masses) Party, the Communist political party in Iran, outlawed for alleged involvement in an attempt to assassinate the Shah.

1951
March
British-owned oil industry nationalized; oil production ceases; anti-British street demonstrations threaten the national security.

April
Mohammad Mosadeq becomes Prime Minister.

1953
August
Mosadeq ousted by coup, and the Shah, who had fled to Europe after an abortive attempt against Mosadeq a few days earlier, returned to Iran.

1955
November
Iran joins Baghdad Pact, which in 1959 became the Central Treaty Organization (CENTO).

1959
March
Bilateral defense agreement signed with United States

1960
July
Iran and the United Arab Republic break diplomatic relations in a dispute over relations with Israel.

October
Male heir born to Shah, named Reza Cyrus Ali.

1961
May
Ali Amini appointed Prime Minister, initiates widespread political, economic, and social reforms at Shah's behest.

1962
September
Unilateral declaration by Iran, for the benefit of the USSR, that Iranian soil will not be used by foreign powers for missile bases.

1963
January
National referendum on Shah's six-point reform program results in overwhelming vote in favor of program.

September
Parliamentary elections held for 21st Majlis.

1964

July

Iran, Pakistan, and Turkey establish Regional Cöoperation for Development (RCD).

1965

January

Prime Minister Hasan-Ali Mansur assassinated by a member of a fanatical Muslim group; Amir Abbas Hoveyda appointed Prime Minister.

April

Attempt on Shah's life by a conscript member of Imperial Guard.

June

The Shah makes official visit to USSR.

1966

January

Iran and USSR agree that USSR will build a steel mill, develop iron and coal, and build a pipeline for Iranian natural gas to USSR.

1967

January

Soviet military credit of US$110 million extended to Iran.

August

Parliamentary elections held for 22nd Majlis.

September

Constituent assembly amends constitution to provide for succession to Shah; Empress named Regent.

October

Coronation of Mohammad Reza Shah.

November

US economic aid to Iran officially ends.

1968

January

British announce they will pull forces out of Persian Gulf at end of 1971.

1968

February

Shah cancels trip to Saudi Arabia in dispute over status of Bahrain as competition in the Persian Gulf mounts.

September

Shah visits USSR.

October

Municipal council elections held in larger cities and towns.

November

Shah visits Saudi Arabia and Kuwait.

1969

April

Iran breaks diplomatic relations with Lebanon over Lebanese refusal to extradite Lt. Gen. Timur Bahktiar, wanted for trial in Iran.

Iran abrogates 1937 agreement with Iraq over border in the Shatt al Arab because of alleged Iraqi violations.

October

Shah visits United States.

1970

July

General Timur Bahktiar assassinated in Iraq by Iranian agents.

1971

July

Parliamentary elections for 23rd Majlis.

October

Celebration of 2,500th anniversary by Persian Monarchy.

November

Iranian forces occupy Persian Gulf Islands of Abu Musa and the Tunbs.

1972

October

Shah and Empress visit USSR.

Area Brief*

LAND:

636,000 sq. mi.; 14% agricultural, 11% forested, 16% cultivable with adequate irrigation, 51% desert, waste, or urban, 8% migratory grazing and other

Land boundaries: 3,305 mi.

WATER:

Limits of territorial waters (claimed): 12 n. mi.

Coastline: 1,560 mi. (includes off-lying islands)

PEOPLE:

Population: 30,805,000 estimated 1 January 1973; density, 48 persons per square mile; 43% urban, 57% rural

Ethnic composition: Over 50% of the population can be described as Persian, while 22% are also ethnic Iranians, including the Kurds (6%); Turkic peoples comprise 22%, Arabs, 5%, and others 1%

Religion: 90% nominally Shia Muslim; 8% Sunni Muslim; 2% Christian, Jewish, Zoroastrian, and other

Languages: Persian (Farsi), Turki, Kurdish, Arabic

Literacy: About 33% of population age 10 and over (1972 estimate)

Labor force: 8.3 million, including: 37% in agriculture, 27% in industry, 25% in services

Health, nutrition, and sanitation levels: Low

GOVERNMENT:

Legal name: Empire of Iran

Type: Constitutional monarchy controlled by the Shah

Capital: Tehran

Political subdivisions: 14 provinces and nine independent governorates, subdivided into districts, subdistricts, counties, and villages; major provincial rearrangement planned (C)

Legal system: Based largely on French law, with elements drawn from other continental systems and Islamic law, constitution adopted 1906; Supreme Court operates merely as highest appellate court; legal education at University of Tehran; has not accepted compulsory ICJ jurisdiction

Branches: Executive power rests in Shah, Prime Minister, appointed by Shah, must be approved by lower house (Majlis); while Cabinet theoretically responsibility of Prime Minister, Shah usually exerts strong influence over its selection; bicameral legislature; Majlis has 268 seats (with 2 vacant for Islands of the Persian Gulf) elected to 4-year terms; half of Senate members appointed by Shah, other half elected; no provision for judicial review of constitutionality of legislative acts

Government leader: Shah Mohammad Reza Pahlavi

Suffrage: Universal over age 20

Elections: Majlis every 4 years; Senate every 4 years; latest national election: July 1971; local in October 1972

Political parties: Iran Novin Party; Mardom (Peoples) Party; Iranian Party

Voting strength: Majlis—Iran Novin Party, 230 seats; Mardom Party, 37 seats; Iranian Party, 1 seat; Senate—Iran Novin Party, 28 seats, Mardom Party, 2 seats; plus 30 seats appointed by Shah; all candidates government approved

Communists: 500-4,500 (hard-core, est.); some sympathizers among workers and intellectuals; mostly pro-U.S.S.R. but pro-Chinese faction developing (S)

Other political or pressure groups: Tudeh Party (Communist, illegal); Confederation of Iranian Students (illegal)

Member of: CENTO, Colombo Plan, FAO, IAEA, IBRD, ICAO, IDA, IFC, IHB, ILO, IMCO, IMF, ITU, OPEC, RCD, U.N., UNESCO, UPU, WHO, WMO

ECONOMY:

GNP: $12 billion (Iranian FY71-72 est.), $400 per capita; real GNP growth, Iranian FY71-72, 14% est.

Agriculture: Wheat, barley, rice, sugar beets, cotton, dates, raisins, tea, tobacco, sheep, and goats

Major industries: Crude oil production (1,655 million barrels in 1971) and refining, textiles, cement and other building materials, food processing (particularly sugar refining and vegetable oil production), metal fabricating (C)

Electric power: 2,800,000 kw. capacity (1972); 8.3 billion kw.-hr. produced (1971)

Exports: $356 million (nonoil, Iranian FY71-72): 89% petroleum; also carpets, raw cotton, fruits, nuts, hide and leather items, ores; Communist countries (primarily U.S.S.R.) took about 31% of nonoil exports

Imports: $1,872 (Iranian FY71-72); machinery, iron and steel products, chemicals, pharmaceuticals, electrical equipment; Communist countries supplied about 13% of commodity imports

Major trade partners: Exports—West Germany, U.S., Japan, U.S.S.R. and other Communist countries; imports—U.S., West Germany, U.K., Japan, U.S.S.R.

Aid:

Economic—$1,029 million in economic credits extended by Communist countries 1958 to 1971 ($601 million from U.S.S.R.); total U.S. aid (FY46-71), $1,131 million; AID program which reached $603.9 million (FY46-66), terminated in November 1967; assistance from international organizations amounted to $682.1 million (FY49-71)

*The material in this brief is drawn from the January 1973 issue of the semiannual NIS Basic Intelligence Factbook; it is Unclassified/Official Use Only unless otherwise indicated.

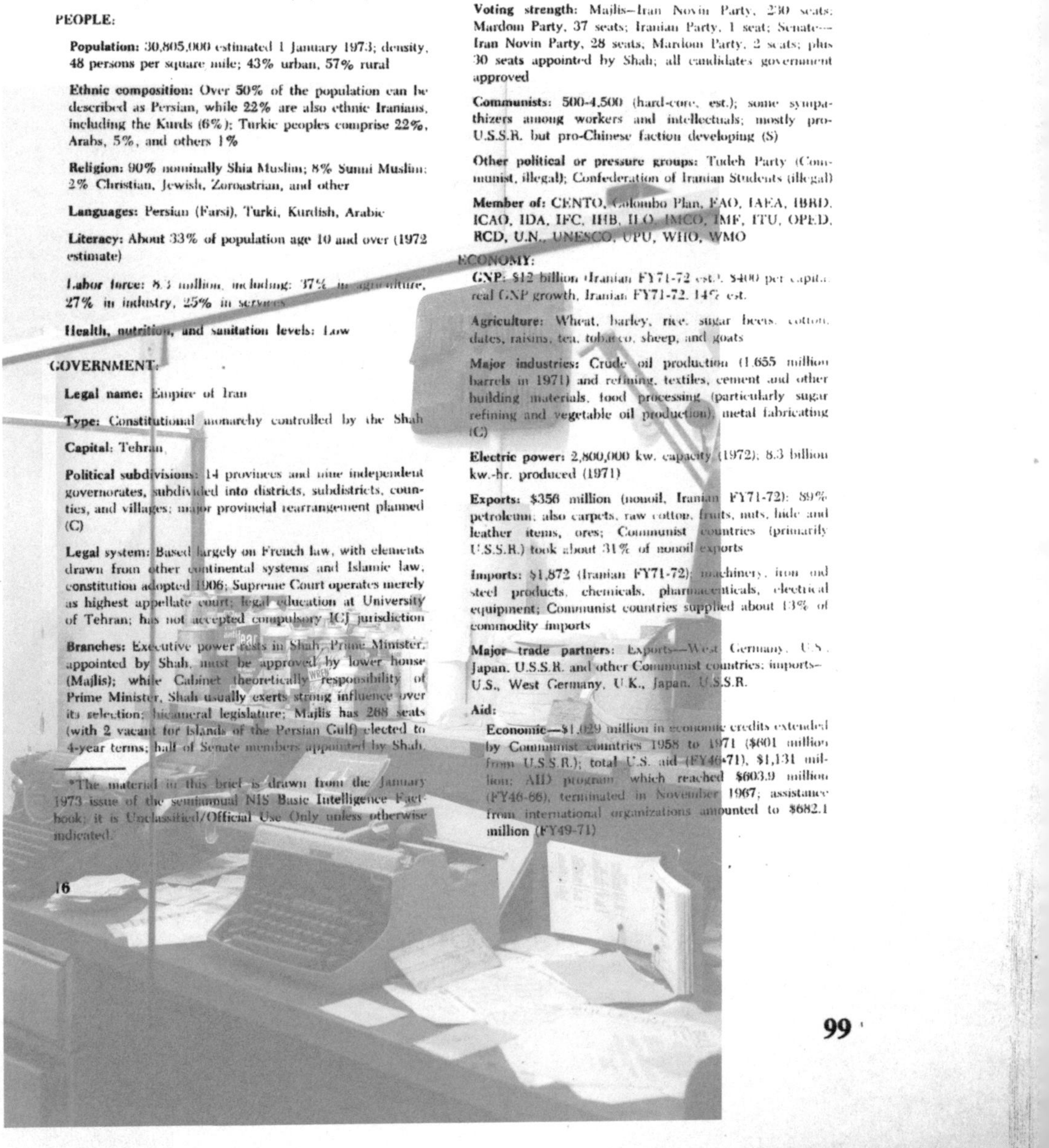

ECONOMY: (Continued)

Aid (Continued)

Military—$325 million in aid extended by U.S.S.R. (1967-71); total U.S. aid 1946-72 amounted to $1,700 million (S)

Monetary conversion rate: 75.75 rials = US$1 (1972)

Fiscal year: 21 March—20 March

COMMUNICATIONS:

Railroads: 2,875 miles 4'8½" gage, 57 miles 5'6" gage

Highways: 26,500 miles; 7,100 miles paved, 12,900 miles gravel and crushed stone, 6,500 miles improved earth

Inland waterways: 565 miles, not including Caspian Sea, Shatt al Arab, and Lake Urmia

Pipelines: Crude oil, 3,300 miles; refined products, 2,785 miles; natural gas, 1,760 miles

Ports: 7 major, 6 minor

Merchant marine: 15 ships (1,000 GRT or over) totaling 150,399 GRT, or 219,075 DWT; includes 11 cargo, 4 tanker

Civil air: 18 major transport aircraft

Airfields: 148 usable; 6 have runways over 12,000 ft.; 15 have runways 8,000-11,999 ft.; 49 have runways 4,000-7,999 ft.; 49 fields have permanent-surfaced runways; 82 airfield sites

Telecommunications: Advanced system of high-capacity radio-relay links, open-wire lines, cables, and tropospheric links; principal center Tehran; secondary centers, Esfahan, Mashhad, and Tabriz; 307,500 telephones (1971); 3 million radio receivers (1970) and 700,000 TV receivers (1972); 24 AM, 1 FM, and 18 TV stations (January 1973); satellite ground station

DEFENSE FORCES:

Military manpower: Males 15-49, 7,255,000; about 59% fit for military service; about 317,000 reach military age (21) annually

Personnel: 298,300, as follows: ground forces, 165,000; navy, 13,000 (including 3,000 naval infantry); air force, 50,000 (461 pilots); gendarmerie, 70,300 (S)

Major ground units: 5 divisions (2 infantry, 3 armored), 1 army aviation command, 4 separate brigades (2 infantry, 1 airborne infantry, 1 special forces) (S)

Ships: 1 guided-missile destroyer, 2 guided-missile destroyer escorts, 12 patrol craft, 6 mine warfare, 4 amphibious craft, 21 service craft, 2 yachts; 10 hovercraft (S)

Aircraft: 508, including 320 (212 jet) in air force; 52 nonjet in gendarmerie, 117 nonjet in ground forces, and 19 nonjet in navy (S)

Supply: Produces small arms and ammunition to 105-mm; bulk of equipment from U.S., some antitank missiles from France, some surface-to-air missiles and naval craft from U.K., helicopters from Italy; since 1967 has received significant quantities of armored vehicles, artillery (including self-propelled AA guns), and transport vehicles from the U.S.S.R.; recently procured AA guns and associated radar from Switzerland, and tanks from U.K. (S)

Military budget: For fiscal year ending 20 March 1973, estimated at $1,471.2 million; about 20.3% of total budget

BRIEFING FOR TDY PERSONNEL

Slide #1
ARMISH-MAAG
Logo

(U) GOOD (MORNING) (AFTERNOON) GENTLEMEN. I AM __________ SINCE YOUR STAY IN IRAN WILL BE BRIEF, WE HAVE DESIGNED A BRIEFING WHICH WILL GIVE YOU A BROAD OVERVIEW OF THE SITUATION HERE, WITH THE HOPE THAT IT WILL ASSIST YOU IN PERFORMING YOUR MISSION.

Slide #2
BRIEFING OUTLINE

(C) INTRODUCTION: THIS RESUME BEGINS WITH A CONSIDERATION OF U.S. NATIONAL INTERESTS AT STAKE IN IRAN. IT CONTINUES WITH A BIT OF STAGE SETTING BY WEIGHING THE IMPLICATIONS OF IRAN'S GEOGRAPHIC LOCATION IN THE MIDDLE EAST AND BY EXAMINING THE PRINCIPAL PHYSICAL FEATURES OF THE COUNTRY, SINCE THEY HELP TO EXPLAIN IRAN'S DEFENSE REQUIREMENTS AND DEFENSE POSTURE. WE WILL ALSO TAKE A LOOK AT IRAN'S SOCIAL AND INDUSTRIAL DEVELOPMENT, ITS PEOPLE AND THEIR RELIGION, AND COMMENT BRIEFLY ON A FEW IMPORTANT CULTURAL FACTORS. THIS SERVES AS A PRELUDE TO A STATEMENT OF THE EXTERNAL THREAT AS IT IS PERCEIVED BY IRAN AND THE STRATEGY THAT THE SHAH HAS DEVISED TO COUNTERACT THIS THREAT. AN ANALYSIS OF IRAN'S DEFENSE DECISION-MAKING APPARATUS IS THEN INCLUDED AND FOLLOWED BY A SUMMARY OF THE STRENGTH, DISPOSITION, AND EXPANSION PLANS OF THE THREE MILITARY SERVICES. NEXT, THE REVIEW OUTLINES THE U.S. SECURITY ASSISTANCE PROGRAM OPERATING IN SUPPORT OF THE IRANIAN FORCES AND COVERS IN DETAIL ITS TWO PRINCIPAL COMPONENTS: ARMISH-MAAG, THE MILITARY ASSISTANCE ADVISORY GROUP, AND TAFT, THE TECHNICAL ASSISTANCE FIELD TEAMS.

CONFIDENTIAL

Slide #40
TRIBAL COSTUMES

(U) THE MAJOR TRIBAL GROUPS ARE THE KURDS, THE BAKHTIARIS, THE GASHGHAI, THE BALUCHIS AND THE TURKOMANS. THERE ARE ALSO NUMEROUS SMALLER TRIBES SUCH AS THE LURDS, SHAHSAVANS, AFSHARS AND OTHER MINOR TRIBAL ELEMENTS. OF THOSE MENTIONED, THE KURDS AND THE BAKHTIARIS ARE THE LARGEST, NUMBERING ABOUT TWO MILLION AND ONE MILLION RESPECTIVELY. EXCEPT FOR AN ABORTIVE RUSSIAN ATTEMPT AFTER WORLD WAR II, THE KURDS HAVE NEVER BEEN A NATION, BUT HAVE BEEN A DISTINCT ETHNIC GROUP FOR ABOUT 3,000 YEARS. THE IRANIAN KURDS LIVE IN THE NORTHWESTERN BORDER AREA.

Slide #41
PERSIAN CULTURE

(U) JUST AS THE RELIGION OF IRAN IS DIFFERENT FROM OUR OWN, SO IS THEIR CULTURE. WHILE SOME OF ITS ASPECTS CAN BE PERPLEXING, THERE ARE OTHER FACETS WHICH ARE MOST ENJOYABLE. WITHOUT GOING INTO A COMPREHENSIVE DISCUSSION, LET ME JUST TOUCH ON A FEW POINTS.

(U) MOST IRANIANS LOOK UPON WESTERNERS AS BEING COLD-BLOODED AND UNRESPONSIVE, CARING MORE ABOUT PRIVACY, ACCURACY AND RULES THAN ABOUT PERSONAL LOYALTY, WHILE SEEING THEMSELVES AS WARM, GENEROUS AND KIND.

(U) YET, PROBABLY ONE OF THE THINGS WHICH "BUGS" AMERICANS MOST IS THIS WALLED SOCIETY WHICH IS DIFFICULT TO PENETRATE. THE IRANIAN FAMILY IS THE CENTER OF THIS SOCIETY. BEHIND THESE WALLS THEY LIVE IN LITTLE OASES OF SAFETY SURROUNDED BY THEIR RELATIVES AND FRIENDS, THOSE THEY KNOW THEY CAN TRUST, PEOPLE WHO ARE "KHODI"---OR "ONE OF US."

10

CONFIDENTIAL

Slide #42
PERSONAL DIGNITY

(U) JUST AS IRANIANS VALUE THEIR FAMILY AND FRIENDS, IRANIANS ALSO VALUE THEIR SELF-RESPECT. THOSE WHO HAVE SERVED IN THE ORIENT KNOW HOW IMPORTANT "FACE" IS. IRANIANS CALL THIS "AB-E-RU,"---"THE WATER OF HIS FACE." IF YOU GIVE SOMEONE A DRESSING DOWN IN FRONT OF OTHERS, YOUR WORDS CAN HURT HIM MORE THAN IF YOU HIT HIM. INSULTS REALLY HURT HERE. AND SOME OF THE THINGS YOU MIGHT CALL HIM CASUALLY, EVEN IN ENGLISH, REALLY HIT HOME. YOU JUST HAVE NO WAY OF KNOWING HOW DEEPLY INFURIATING OR HURTFUL A PARTICULAR PHRASE MAY BE.

(U) AND BY THE WAY, GESTURES HAVE A WHOLE NEW WORLD OF MEANING HERE. EVEN THE HARMLESS "THUMBS UP" SIGN HAS A VERY INSULTING CONNOTATION. IRANIANS TALK WITH THEIR HANDS. LEARN THE LANGUAGE BEFORE YOU TRY TO TALK WITH YOURS.

(U) YOU CAN INSULT PEOPLE IN OTHER WAYS BESIDES CRITICISM. PEOPLE OF LOWER STATUS WILL GREET YOU FIRST, BUT YOU SHOULD ALWAYS SAY "SALAM" BACK. IN IRAN, IT'S POLITE TO RISE WHEN AN EQUAL OR SOMEONE OF HIGHER STATUS ENTERS THE ROOM. SOME WOMEN WILL ALSO RISE FOR OTHER WOMEN OR FOR IMPORTANT OLDER MEN. AND WHEN A GUEST IS LEAVING YOUR HOUSE, ALWAYS SEE HIM OUT TO THE STREET OR AT LEAST ACCOMPANY HIM PART WAY. IF YOU DON'T, IT WILL SEEM YOU LOOK DOWN ON HIM.

Slide #43
NO WORD FOR NO

(U) THE IRANIAN CONCERN FOR SELF-RESPECT LEADS TO ANOTHER CHARACTERISTIC WHICH WESTERNERS FIND PUZZLING. DID YOU KNOW

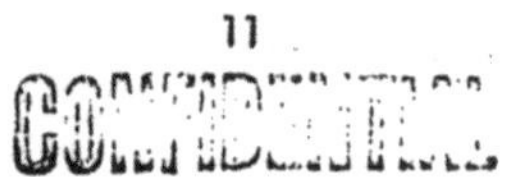

بسم الله الرحمن الرحيم

❊ مرکز نشر اسناد لانه جاسوسی

تقاطع خیابان آیت‌ا... طالقانی و دکتر مفتح ــ لانه جاسوسی

صندوق پستی ۳۴۸۹ ــ ۱۵۸۱۵ تلفن ۸۲۴۰۰۵

اسناد لانه جاسوسی ۶۰

دخالتهای آمریکا در ایران (۹)

دانشجویان مسلمان پیرو خط امام

اسناد لانه جاسوسی ۶۰

فعالیتهای آمریکا در ایران (۹)

SECRET

NOFORN

COVER SHEET

BASIC SECURITY REQUIREMENTS ARE CONTAINED IN AR 380-5

THE UNAUTHORIZED DISCLOSURE OF THE INFORMATION CONTAINED IN THE ATTACHED DOCUMENT(S) COULD RESULT IN SERIOUS DAMAGE TO THE UNITED STATES

RESPONSIBILITY OF PERSONS HANDLING THE ATTACHED DOCUMENT(S)

1. Exercise the necessary safeguards to prevent unauthorized disclosure by never leaving the document(s) unattended except when properly secured in a locked safe.
2. Transfer document(s) only to persons who need to know and who possess the required security clearance.
3. Obtain receipt whenever relinquishing control of the document(s).

STORAGE

Store as prescribed in AR 380-5.

REPRODUCTION

1. SECRET material originating in an agency outside the Department of Defense will not be reproduced, copied, or extracted without the consent of the originating agency.
2. The reproduction, extraction or copying of SECRET material originating within the Department of Defense is authorized except when the originator or higher authority has specifically denied this authority.
3. Reproduction of Joint Chiefs of Staff papers is not authorized.

DISPOSITION

This cover sheet should be removed when document(s) are filed in a permanent file, declassified, destroyed, or mailed.

(This cover sheet is unclassified when separated from classified documents)

SECRET

PREVIOUS EDITIONS OF THIS LABEL ARE OBSOLETE

DA LABEL 23
1 FEB 77

دانشجویان مسلمان پیرو خط امام

* 444 days or 1 year, 2 months, 2 weeks and 2 days
November 4, 1979 – January 20, 1981

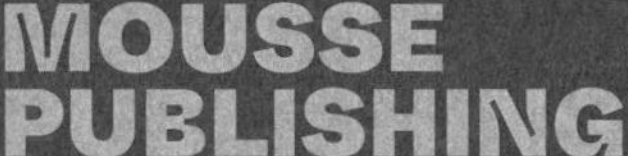

GIOVANNA SILVA
KAKOL
A LOCK OF PHOTOGRAPHS

NARRATIVES – RELAZIONI N.7

To Cesare,
who was waiting for me behind the buses

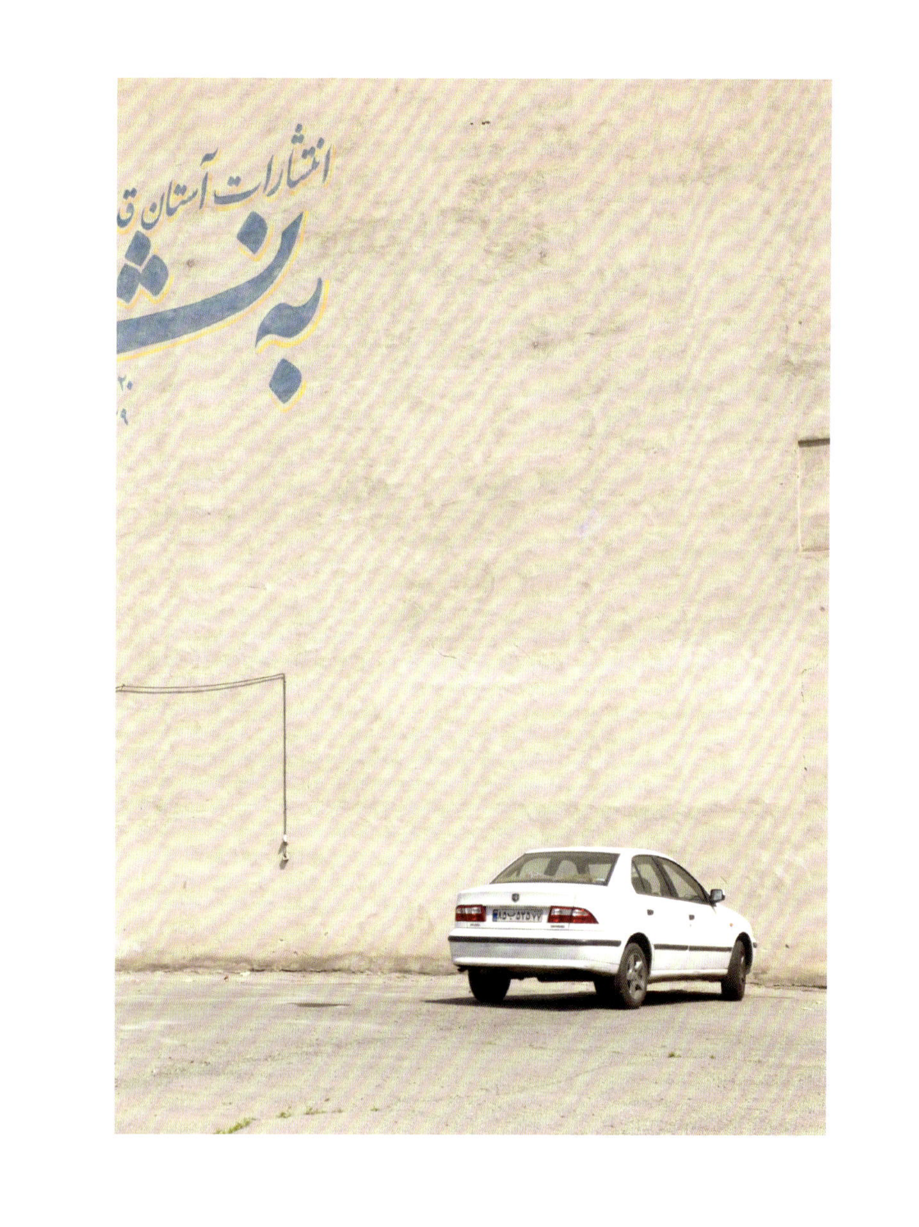
انتشارات آستان

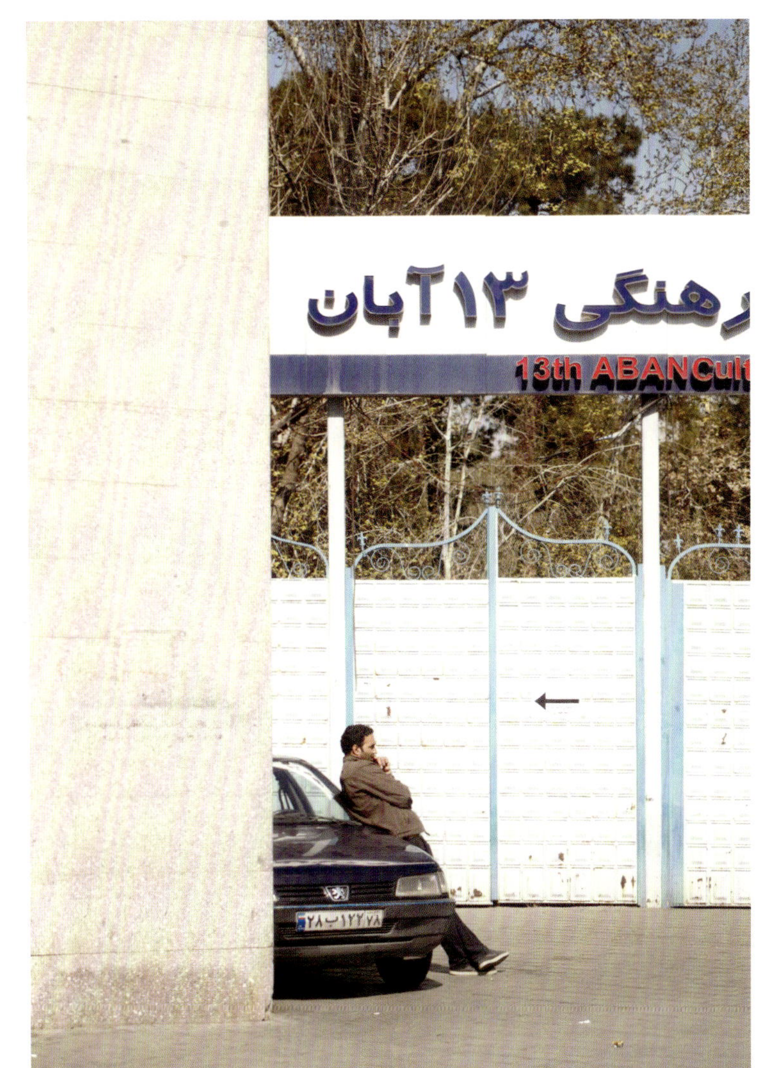
رهنگی ۱۳ آبان
13th ABANCult

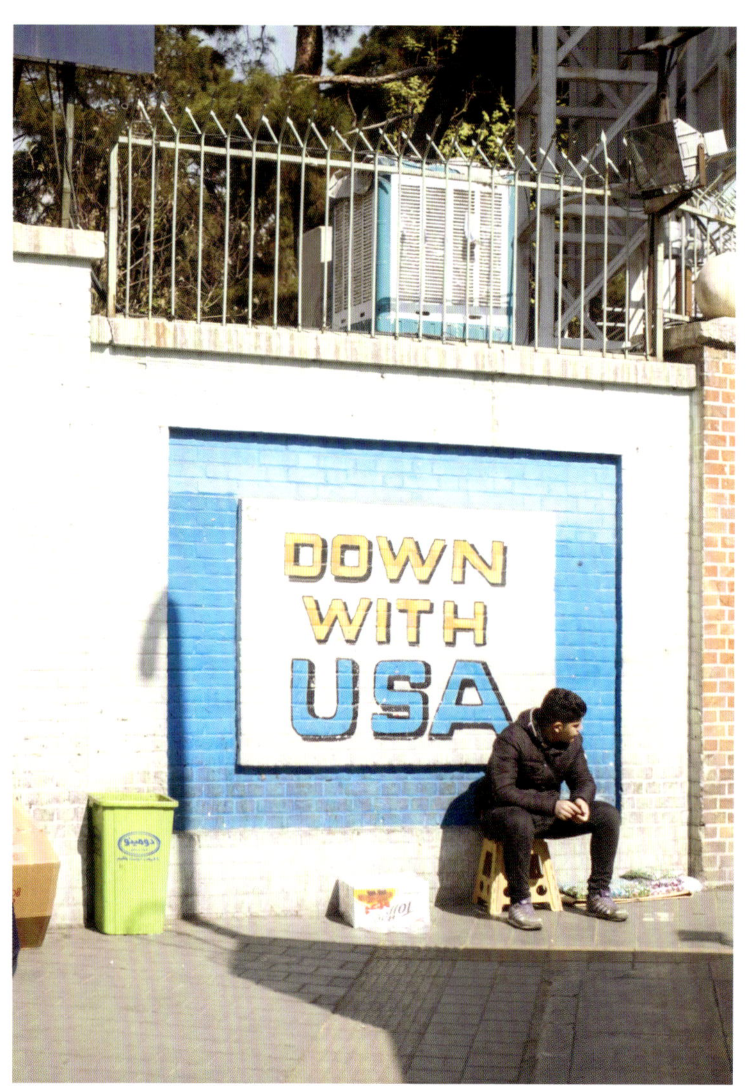
DOWN
WITH
USA

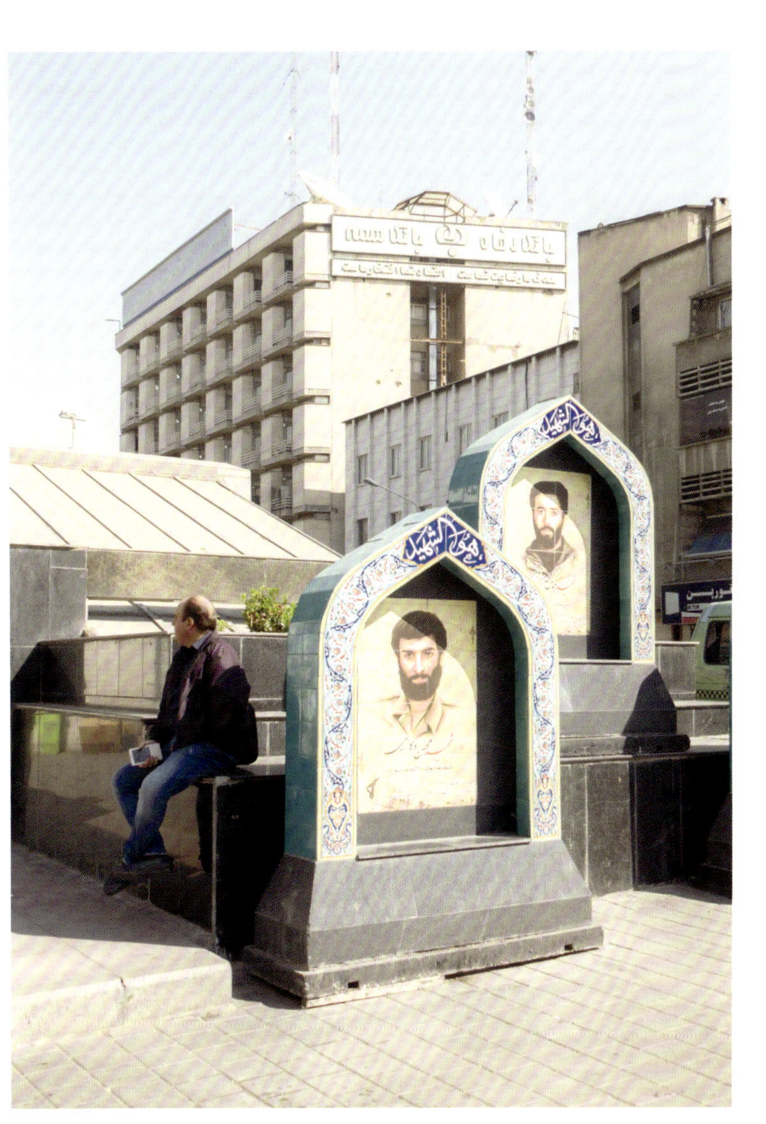
هو الشهید
هو الشهید

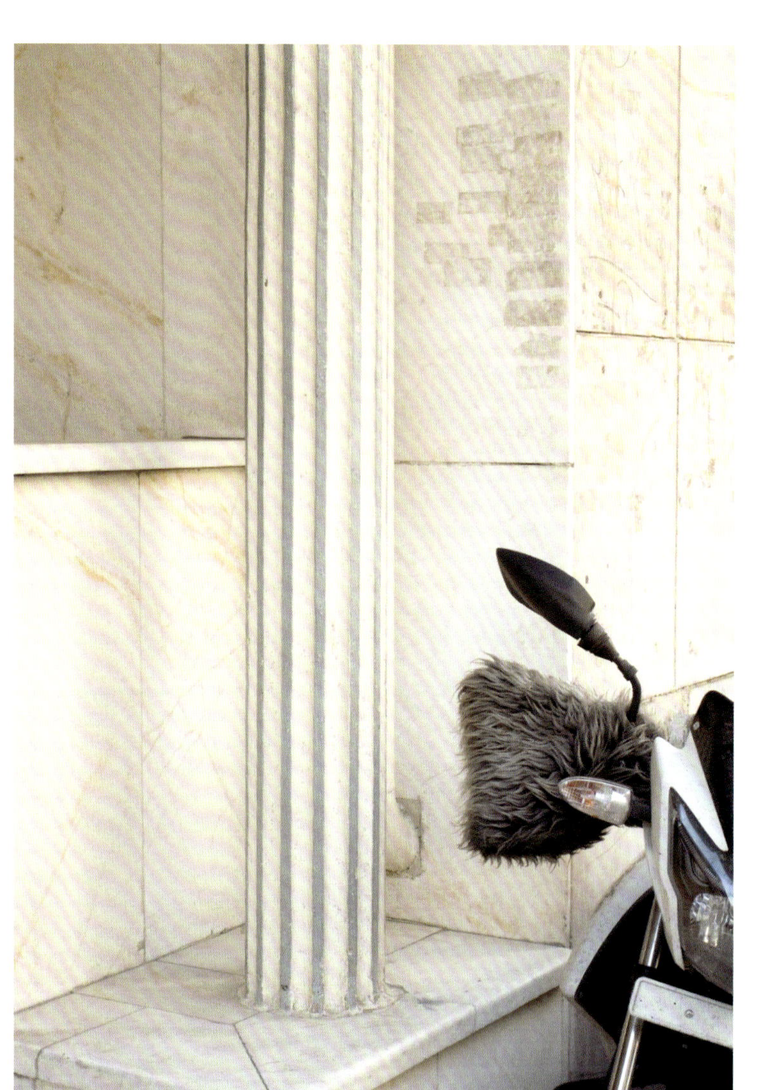

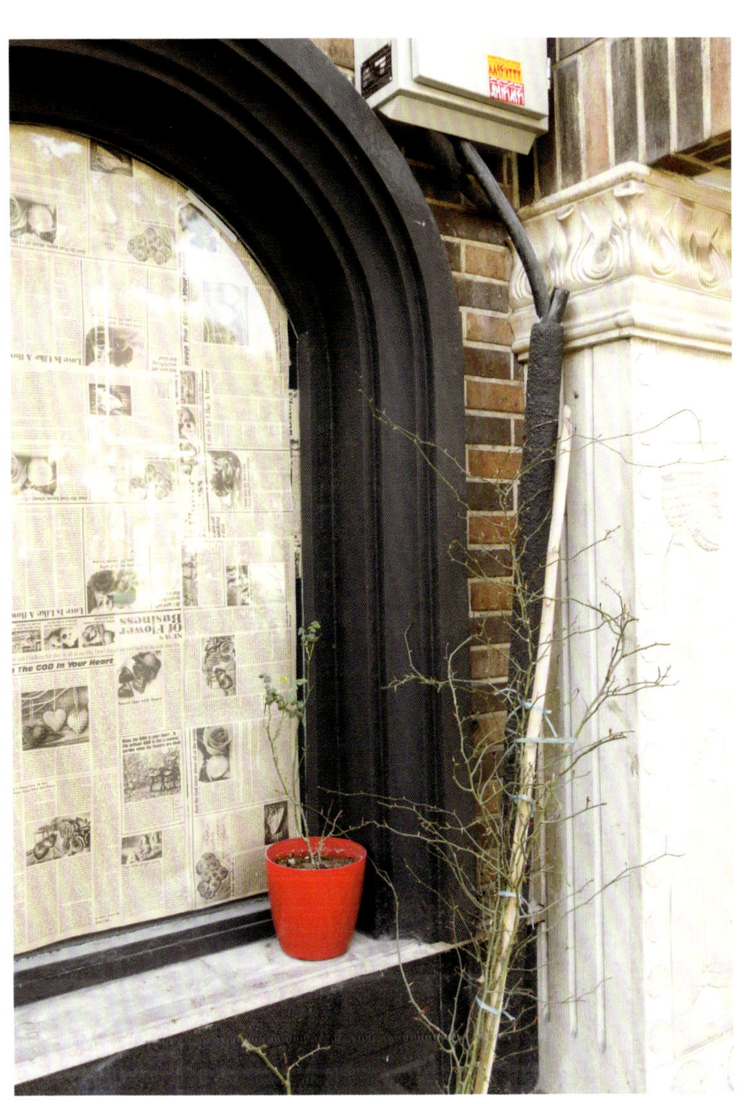
The GOD In Your Heart

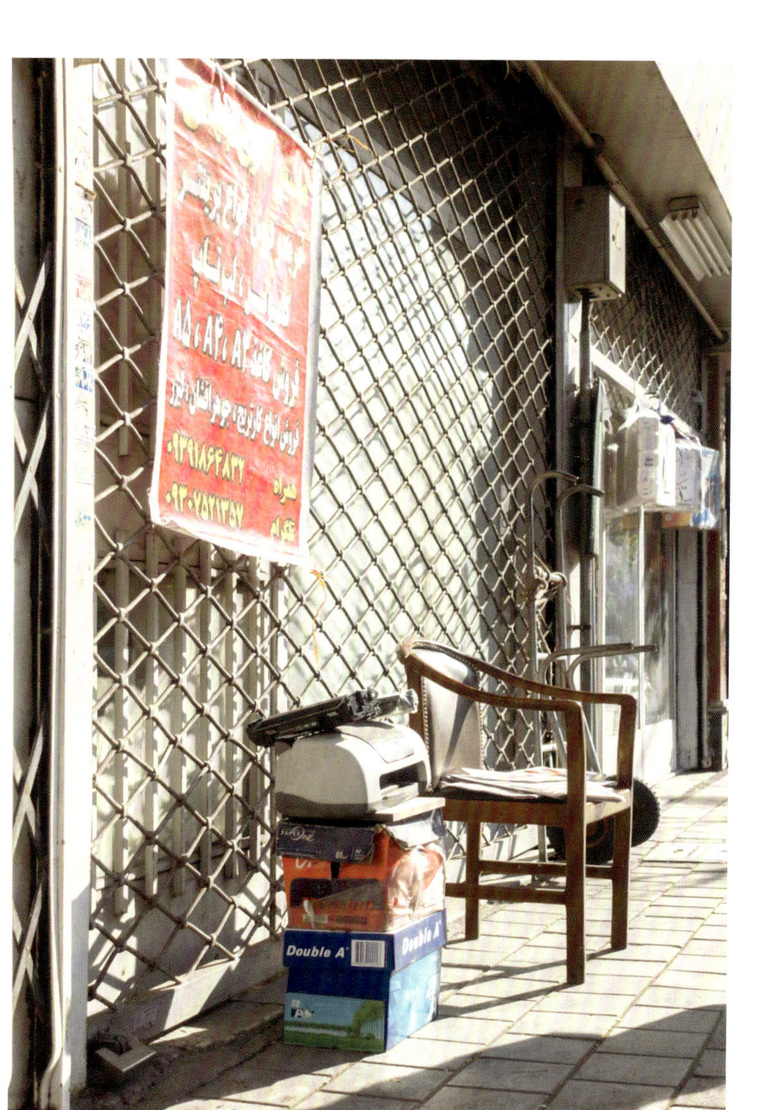
فروش کاغذ A۳ ، A۴ ، A۵
فروش انواع کارتریج، جوهر افشان و لیزر
همراه ۰۹۳۹۱۸۶۴۸۳۲
۰۹۳۰۷۵۲۱۳۵۷
Double A
Double A

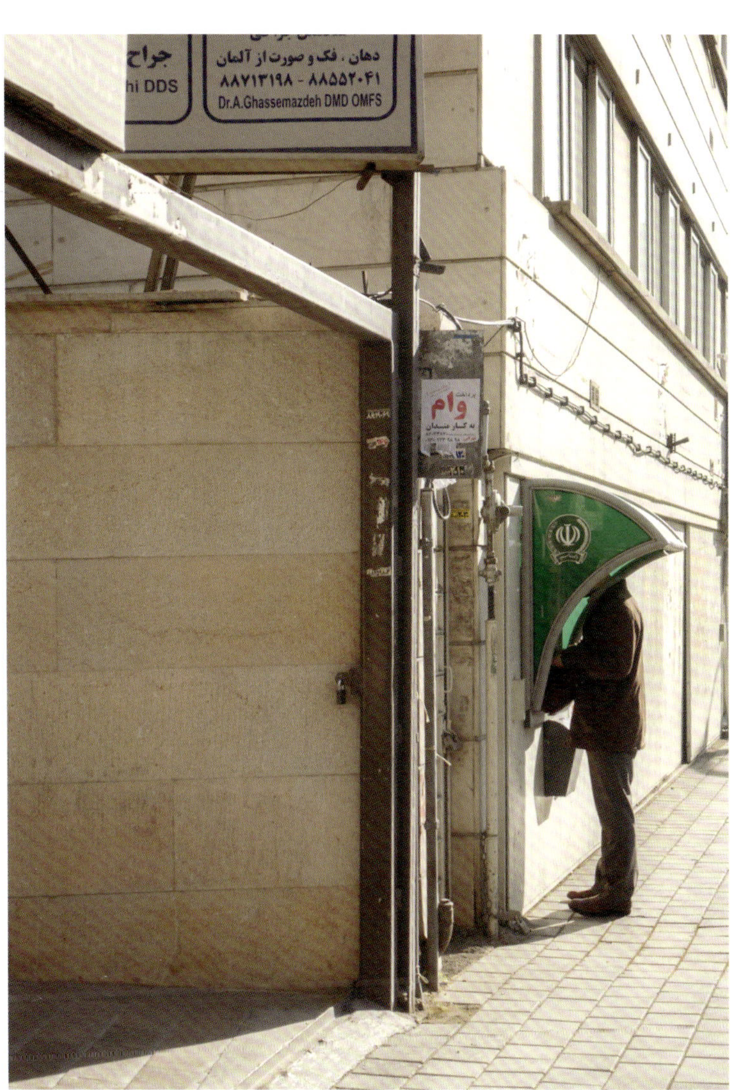
جراح
hi DDS
دهان ، فک و صورت از آلمان
۸۸۷۱۳۱۹۸ - ۸۸۵۵۲۰۴۱
Dr.A.Ghassemazdeh DMD OMFS
پرداخت
وام
به کارمندان

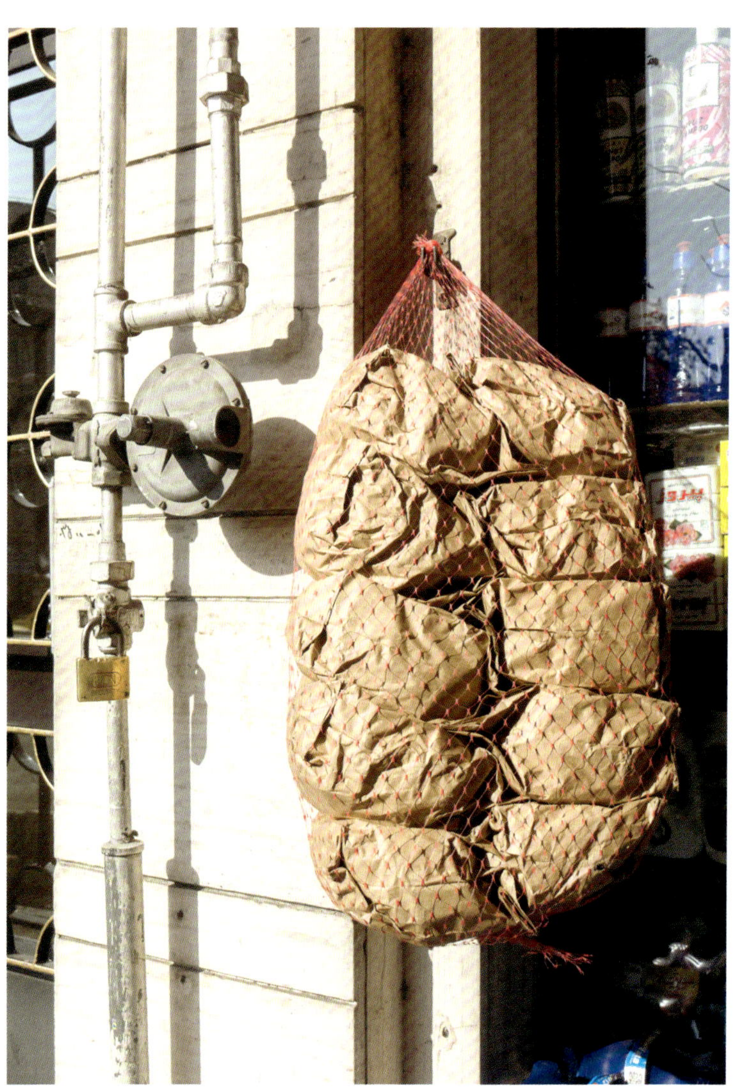

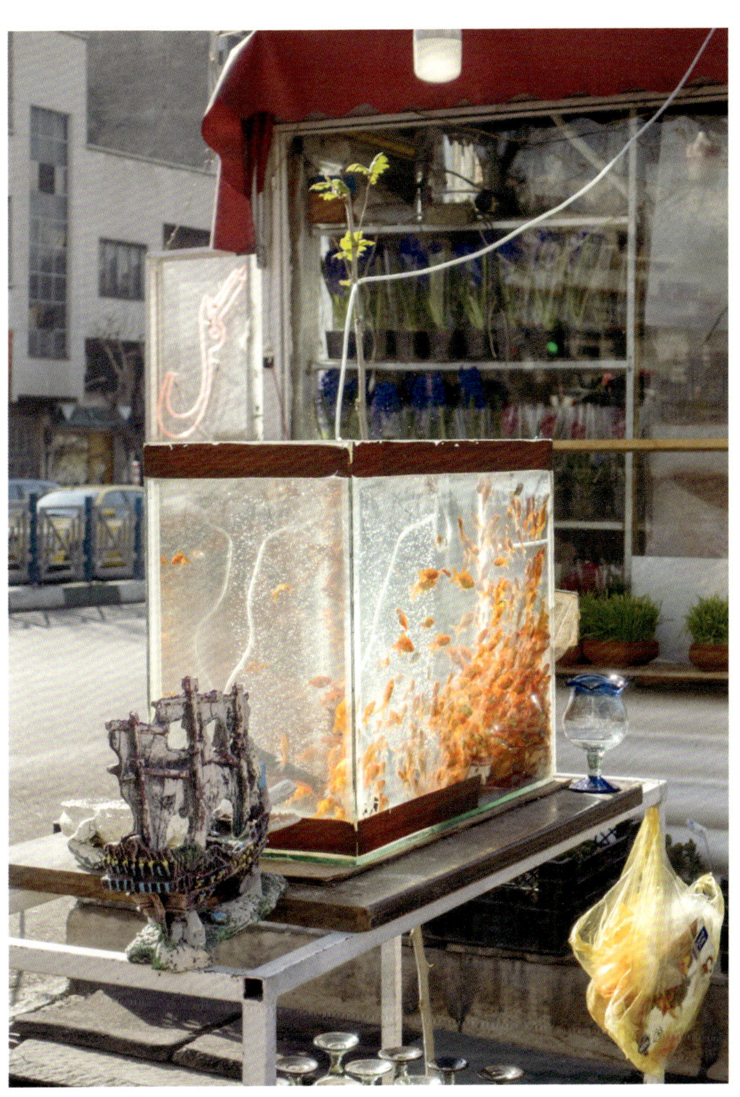

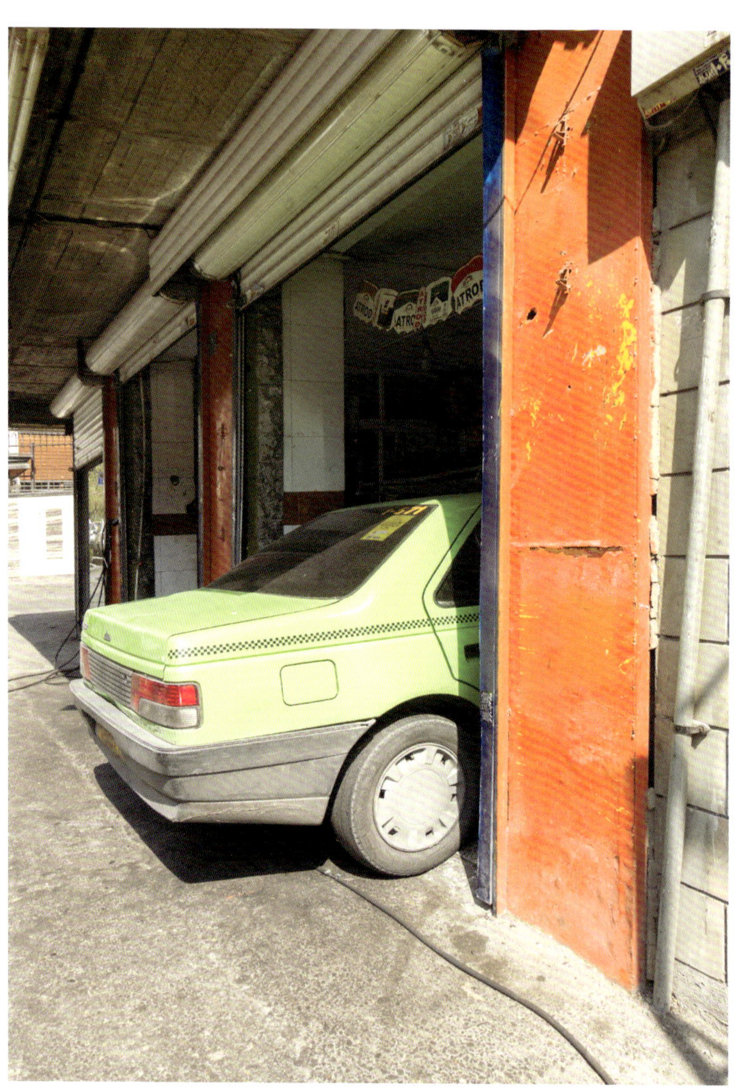

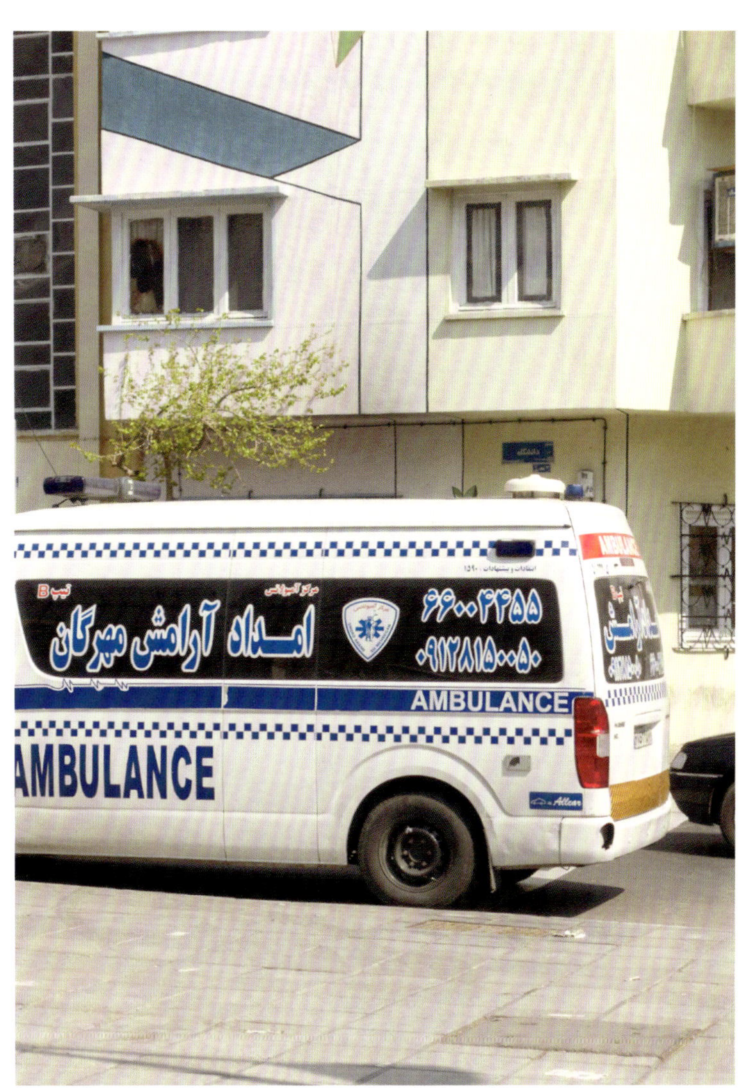
انتقادات و پیشنهادات : ۱۵۹۰
تیپ B
مرکز آمبولانس
امداد آرامش مهرگان
۶۶۰۰۴۴۵۵
۰۹۱۲۸۱۵۰۰۵۰
AMBULANCE
AMBULANCE

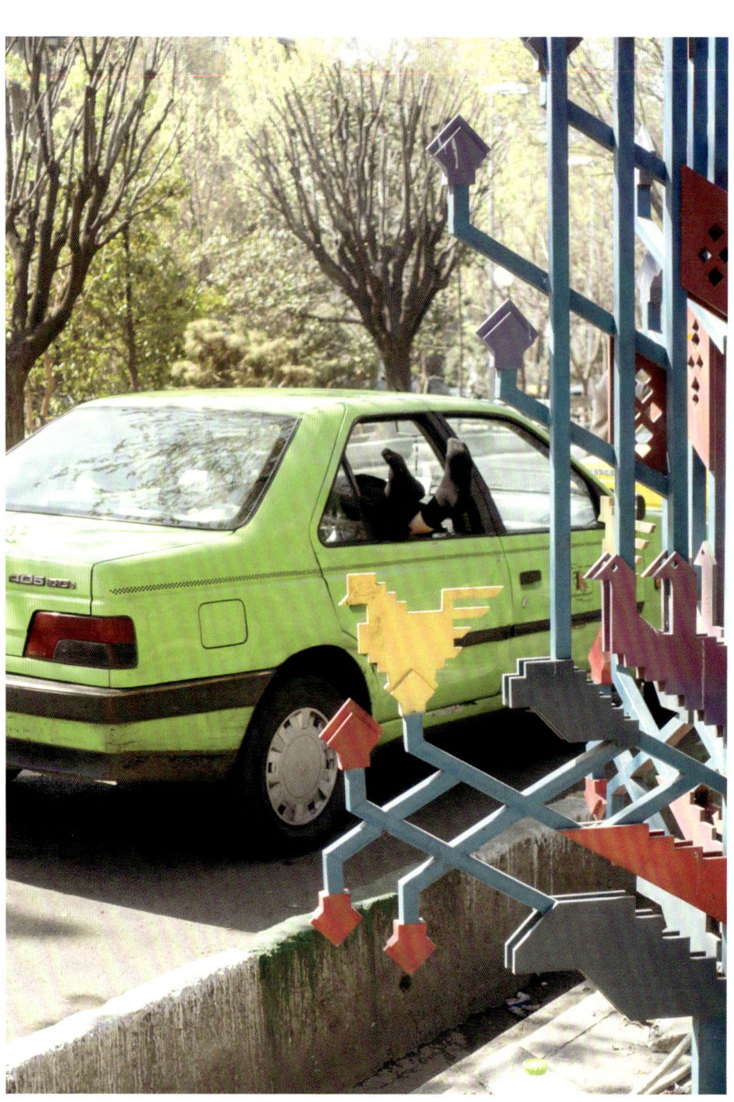

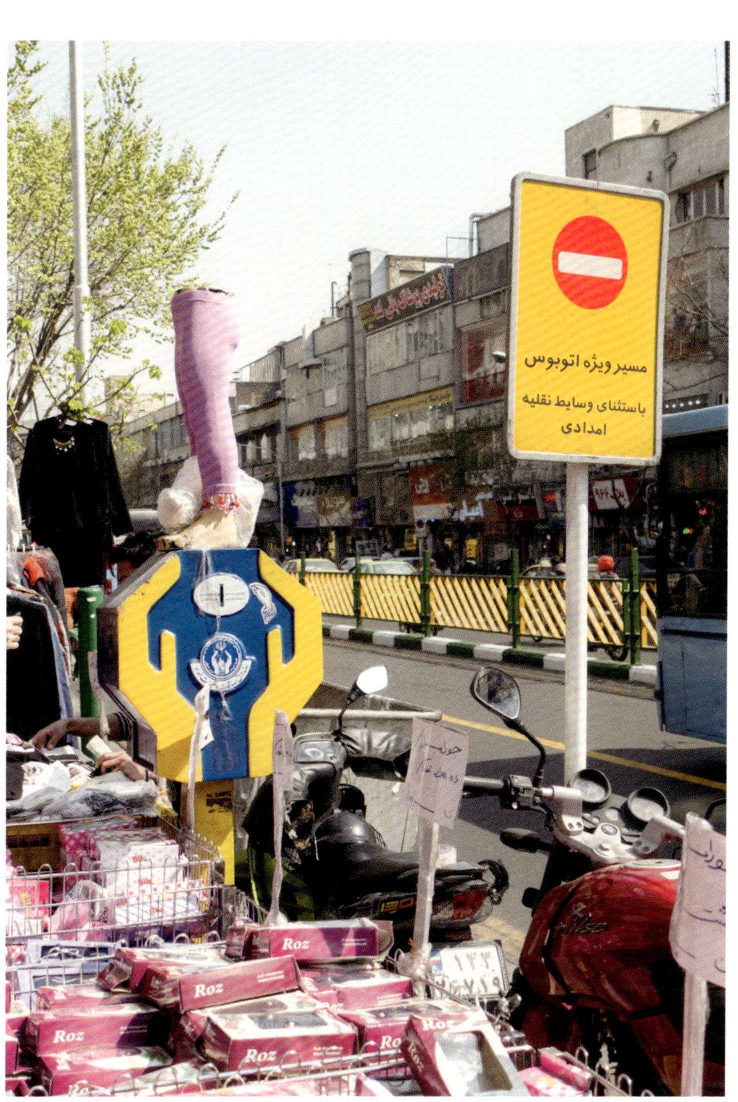
مسیر ویژه اتوبوس
باستثنای وسایط نقلیه
امدادی
Roz

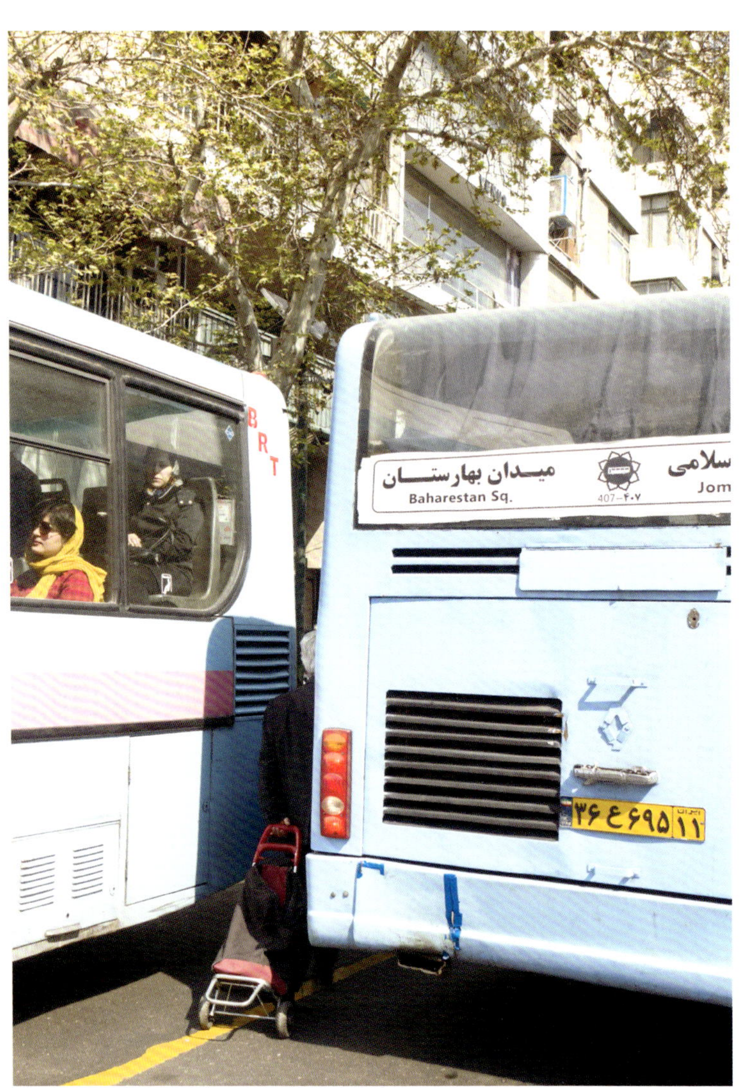
BRT
میدان بهارستان
Baharestan Sq.
407-۴۰۷
۳۶ع۶۹۵ ۱۱

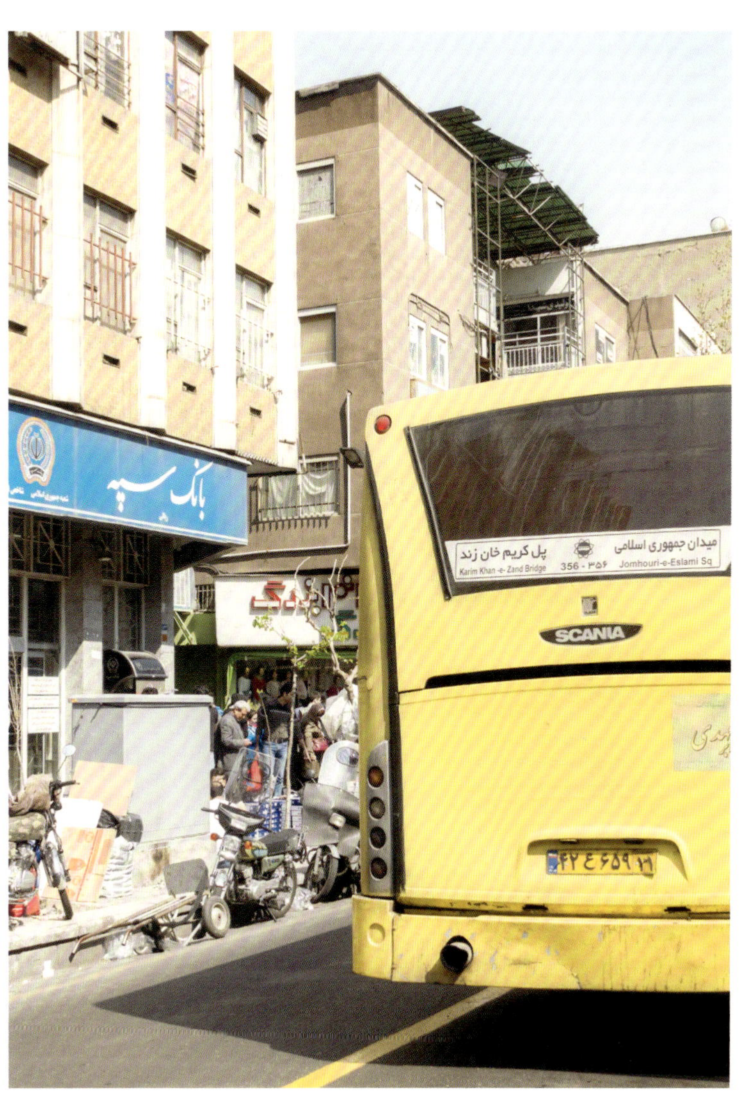
بانک سپه
میدان جمهوری اسلامی
پل کریم خان زند
356 - ۳۵۶
Karim Khan -e- Zand Bridge
Jomhouri-e-Eslami Sq
SCANIA

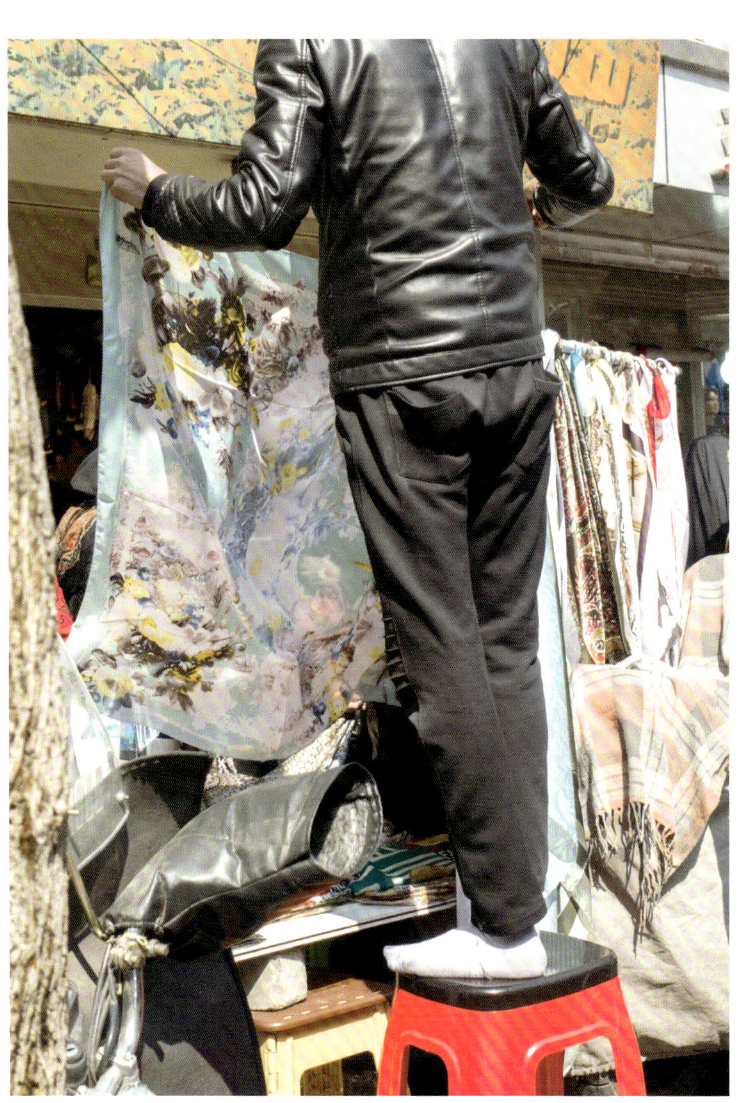

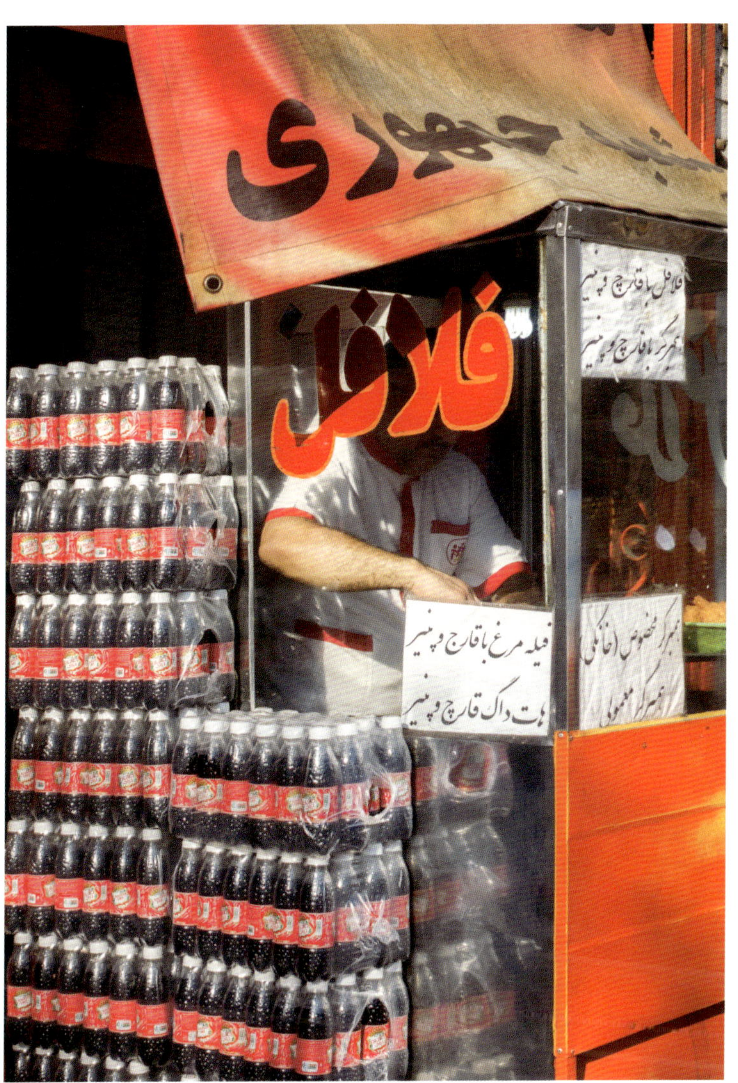
جمهوری
فلافل
فلافل با قارچ و پنیر
همبرگر با قارچ و پنیر
فیله مرغ با قارچ و پنیر
هت داگ قارچ و پنیر
همبرگر مخصوص (خانگی
همبرگر معمولی

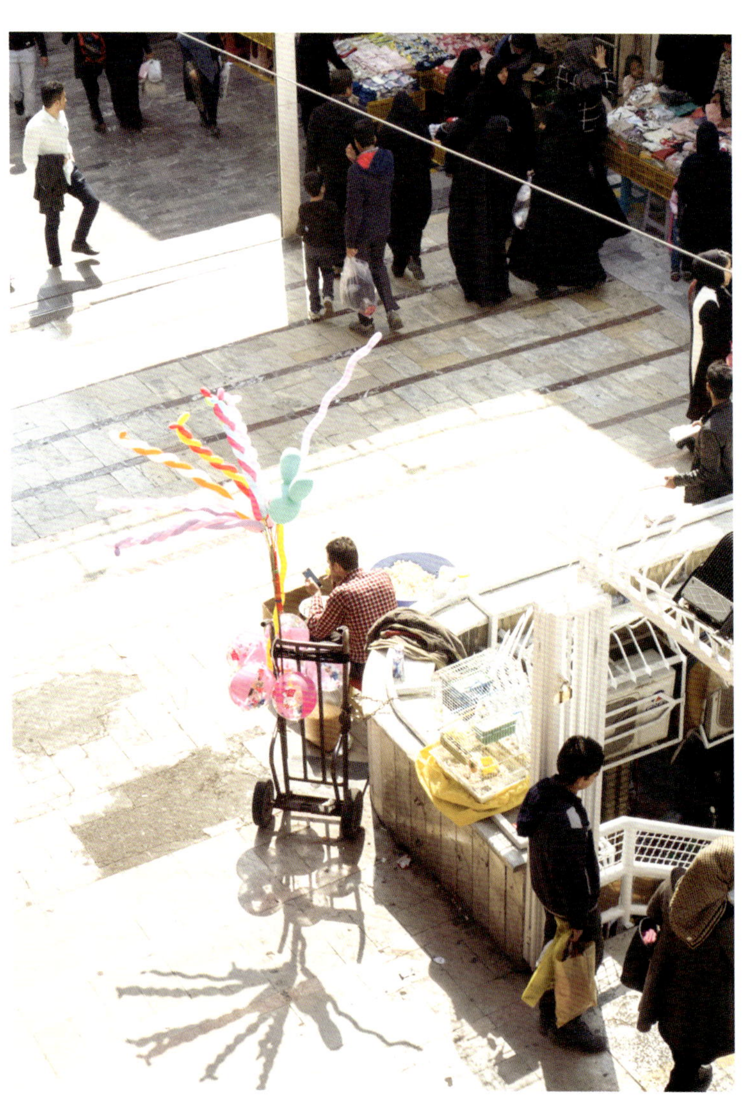

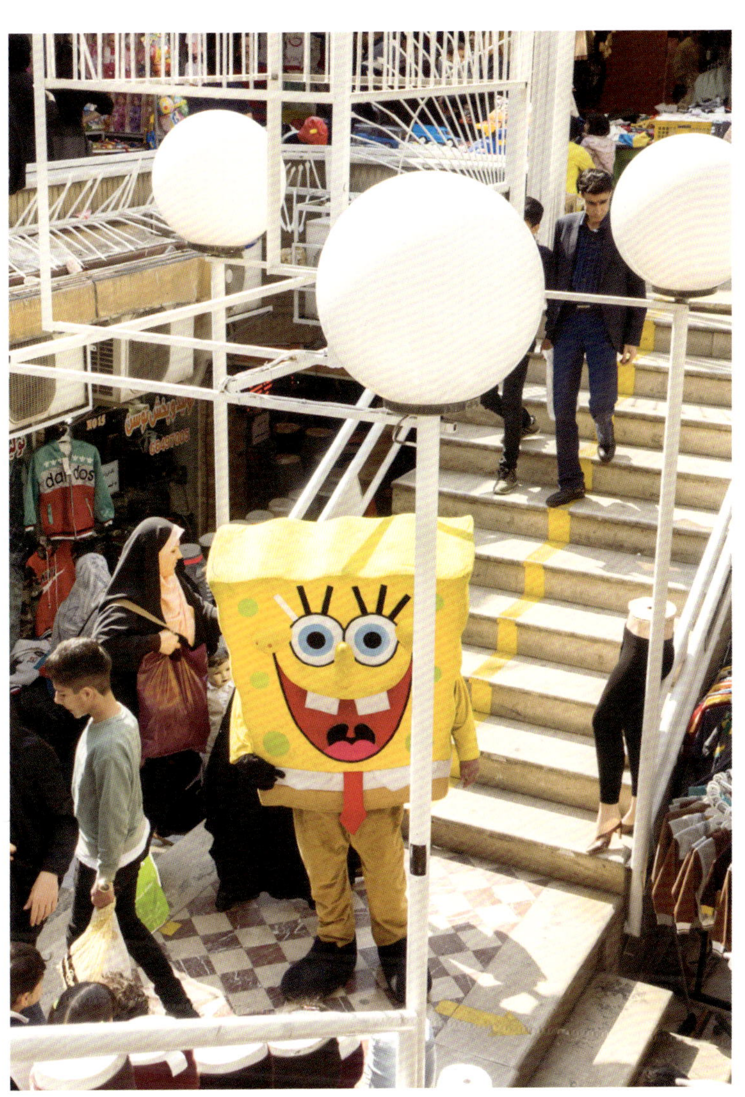

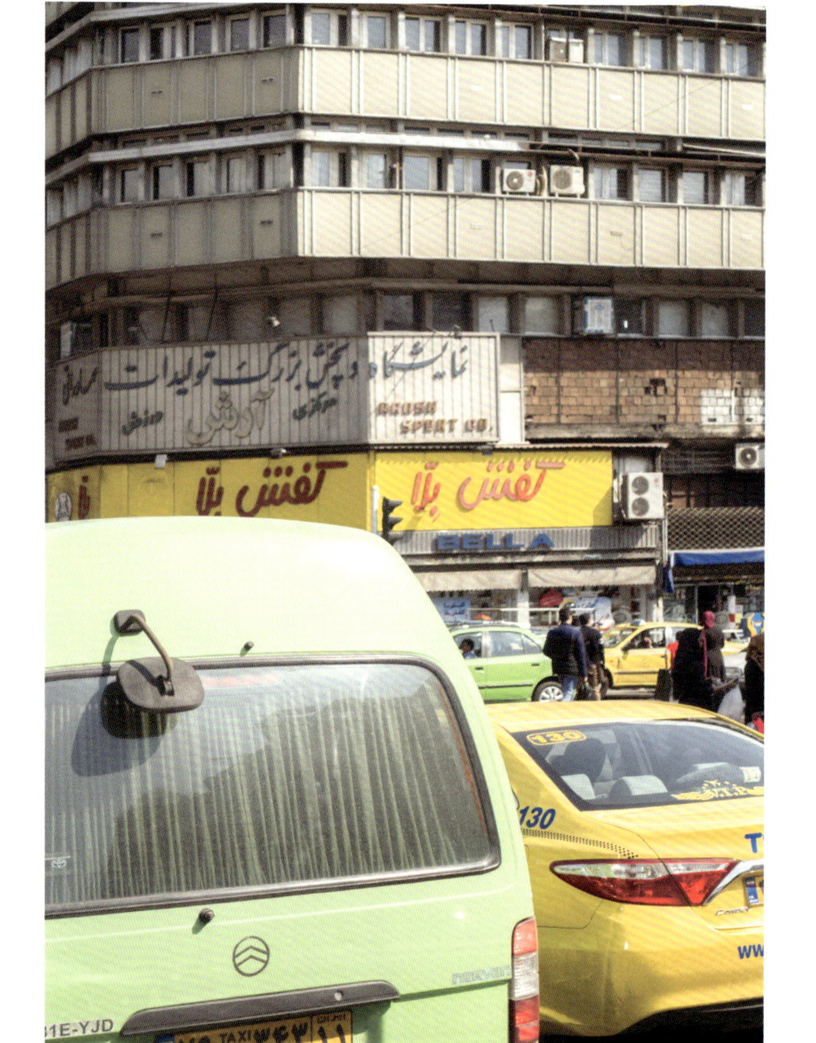
نمایشگاه و پخش بزرگ تولیدات
کفش بلا
کفش بلا
BELLA
130
TAXI

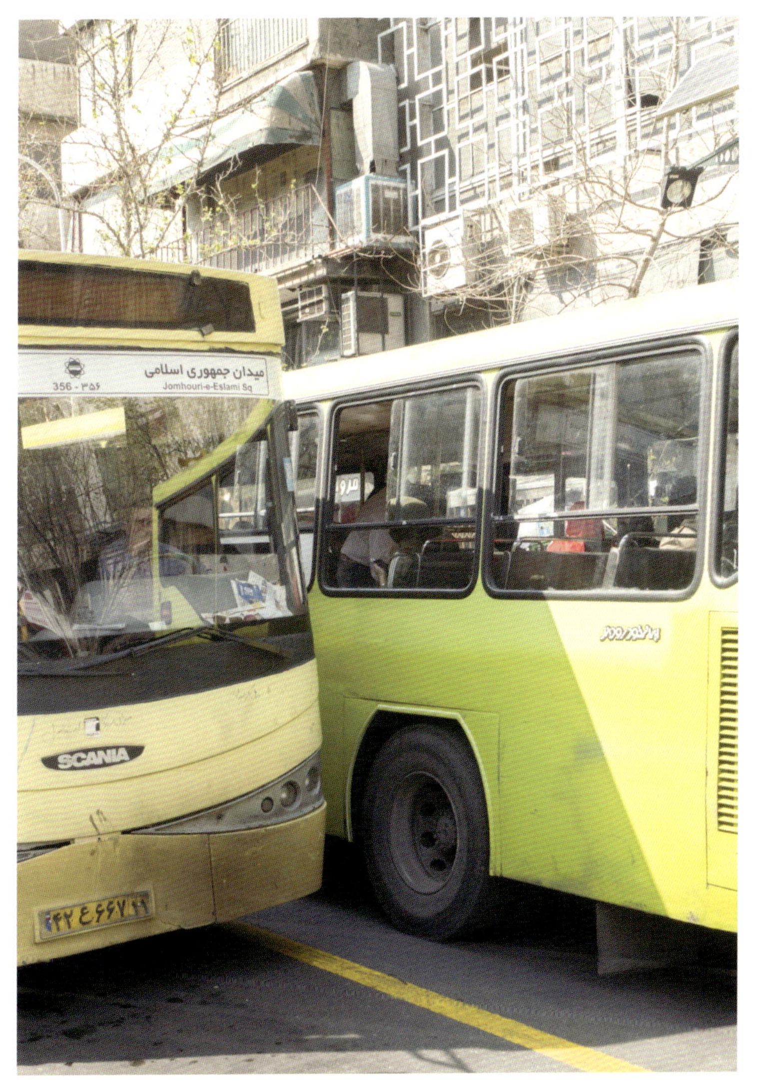

میدان جمهوری اسلامی
Jomhouri-e-Eslami Sq
356 - ۳۵۶
SCANIA

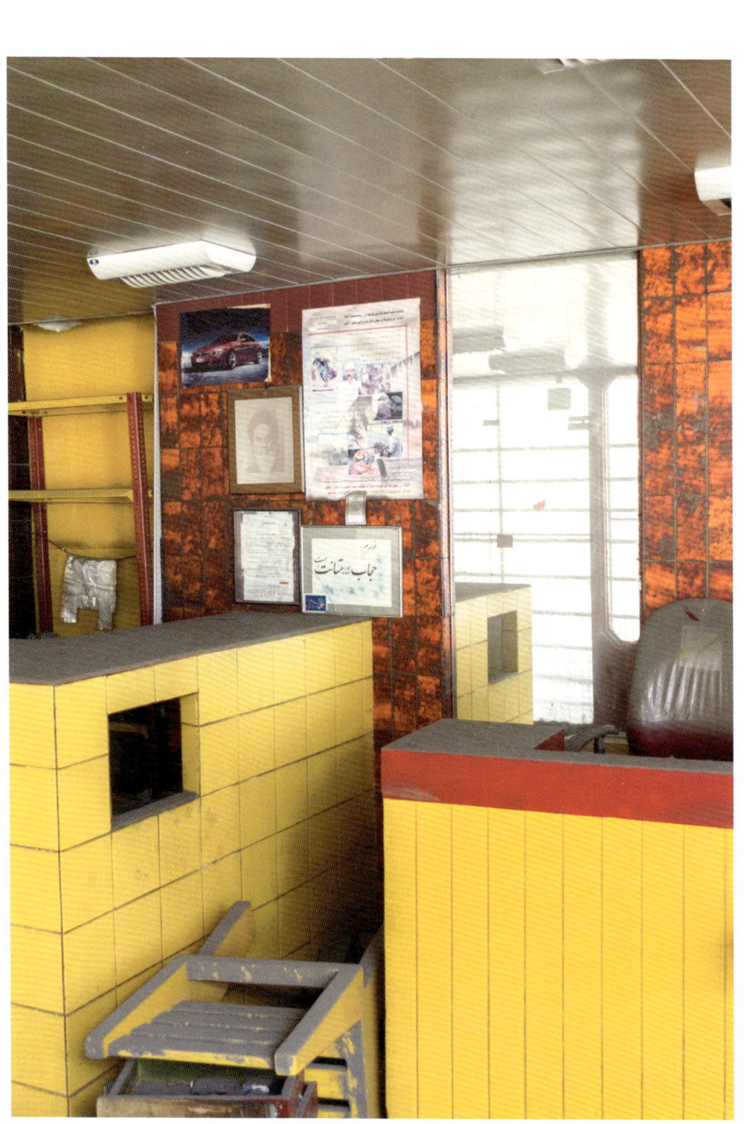
حجاب متانت

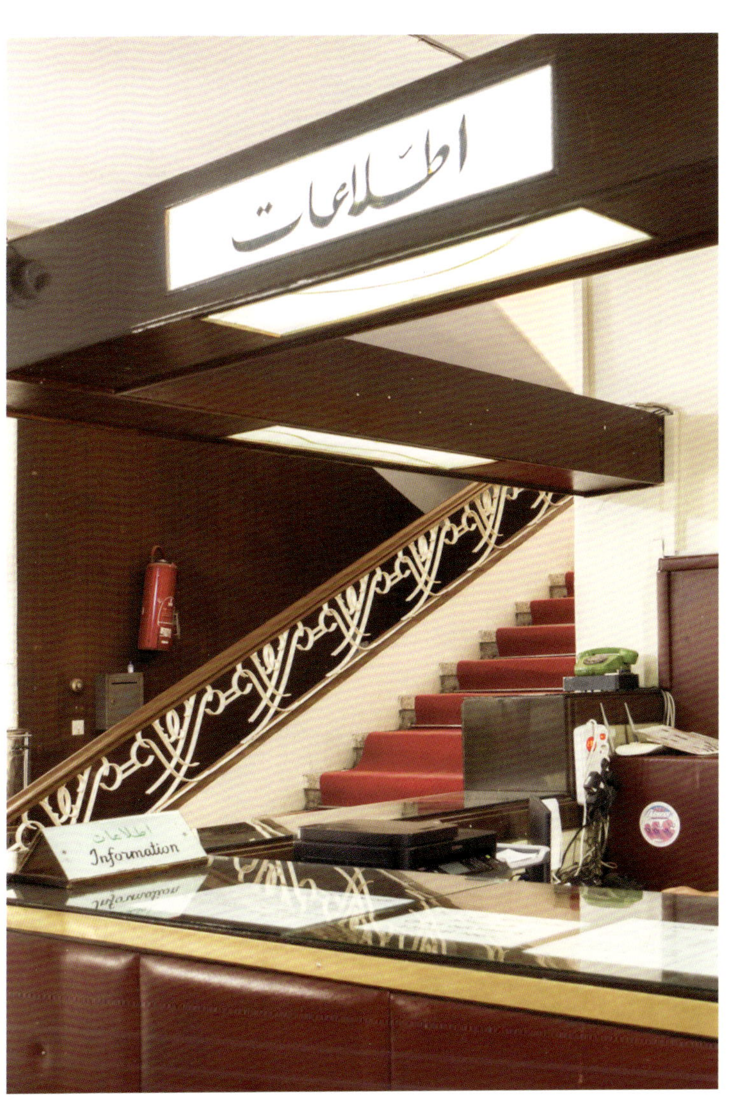

اطلاعات
اطلاعات
Information

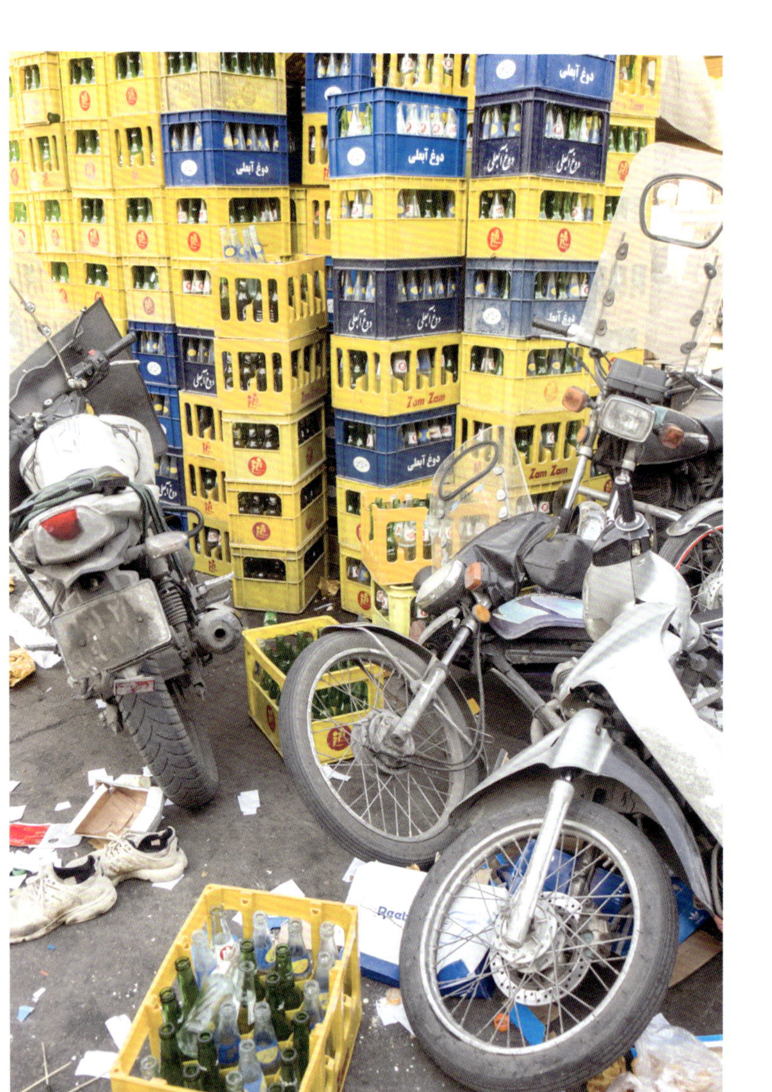
دوغ آبعلی
Zam Zam

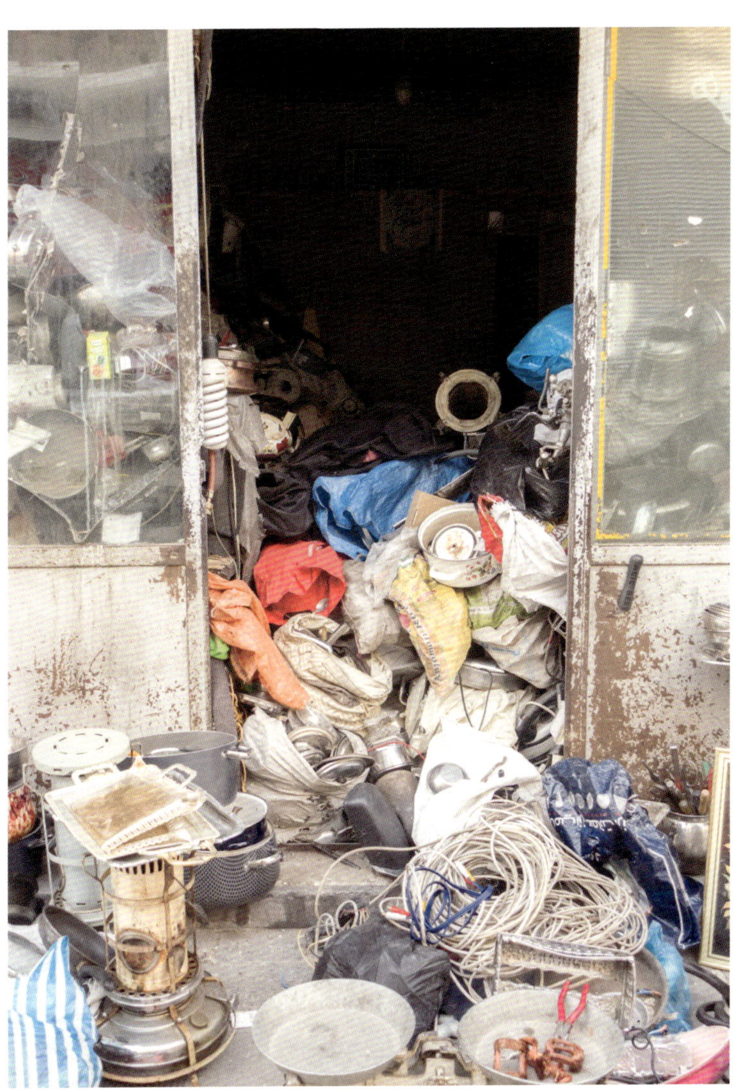

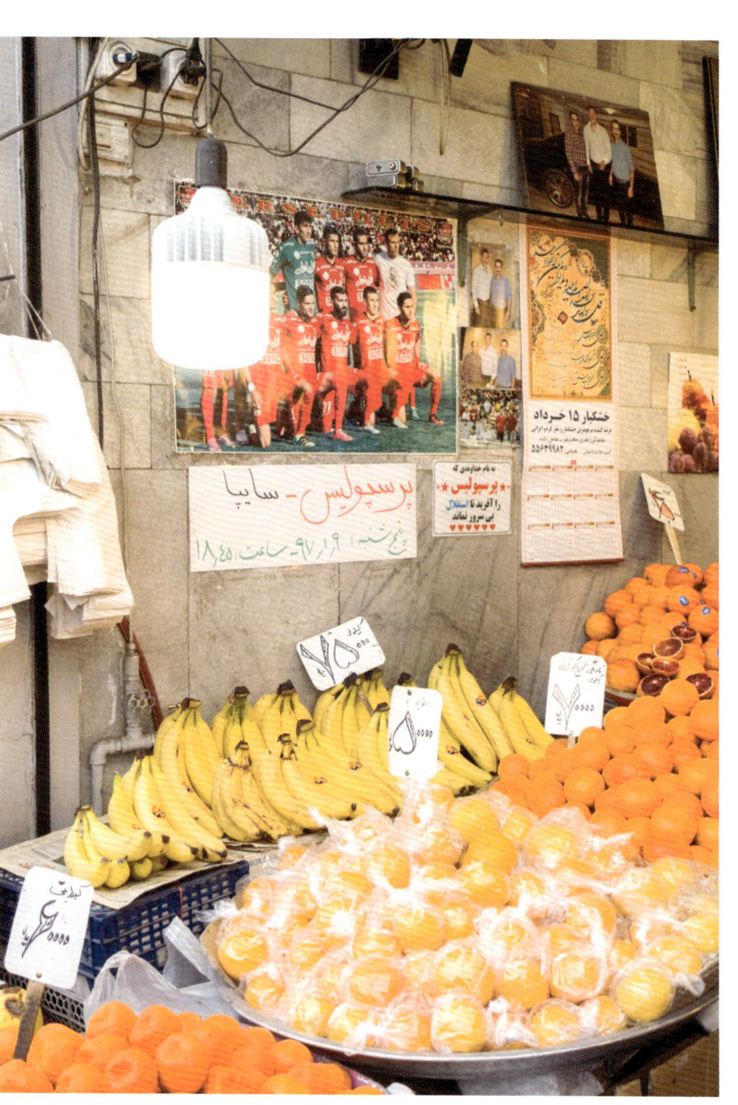

خشکبار ۱۵ خرداد
۵۵۶۳۹۹۸۲
پرسپولیس - سایپا
پنج شنبه : ۹/۱/۹۷ - ساعت : ۱۸/۴۵
به نام خداوندی که
پرسپولیس
را آفرید تا استقلال
بی سرور نماند

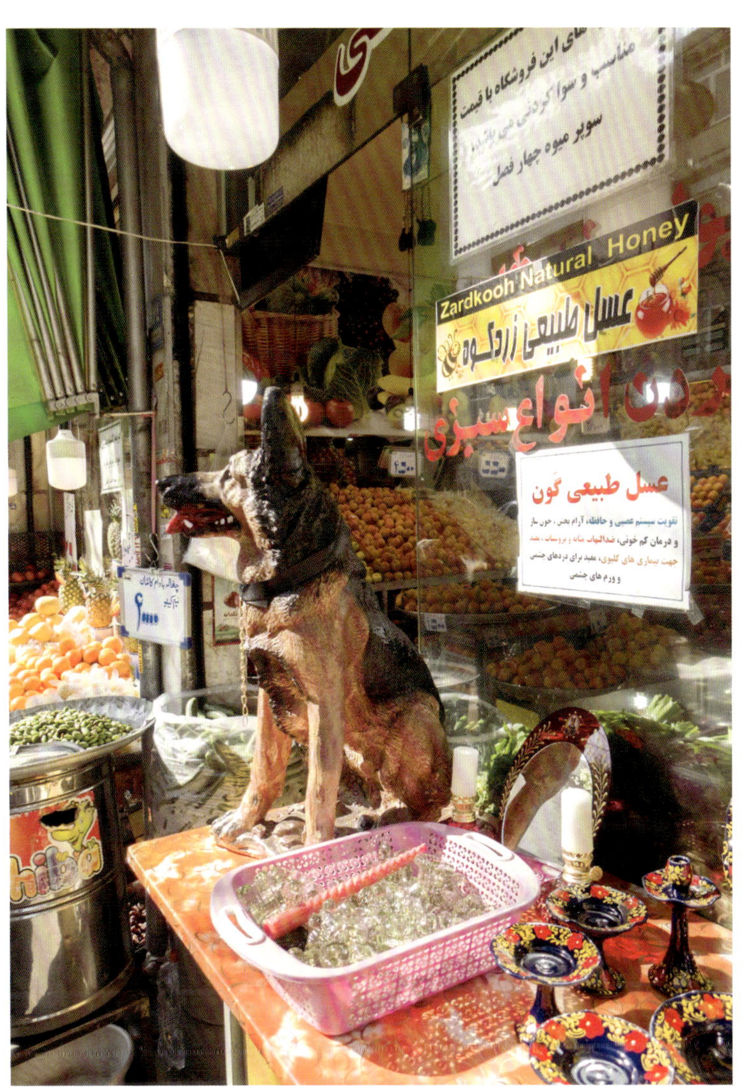
سوپر میوه چهار فصل
Zardkooh Natural Honey
عسل طبیعی زردکوه
انواع سبزی
عسل طبیعی گَون
تقویت سیستم عصبی و حافظه، آرام بخش، خون ساز
و درمان کم خونی، ضدالتهاب مثانه و پروستات، مفید
جهت بیماری های کلیوی، مفید برای دردهای جسمی
و ورم های جسمی

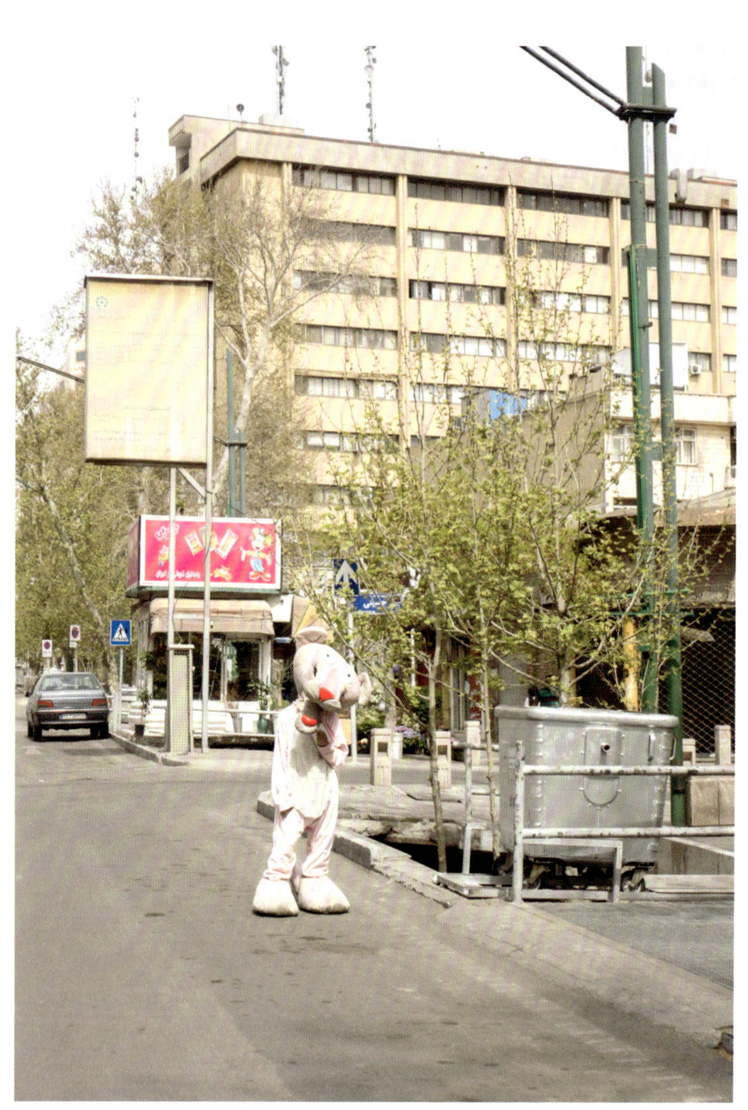

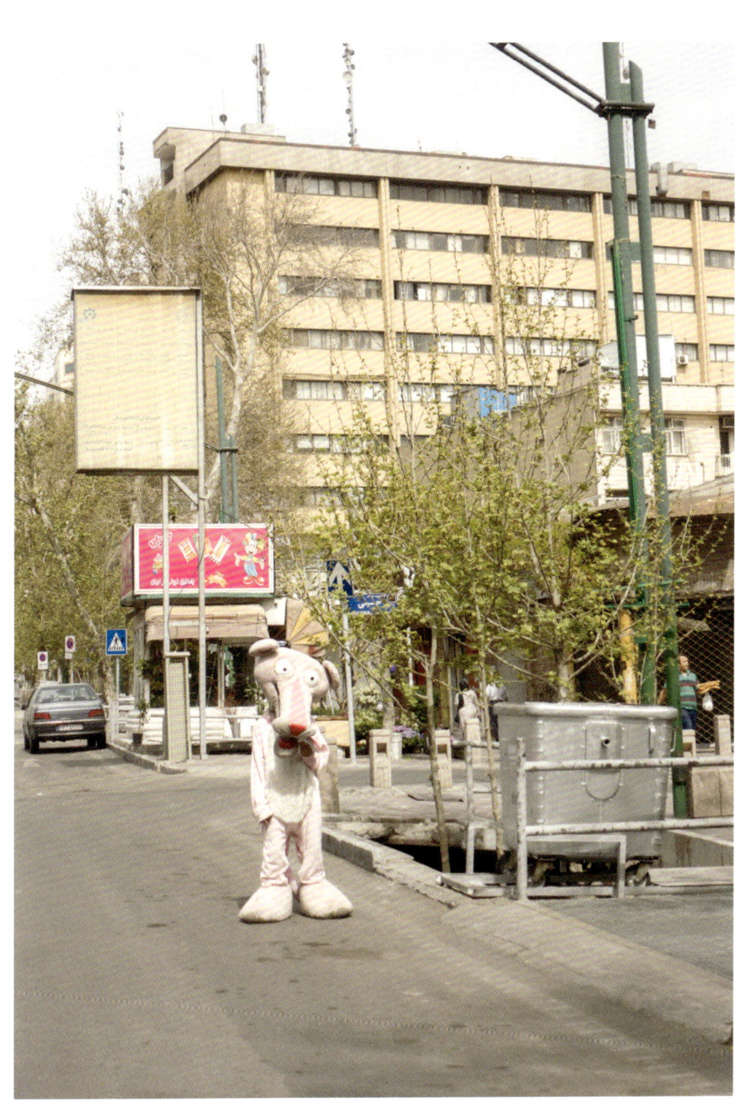

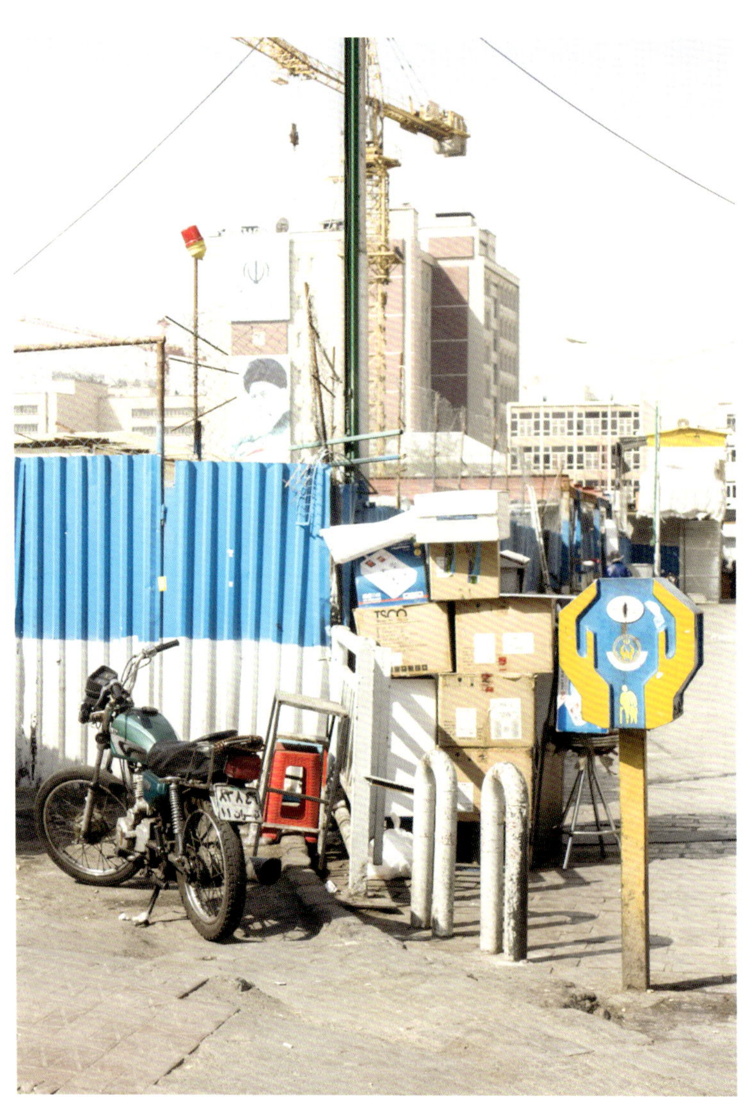
TSCO

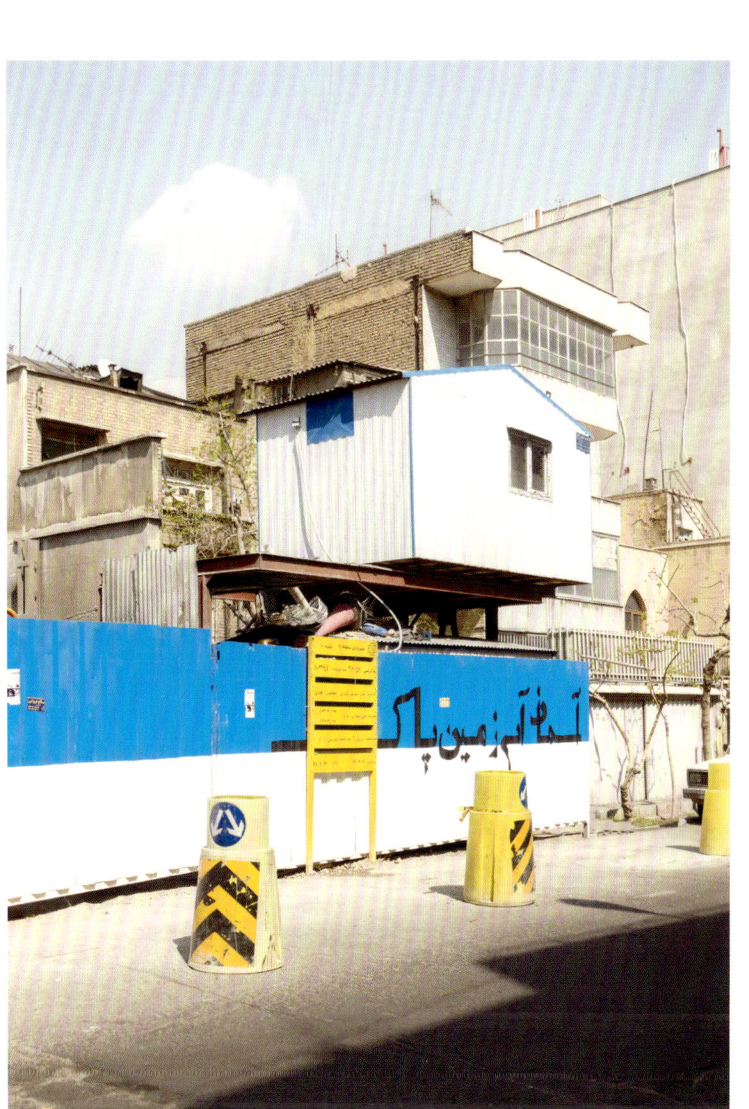

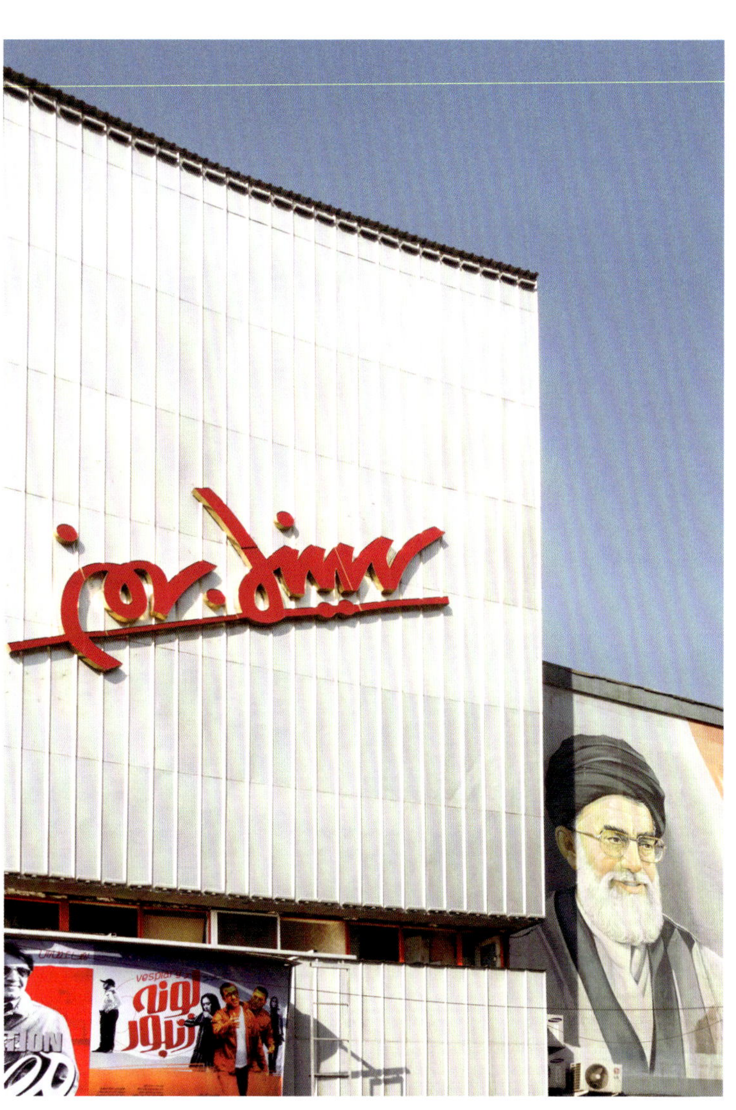

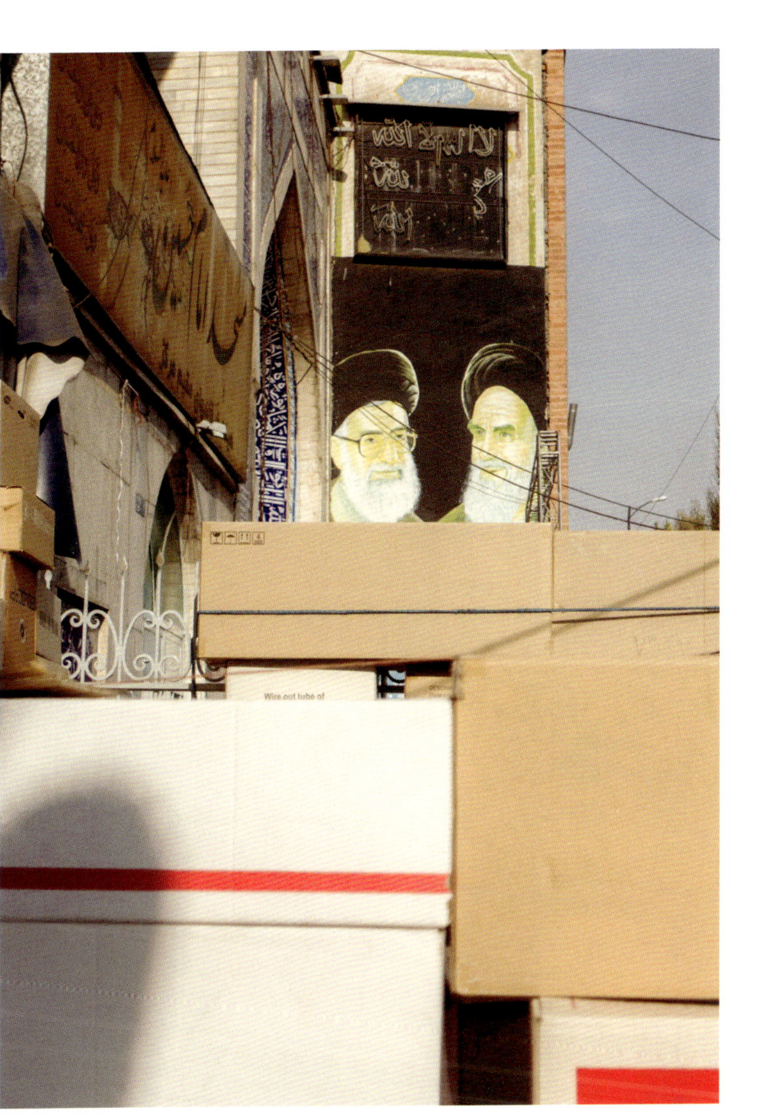
Wire out tube of

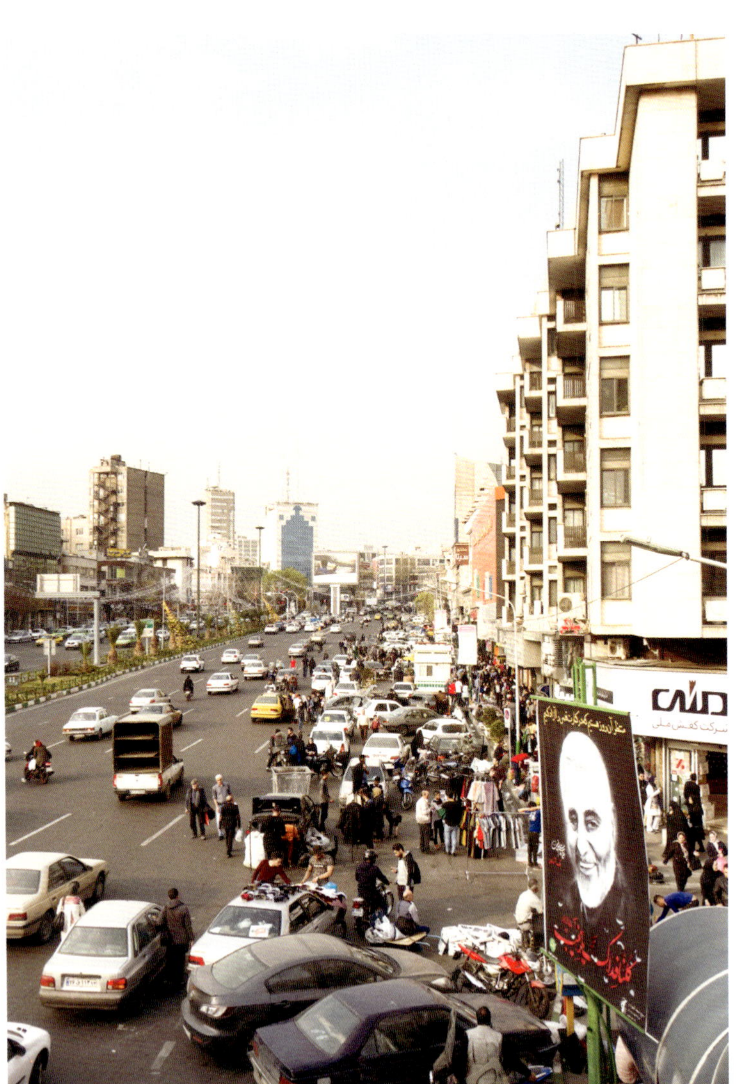
ملی
کفش ملی

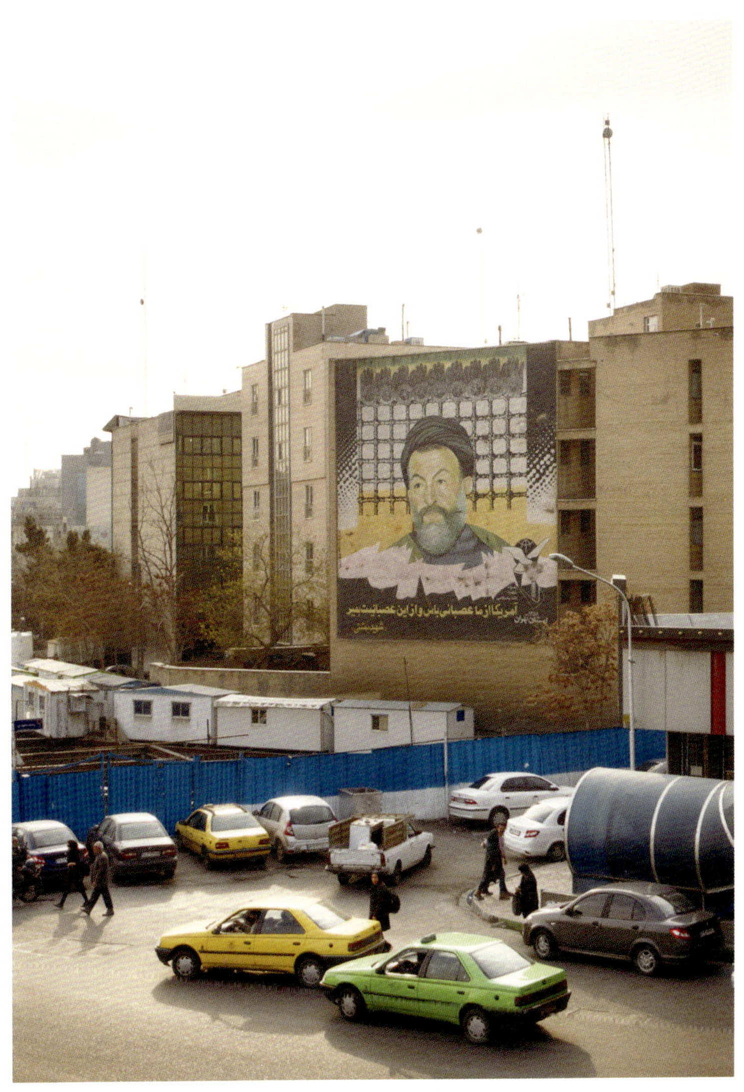
آمریکا از ما عصبانی باش و از این عصبانیت بمیر

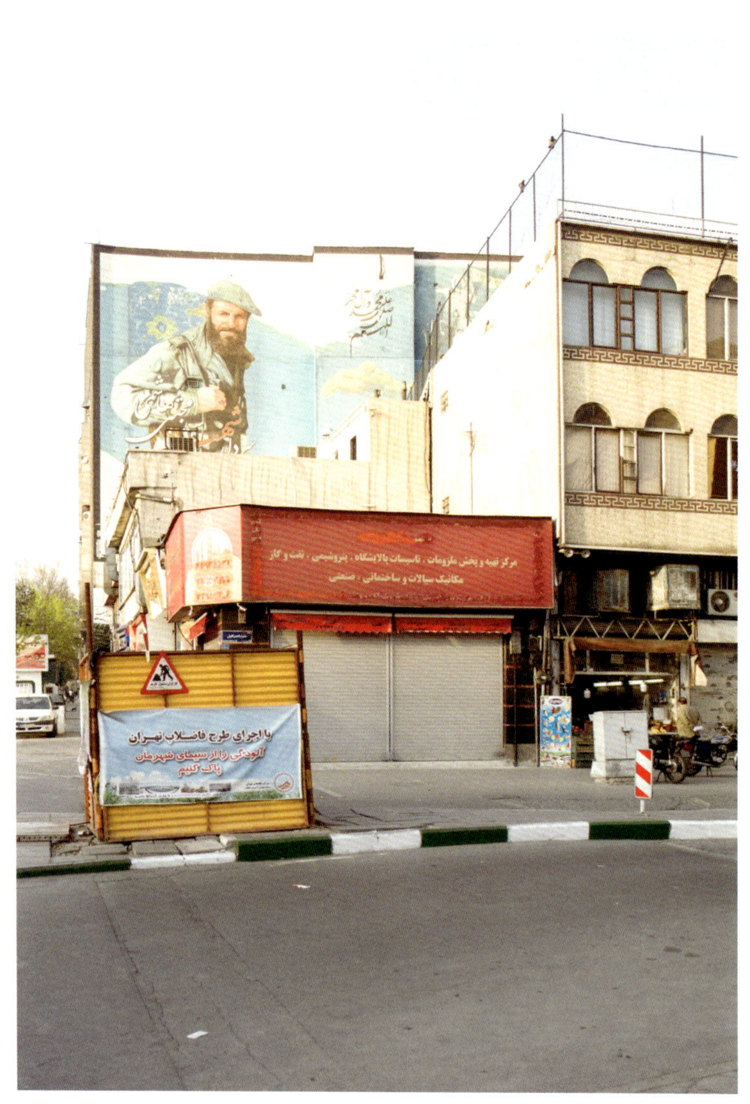
مرکز تهیه و پخش ملزومات ، تاسیسات پالایشگاه ، پتروشیمی ، نفت و گاز
مکانیک سیالات و ساختمانی ، صنعتی
با اجرای طرح فاضلاب تهران
آلودگی را از سیمای شهرمان
پاک کنیم

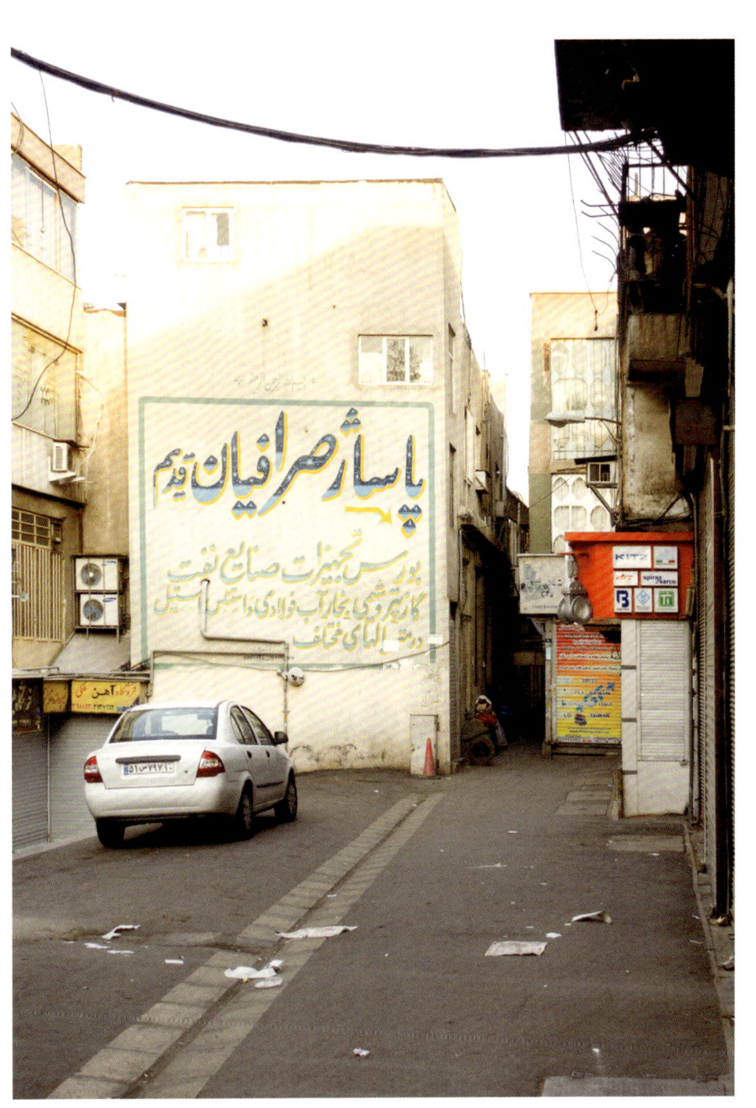

پاساژ صرافیان قدیم
بورس تجهیزات صنایع نفت

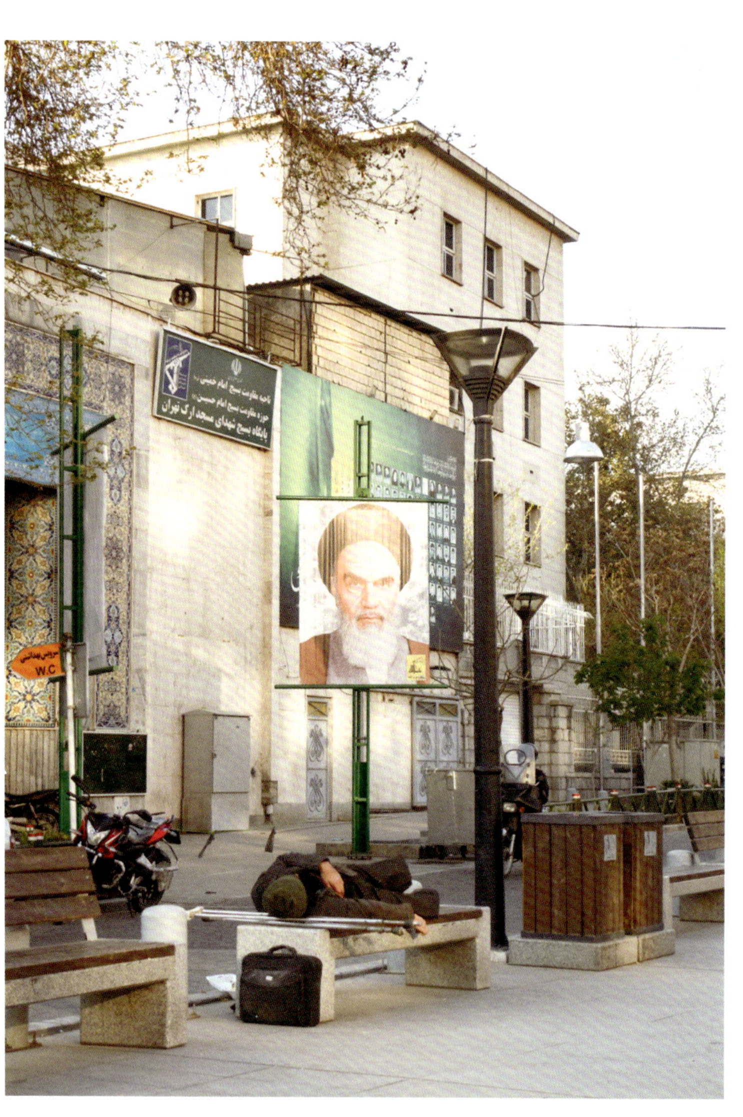

ناحیه مقاومت بسیج امام خمینی
حوزه مقاومت بسیج امام حسین
پایگاه بسیج شهدای مسجد ارک تهران
سرویس بهداشتی
W.C

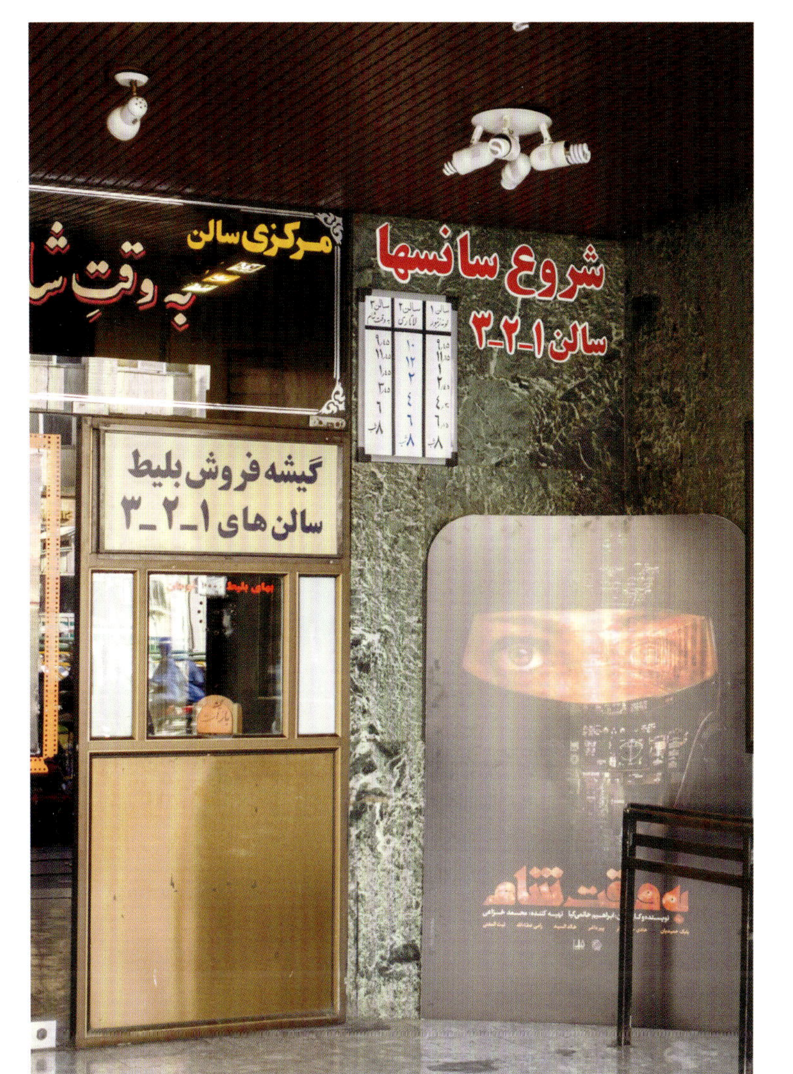
مرکزی سالن
شروع سانسها
سالن ۱_۲_۳
گیشه فروش بلیط
سالن های ۱_۲_۳

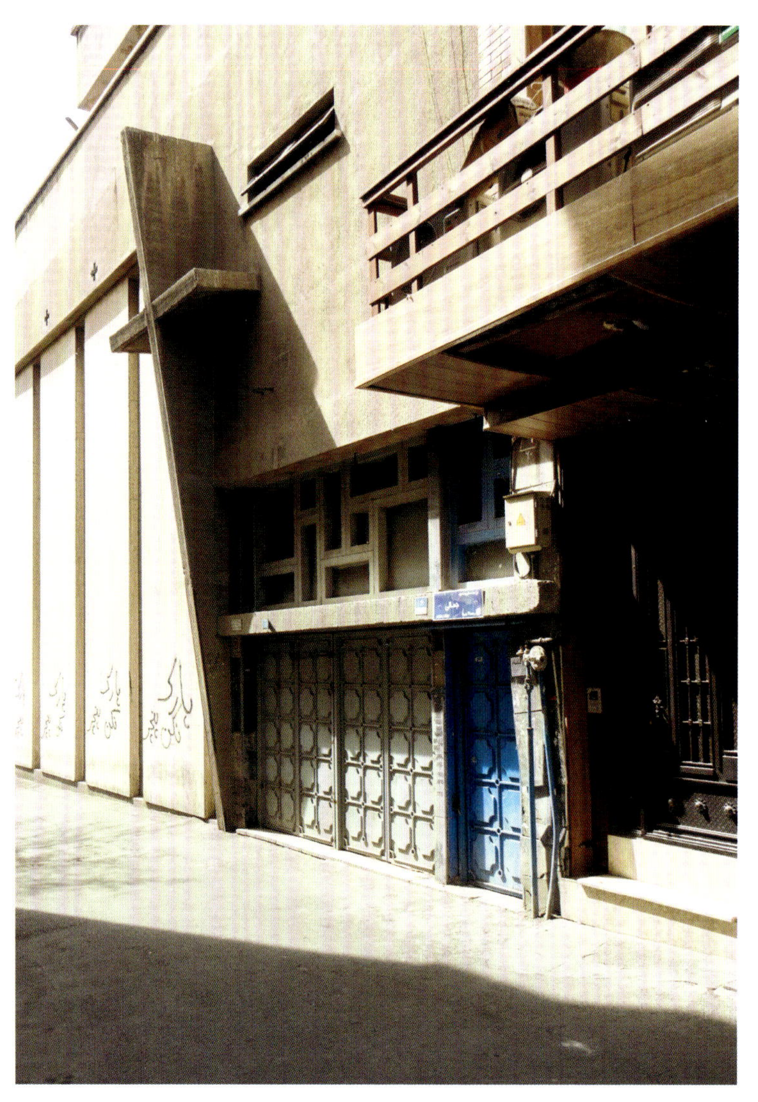

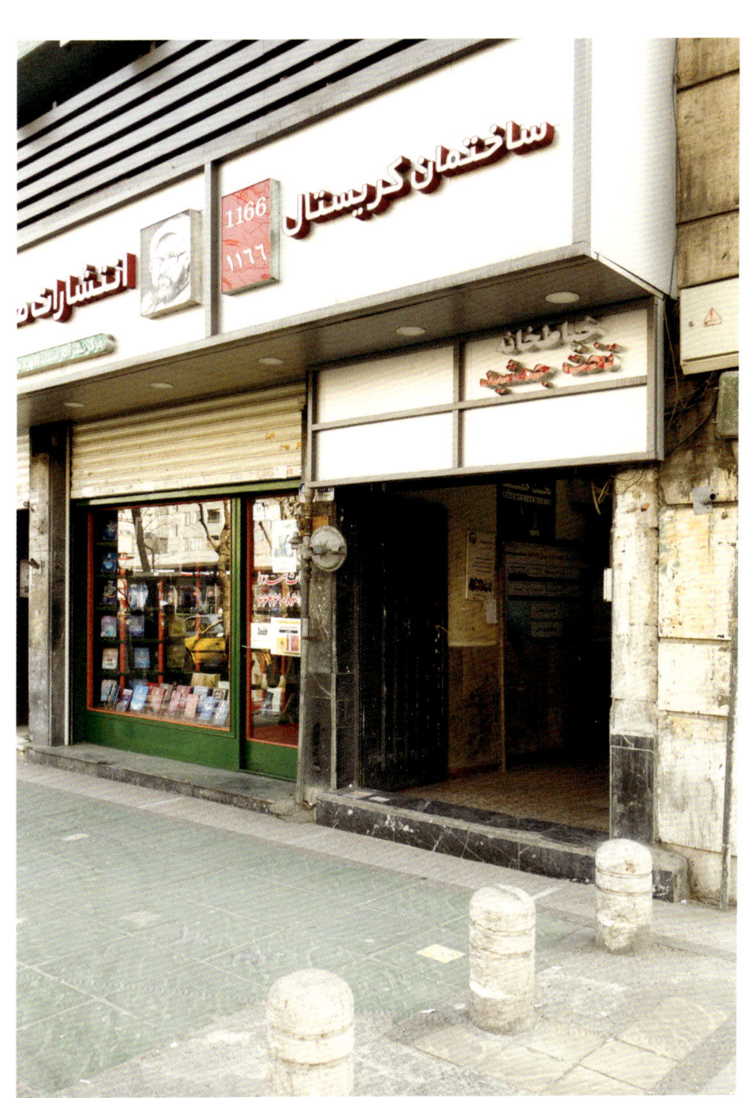
ساختمان کریستال
1166
۱۱۶۶
انتشارات

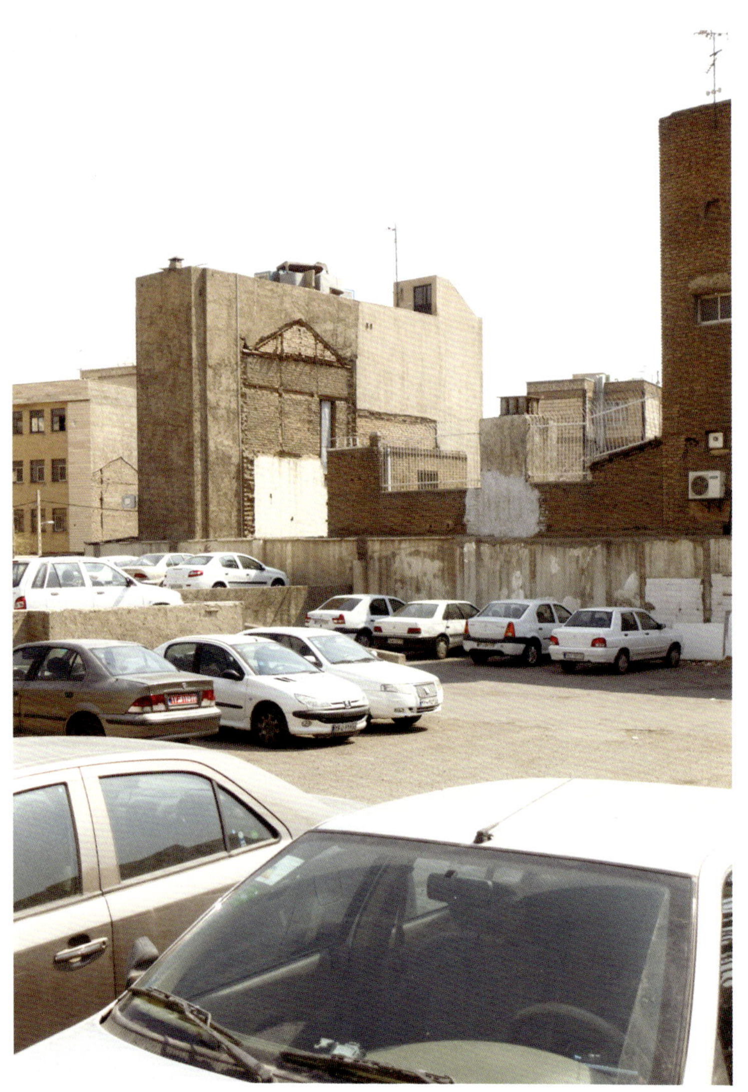

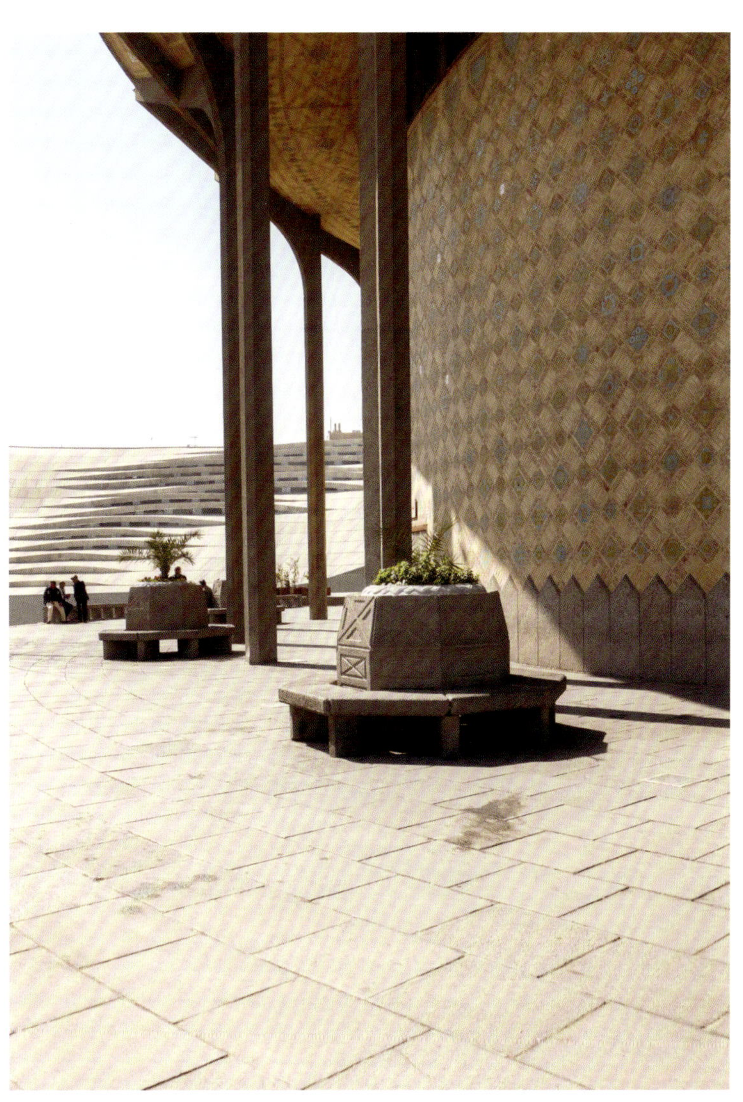

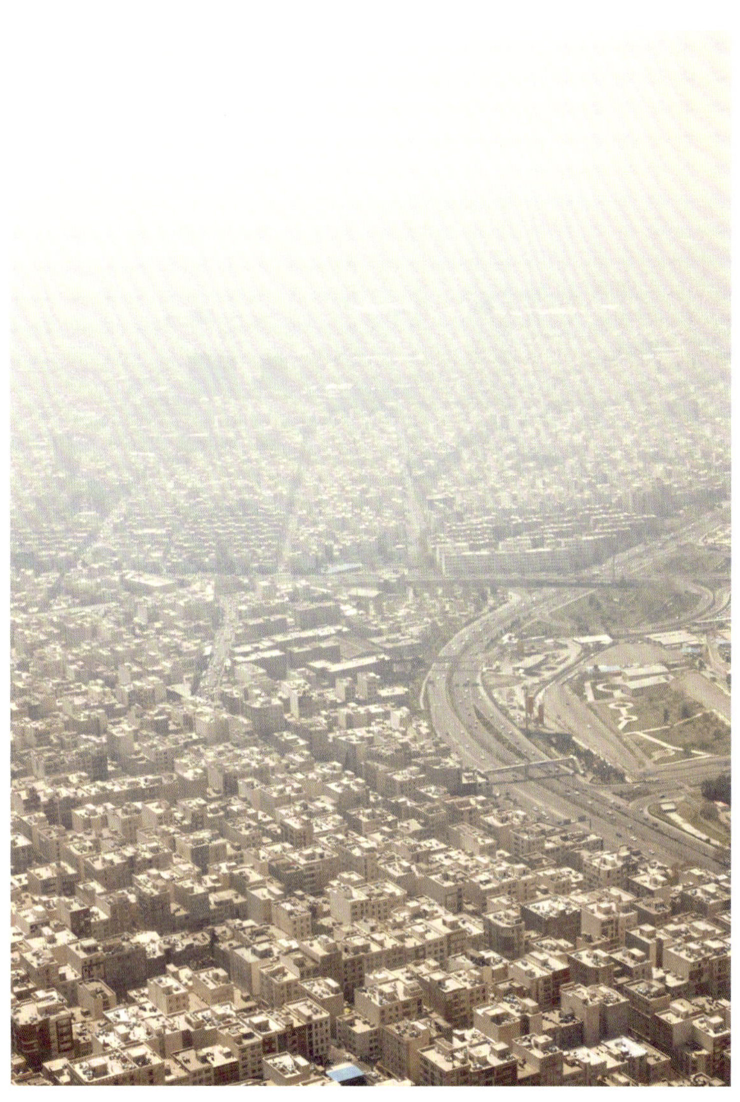

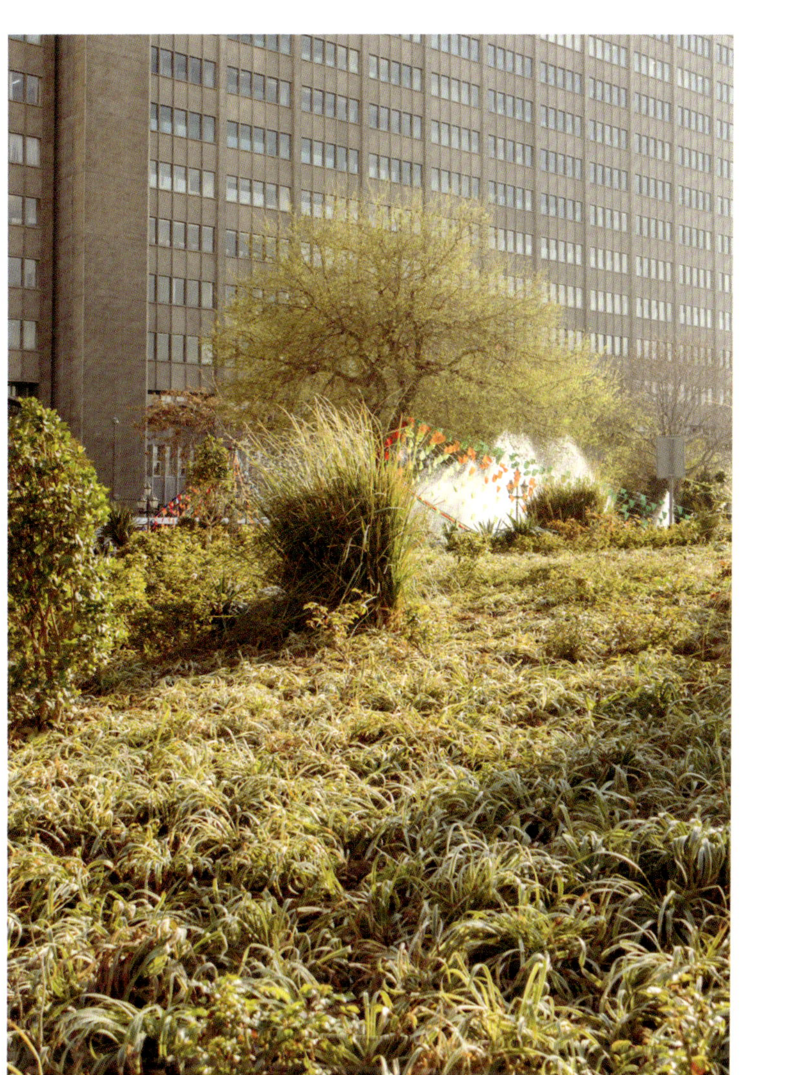

These pictures were shot on New Year's Eve 1358, according to the Jalāl Calendar

* Kakol: a fringe or lock of hair showing from under a scarf and falling across a girl's or woman's forehead

MOUSSE
PUBLISHING

HAMED KHOSRAVI

WAKE UP! AN ANTHOLOGY OF BIDARI-E MA

NARRATIVES – RELAZIONI N.7

We Have Rights in this House, Hamed Khosravi 2

Bidari-e Ma 14

Wake Up!, Maryam Firouz 15
Bidari-e Ma vol.1 no.1 (July 1944), 9–13

Our Mission, Maryam Firouz 18
Bidari-e Ma vol.1 no.10 (March 1945), 16–21

Our Sisters and Daughters!, Maryam Firouz 23
Bidari-e Ma vol.1 no.9 (February 1945), 6–11

House, Household, and their Constraints in the Contemporary Time, Farrokh-Laqa Alavi 29
Bidari-e Ma vol.1 no.4 (September 1944), 13–14

Iranian Women Must Turn Out at Ballot Boxes, Maryam Firouz 30
Bidari-e Ma vol.1 no.7 (January 1945), 15–17

The Life of Women Workers, Homayoun Eskandari 32
Bidari-e Ma vol.2 no.8 (June 1946), 21–25

Lustful Dolls, Editorial Team, *Bidari-e Ma* 34
Bidari-e Ma vol.4 no.2 (May 1948), 38–39

The Simpler, The Prettier, Editorial Team, *Bidari-e Ma* 36
Bidari-e Ma vol.4 no.2 (May 1948), 38–39

Original Pages of *Bidari-e Ma* 39

WE HAVE RIGHTS IN THIS HOUSE

HAMED KHOSRAVI

The aftermath of World War II not only marked the beginning of a new geopolitical order but also once again brought discourses of architecture and domesticity back to the front line of these confrontations. Although the immediate need for postwar reconstruction left almost no time for comprehensive theoretical development in architectural and planning principles, the "occupied" and "liberated" territories became laboratories in which new concepts of territory, city, and forms of life were tested. At the heart of the discourse was the significance of domestic spaces as spaces of resistance and of cultivation of community bonds and individual freedom. Domestic space has been described as a collective sphere, a breeding ground in which narratives of liberation and radical ideas could develop, as well as a nurturing place for collective memories and cultures. Such a task was mainly performed by women. This was a true process of the construction of political consciousness—not because of a supposedly "natural" disposition of women toward care and nurture but as an active space of resistance.

Experiments in the collectivization of domestic spaces such as kitchens and laundries and, in some cases, of childcare had already been tested in parallel to social movements in Eastern Europe, Western Europe, and the United States until the 1930s, but the experiments came to an end in the postwar period. However, in countries like Iran, it was the second wave of the Modern Movement that aided post–World War II social movements and revitalized the discourse. Being located on the fault line between the communist and capitalist worlds, Iran became a laboratory in which such ideological projects were tested.

Back in August 1941, the Anglo-Soviet invasion of Iran had inaugurated an interregnum that lasted a full twelve years. It was the beginning of a period in which the new monarch, Mohammad Reza Shah, continued to hang on to much of the armed forces but lost control over the bureaucracy and the system of patronage. This interregnum was first challenged in January 1949 when President Truman launched his Point Four Program in the Middle East, and in particular Iran, to take back control of the strategic territories over which the Soviet influence had expanded. If the 1949 Point Four Program was a "soft counterproject," August 1953 marked the violent end of the twelve-year interlude, when the shah, through a coup engineered by the Americans and the British, reestablished royal authority, thereby recreating his father's regime and enabling him to act as an executive monarch for the next twenty-five years. In this twelve-year interregnum, power was not concentrated in one place. On the contrary, it was hotly contested between the royal palace, the cabinet, the parliament, and most importantly the urban masses, who were mobilized first by socialist movements and then by a nationalist one. Indeed, in this period the masses, mainly made up of the urban middle and working class, constituted a major threat to the Pahlavi dynasty.

The first real challenge to the state came from labor movements. On September 29, 1941, within a month of Reza Shah's abdication, a group of recent graduates from European universities and former political activists announced the formation of an Iranian communist party: the Tudeh Party (the Party of the Masses). Besides their political activities in the form of demonstrations and gatherings, they set out to train and educate the public, specifically the working and middle classes. During 1946 the Tudeh Party extended its activities with a view to mobilizing middle-class intellectuals. The mission resulted in the formation of numerous groups, circles, and clubs as subbranches, if not sympathizers, of the Tudeh Party, namely the Women's Association, Youth Association, Officers' Organization, Students' Association, and affiliated groups such as the Writers' Association and the Association of Iranian Architects.

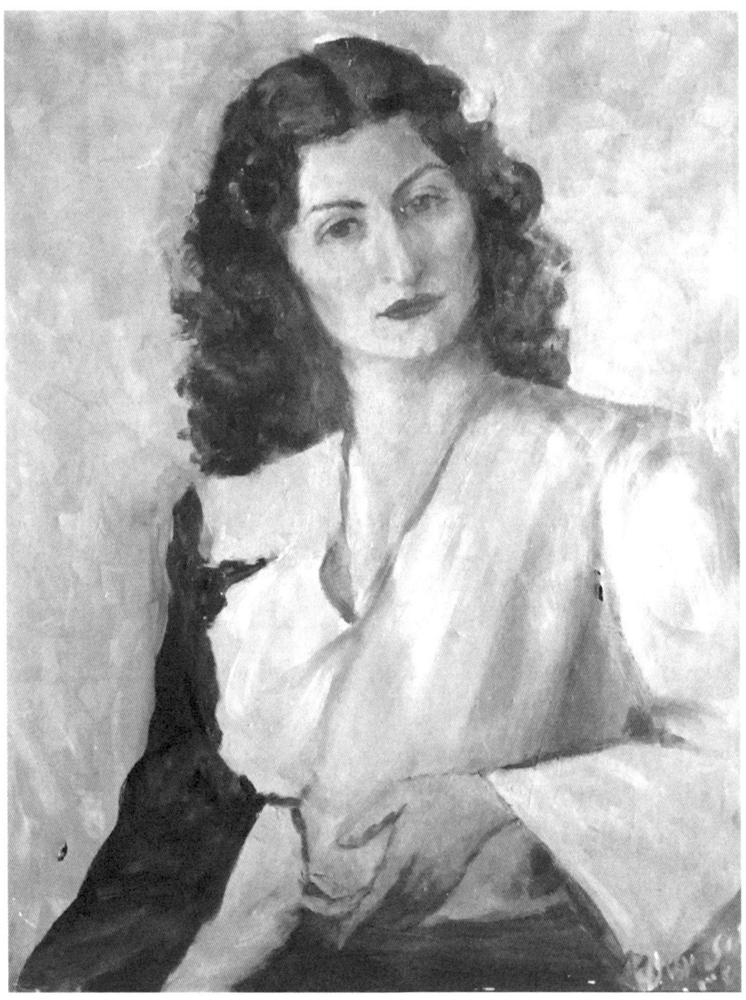

Portrait of Maryam Firouz by Mehdi Vishkaei, 1945
Courtesy of Afsaneh Gidfar

The role of the Women's Association and the Association of Iranian Architects was quite fundamental, the discourse of domesticity was at the center of their political program to activate urban society, addressing women in particular as a forgotten half of the active political mass. Their ideology was influential in the design and construction of mass housing projects in Tehran during the late 1940s and 1950s. Each association ran its own publication in order to reach a larger audience. The journals *Bidari-e Ma* (Our awakening) and *The Architect* soon became quite popular and were distributed countrywide. The two leading figures behind the organizations were the writer Maryam Firouz and the architect Noureddin Kianouri.

Bidari-e Ma was launched in June 1944—a year after the foundation of the Women's Association—and ran until December 1948. Every issue had the same front cover, it was a lithograph illustration signed Sarvari, depicting a female figure, dressed in an unorthodox fashion, waving a large flag with her left hand against the rising sun of the East. On the ground, there were broken chains signifying freedom and emancipation of the Iranian women. Beyond its name, the inner cover bore the motto of the journal: "We Have a Right in this House Too," referring to both the country and the domestic space. In the editorial essay of the second issue, the author(s) wrote:

> As it is evident from the title of the journal, our mission is to wake half of the nation up, the women. Although in many circumstances both men and women are deadened and are incapable of claiming their rights, we must admit that these conditions, coupled with other forces, have pushed women back more than men.[1]

The authors made a clear statement addressing their target group and distinguishing themselves from the decrees of Reza Shah when he banned the wearing of traditional clothes in public, including veils, in 1936. They criticized these state-initiated policies:

> If in the twenty dark years of the former shah's [Reza Shah's] rule, in the name of a privileged group of women a so-called "Women's Movement" was propagated, it was to exploit more of those women who were working in factories, [...] this was a fake movement! The true movement is the one that is mobilized by the nation itself or emerges out of a serious class struggle, the one that is a continuous movement toward fulfilling the real goals. A true movement cannot go on without high expectation.[2]

Their mission was clear and explicit:

> *Bidari-e Ma* wants to initiate a true women's movement in Iran, whose aims are claiming equal rights for women, women's education, and their economic empowerment, a movement that embraces modesty and belief, as well as a sense of solidarity among women, a movement that unites women, turning individuals into socially confident, skillful, and independent members of the society.[3]

The journal was carefully structured to communicate to the widest audience possible, from a housewife to a worker, a traditional or an intellectual one. Manifestos and statements usually were the opening titles, they were followed by sociopolitical critiques of society, reports of the association's activities, short stories and poems, essays on women's hygiene and health, and translated articles on international women's movements from around the world, and they usually ended with a series of advice on housekeeping, home economics, and low-budget food recipes. The tone was both critical and seditious, however, the language was culturally appropriate and comprehensible. The editorial

1 Editorial, *Bidari-e Ma 1*, no. 2 (August 1944): 1.

2 *Ibid.*, 2.

3 *Ibid.*, 3.

team was mainly composed of the same members of the Women's Association: the Alavi sisters (Badri, Najmi, and Shah-Zanan), Zahra Eskandari (Bayat), Mehrangiz Eskandari, Aalieh Shermini, A'azam Soroush, and perhaps the most fundamental figure, Maryam Firouz.[4]

Maryam Firouz (also known as Princess Maryam Firouz Farman-Farmaian) was a linguist, writer, and poet. She was born in 1914 into one of the most influential aristocratic families on the Iranian political scene. Educated at the French school in Tehran, Maryam grew up as an independent thinker and entered the circles of the Iranian intelligentsia in Tehran, which included figures such as Bozorg Alavi, Sadegh Hedayat, and Abdolhossein Noushin, all of whom were left-wing by inclination, if not officially associated with the Iranian Communist Party and later the Tudeh Party. Through her circle of comrades, she was officially introduced to the Tudeh Party and became one of the founders of the Women's Association of the party in June 1943. Najmi Alavi, in her memoir, recalls the day that Maryam joined the second meeting:

> We had gathered in Zahra Eskandari's house. After a few minutes, Bozorg Alavi (my brother) joined the meeting together with a lady. She was introduced to us as Maryam Firouz. [...] The twenty-nine-year-old Maryam was one of most beautiful ladies of those days. Her look, her clothes, and her style caught everybody's attention immediately. When Bozorg left the room, Aalieh Shermini followed him and asked: "Who is this girl?" She added, "Remember, Mr. Alavi! We are here to fight against this class!"[5]

Not only was Maryam received very well by the other members, but soon she took the lead and became the most influential figure of the association. She sponsored the publication of the journal and rented an office for the association in Baharestan Square, in front of the parliament.[6] She eventually took over the task of the editorial responsibilities of *Bidari-e Ma* and frequently wrote essays, manifestos, and poems and translated articles. The journal found its ground in the social and political limbo of Iran in the mid-1940s. The association successfully attracted many active and affiliated members and enabled a large body of committed readers.

Maryam Firouz became a fundamental figure in making the Women's Association an official part of the Tudeh Party. Together with Zahra Eskandari and Aalieh Shermini, they were the only founding members that managed to get involved in the Tudeh Party's activities before the establishment of the association. Although during 1941–42 the central committee of the party, headed by Soleiman Eskandari, was hesitant to accept women as active members, Maryam had her own ties with the party through her friend Noureddin Kianouri, whom she married in 1944.

Maryam had already gotten divorced from her first husband, Abbas-Gholi Esfandiari, in 1939, only a year after that, she met Kianouri, an architect who had been introduced to her to design her house in Shemiran. Kianouri was a graduate of Tehran University. He later moved to Germany and obtained his doctorate in architecture from the Technical University of Aachen in 1939. A year later, he returned to Iran, and in 1945, together with a few other architects, he founded the Association of Iranian Architects. Despite his academic career at the University of Tehran and his professional work as an architect, he was a left-wing activist and already a member of the Communist Party in Germany. Kianouri became one of the founding members of the Iranian Tudeh Party in 1941 after his return.

4 The editorial circle grew very fast. In the coming months, a second group of influential figures and active contributors joined the association: Farrokh-Laqa Alavi (the Alavi sisters' cousin), Jamileh Seddighi, Akhtar Kambakhsh (Kianouri), Afsar Sedghdar, and Homayoun Eskandari, among others.

5 Najmi Alavi, *Ma Ham dar in Khaneh Haqqi Darim* [We have a right in this house too: Najmi Alavi's memoir], ed. Hamid Ahmadi (Tehran: Akhtaran, 2008), 60–61.

6 Maryam Firouz, *Khaterat* [Memoir] (Tehran: Ettelaat Press, 1994), 40.

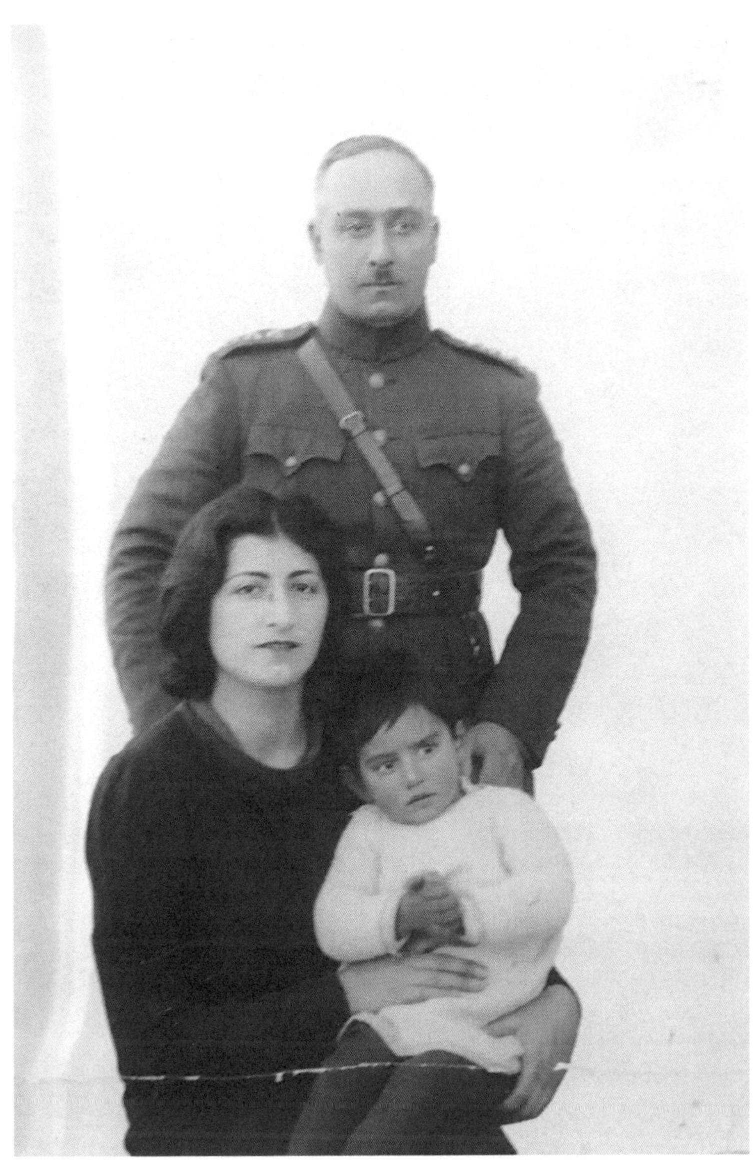

Maryam Firouz with Abbas-Gholi Esfandiari and their daughter Afsaneh, 1935
Courtesy of Afsaneh Gidfar

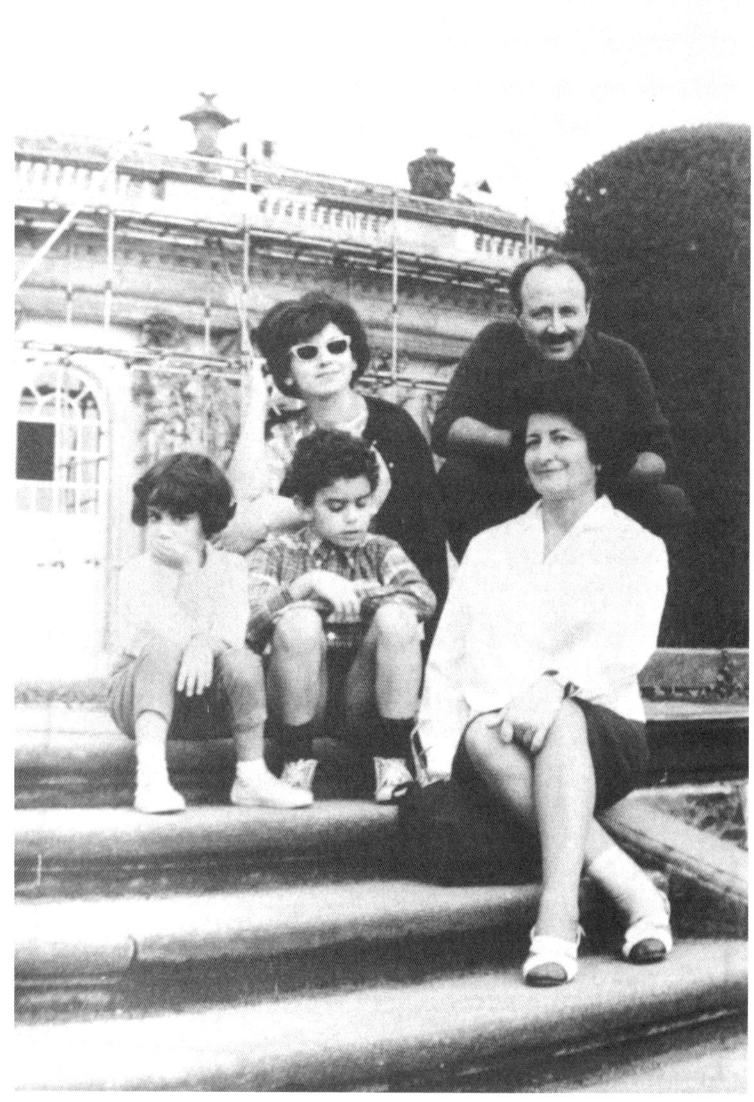

The Macettis with Afsaneh in Berlin, 1960
Courtesy of Afsaneh Gidfar

However, on February 4, 1949, Tudeh was accused of the assassination attempt on the shah during an annual ceremony to commemorate the founding of the University of Tehran. The party was subsequently banned, and most of the party leaders were imprisoned. After two years in jail, Kianouri escaped from prison and lived undercover. After a couple of years, he fled, first to Iraq and then to Italy. There, with the help of the Italian Communist Party, he was given a new identity as Dr. Silvio Macetti.[7] Maryam Firouz followed him after a few months, and she subsequently became known as Mrs. Maria Macetti.

In 1957 Silvio Macetti (that is, Kianouri) moved to Moscow and started working with the architect and urban planner Georgy Alexandrovich Gradov. Their collaborations were mainly focused on designing large-scale housing projects, the initial phase of a larger institutional research project that continued in the following years. After their time in Moscow, in 1959 the Macettis moved to East Germany and settled in Berlin, where Silvio was later appointed as one of the research directors of the Bauakademie to run a project in collaboration with the research institute at the Academy of Architecture in Moscow, directed by Gradov. In Berlin, Maryam gradually got acquainted with cultural scenes and organizations. She became friends with the Jewish painter and activist Lea Grundig and her husband, Hans. Both Lea and Hans had been active members of the German Communist Party during the 1920s and, after the war, they became affiliated with the newly established Socialist Unity Party. Lea was a full member of Akademie der Künste der DDR (East German Academy of Culture) and served as the president of Verband Bildender Künstler der DDR (East German Visual Artists' Association). Maryam and Lea had shared interests and dedication to both culture and political activism.[8] Through Lea, Maryam was introduced to the professors in the Department of Philology at Leipzig University. She started teaching eighteenth-century French literature and in parallel began working on her doctoral research on three influential French figures in eighteenth-century Iranian literature: Montesquieu, Voltaire, and Diderot.[9] After finishing her PhD, Maryam began to teach French literature at Humboldt University in Berlin.[10]

Firouz and Kianouri dedicated the next two decades to research and writing. Their form of political activism was tuned in to the linguistic and architectural apparatuses. They both believed that the key aspects that could possibly trigger social mobilization lay in domestic space. Kianouri (Silvio Macetti) and Gradov worked on an extensive research project whose purpose was to establish and promote the theory of what was to be called a "new socialist architecture," aligned with the new social structure and technological advancements of the time and a vision for the future. The two architects were tasked with revising the fundamental ideology of socialism and applying it in a Neufert-like handbook of socialist architecture, proposing new typologies of collective habitation, public institutions, and urban forms and developing new planning principles for the territories. The twenty-year research collaboration resulted in the publication of two books: *Großwohneinheiten* (1968), by S. Macetti, and *Stadt und Lebensweise* (1971), by G. A. Gradov. In the introduction to *Großwohneinheiten* [Large-scale housing units], Macetti writes:

> Today we live in a great era, it is the era of revolutionary transformation for the whole society, the age of a worldwide transition from capitalism to socialism. This transformation of the world opens up new perspectives on the spiritual and material conditions of human life. Like every realm of human activity, architecture is also under the decisive influence of these overall processes. As architects and urban planners [our] first and foremost duty is to adapt the built

7 Noureddin Kianouri, *Khaterat* [Memoir] (Tehran: Ettelaat Press, 1992), 403.

8 Interview with Afsaneh Gidfar (Esfandiari), Maryam Firouz's daughter, on August 15, 2018, Tehran.

9 Firouz, *Khaterat*, 95.

10 Kianouri, *Khaterat*, 401.

environment of the society to the demands of the socialist way of life. [...] To constantly provide housing for more people and to offer them such a cultural and living milieu as affects the development of individuals as well as society. This [new] form of living must comply with the requirements of our time and the socioeconomic performance of the space in order to foster a high degree of socialization in household tasks.[11]

What was pointed out by Macetti was indeed in continuation of *Bidari-e Ma*'s mission, as that publication had clearly stated: "Today, as a result of the evolution of civilization, domestic labor has been limited, and most of women's traditional responsibilities and tasks now are to be assumed by the society at large."[12] Their agenda was clearly in line with the Soviet ideology, in which women's emancipation from domestic labor had been seen as the fundamental factor in the evolution of the society. They wanted women out of houses not only for their capacities in production and the labor force but also as the forgotten half of the society that could be available for a mass mobilization—a revolution toward new socialism. Macetti further elaborates on their aims behind proposing new forms of domestic spaces:[13]

> Among the main objectives, creating the spiritual and material conditions for the comprehensive emancipation of women is a major task in the socialist transformation of society. As Lenin has written explicitly: "The woman, however, remains a house slave, as she was before the oppressive laws were repealed. She is still engrossed in, and stultified by, the petty details of household management, she is still chained to the kitchen and the nursery, still engaged in the same unproductive and nerve-destroying labour. The real emancipation of women, real Communism, can only begin when the proletariat, at the helm of State, leads the fight of the masses against the system of small housekeeping, it can only begin with the transformation to Socialist great economy."[14]

Both Macetti and Gradov published many journal articles and research reports, a number of which appeared in *Deutsche Architektur*. However, most of their extensive joint project was never published and has remained as manuscripts dispersed in various archives in Germany, Russia, and Iran. Thus, it is difficult to evaluate to what extent such a theoretical project was actually implemented and promoted by the two institutions in planning new settlements and developing architectural typologies. However, one can trace the migration of the ideas and application of these principles of cohabitation and a new socialist way of living along with the movement of the two leading figures.

Gradov was tasked with moving to the southern republics of the Soviet Union to plan new settlements and to develop new public architecture for the capital cities. His legacy is quite visible in the planning and design of the city of Frunze (now Bishkek) in the Kirghiz Soviet Socialist Republic and Dushanbe in the Tajik Soviet Socialist Republic. He died in Pamir in 1984. However, for Macetti (that is, Kianouri), the story was a bit different. It could be claimed that he established, if not developed, the discourse of social housing in Iran parallel to the progression of the research project.

Although Kianouri was not personally involved in designing and planning the first social housing projects in Iran, he served the architectural movement

11 Silvio Macetti [N. K.], *Großwohneinheiten* (Berlin: VEB Verlag für Bauwesen, 1968), 8.

12 Farrokh-Laqa Alavi, "House, Household, and Their Constraints in the Contemporary Time," *Bidari-e Ma 1*, no. 4 (1944), 13–14.

13 Macetti, *Großwohneinheiten*, 26.

14 Vladimir Il'ich Lenin, *The Great Initiative: Including the Story of Communist Saturdays*, trans. P. Lavin (Glasgow: Socialist Labour Press, 1919), 23–24.

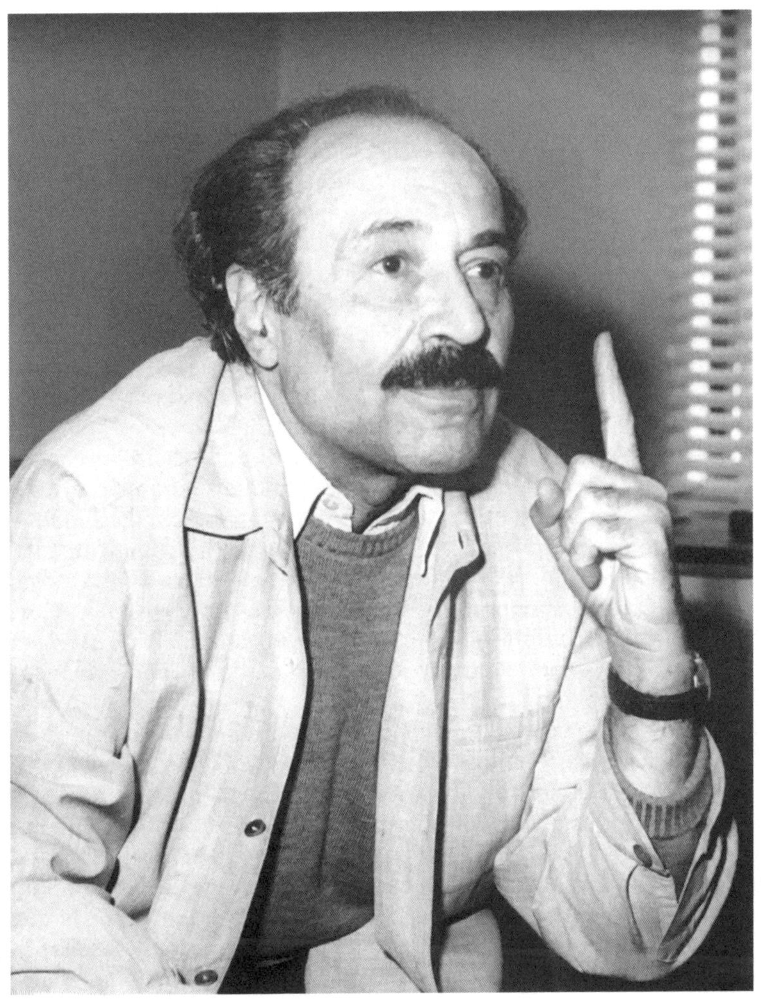

Noureddin Kianouri aka Silvio Macetti, 1980
Courtesy of Afsaneh Gidfar

through his theoretical and ideological inputs. The other members of the Association of Iranian Architects, such as Mohammad Elahi, Manouchehr Khorsand, Ali Sadegh, Iraj Moshiri, Siavash Kasraei, and Nasser Badi'e, most of whom were sympathizers of affiliated members of the Tudeh Party, took the lead.

Following the enactment in 1944 of the Law of Affordable Housing for Working Class and Governmental Employees initiated in parliament by the Tudeh Party fraction, the Association of Iranian Architects developed a series of social housing projects in Tehran: Chaharsad Dastgah (1944–46), Kuy-e Narmak (1951–55), Kuy-e Nazi Abad (1951–58), Kuy-e Nohom-e Aban (1961–63), and Kuy-e Kan (1961–64). The plan of the dwelling units was reduced to a bare minimum of spaces, a series of bedrooms with almost no living room or spacious kitchen, as used to be the case in traditional Iranian houses. The projects were provided with day-care centers, public laundry facilities, and, most importantly, gathering places on the scales of blocks and neighborhoods. For them, the social, political, and economic performance of the projects was the absolute priority, they were planned as breeding grounds for a mass mobilization. The design of the housing typologies thus strictly followed the ideas for the socialization of household tasks promoted by Macetti (Kianouri) and Maryam Firouz in their writings.

Although Kianouri signed his books and articles with his pseudonym, Silvio Macetti, Maryam kept her name on her writings. She did not stop addressing Iranian women in her works. She wrote books such as *Madar-Nameh* (Epic of Motherhood), *Afsaneh va Afsar* (Afsaneh and Afsar), and *Chehreh-haye Derakhshan-e Mobareze Iran* (Prominent Figures in Iran's Activism). But undoubtedly the most influential yet less-known project of hers was the *Bidari-e Ma* journal.

Eight pieces have been selected for this publication from four years of *Bidari-e Ma* that together give an overall image of the structure, language, graphics, and various areas of interests of the journal, from manifestos, statements, and lectures to critique of daily politics, to advice on women's hygiene, beauty, and fashion, to reflection on international women's movements, their strategies and tactics. Maryam Firouz is, of course, the dominant voice behind the articles, however, other writers such as Homayoun Eskandari and Farrokh-Laqa Alavi are also included to demonstrate multiple perspectives within the mission statement of the journal and the association.

The opening article, "Wake Up!," was published in the first issue of the journal (July 1944), wherein Maryam Firouz elaborates on the Women's Association's main critique about Iranian society and in particular Iranian men. She addresses the Iranian women, asking them to act collectively: "Wake up! Society won't turn into a paradise without your participation and effort, it is fundamental, and necessary too, to assess our aims, realize them, and live together in fulfilling our common goals." In the follow-up article, "Our Mission" (March 1945), Firouz departs from the general observations and begins to identify specific issues in regard to women's unjust legal, political, economic, and social powerlessness, bringing up the questions of motherhood, affective and domestic labor, and women workers. She lays out the mission for the organization in this way: "[T]he Women's Association seeks restoration of women's rights in every sense as its ideal. Every single one of us is ready to fight. We have woken up and would like to wake up our other sisters who are bending under the pressure of suppressive laws in this country."

The third piece, "Our Sisters and Daughters!" (February 1945), is a critical response to Ahmad Kasravi's book bearing the same title. In his book—published only a few month before the *Bidari-e Ma*'s article—Kasravi revisits the Iranian women's customs and manners through a historical perspective. He further reflects on the traditional role of women in the Iranian society, their rights, and their social tasks. Firouz cynically calls Kasravi's historical reading normalization of gender violence both at home and in society. She writes, "Don't shackle a woman by tiring and pointless chains of cooking and household chores. Don't tie down women under the name of freedom, which leads to nothing but destruction of her mind and body. The well-being of her child is the responsibility of the society." The short note that follows Maryam's critique is written by Farrokh-Laqa Alavi. "House, Household, and Their Constraints in the Contemporary Time" (September 1944) sees progress of the society through women's emancipation and freedom from domestic labor and household tasks in order to be out as active agents of the society.

"Iranian Women Must Turn Out at Ballot Boxes" (January 1945) is the Women's Association's letter of support to a bill that Fereydoun Keshavarz, member of parliament, presented on August 15, 1944, on behalf of the Tudeh Party fraction. The bill asked for recognition of women's equal rights and social benefits, including the right to vote and the right to be selected as a member of the parliament or the government. "O Iranian women, arise and be happy! Noblemen are out there who would support you," writes Firouz, defending the bill and responding to the oppositional voices who saw such a law as too progressive for Iranian society. They referred to France, where, at the time, women's right to vote was being hotly discussed. However, Maryam Firouz brings up the example of Soviet women who had gained their right to vote back in 1917, and she describes their achievements in the Soviet society. The follow-up article, "The Life of Women Workers" (June 1946), is Homayoun-Taj Eskandari's review of Marie Couette's article in *La Vie Ouvriere*, the magazine of the French General Confederation of Labor, where she discusses the achievements of the French labor unions in supporting the women workers and providing them with facilities such as day care, laundry, and communal kitchens. She recommends it as a successful model that can be employed in Iran.

The last two articles are written by the journal's editorial team. "Lustful Dolls" (May 1948) is a critical reflection on the expanding influence of the American lifestyle through Hollywood movies in Iranian cinemas. The author (whose voice is similar to Firouz's) sees such problems as more threatening to a group, which she calls "modern women," and she asks, "Do these so-called modern women know that what appears on the movie screen is not the true reflection of the reality of life in the United States? It's just a means to deceive the people of the world. Do they know that, more than Hollywood stars, there are women in the States who work hard for their society?" Instead, the last piece advices Iranian women to wear simpler clothes and makeup. The author believes that low-budget clothes can be chosen tastefully and would look more stylish.

The works of Kianouri and Firouz (a.k.a. the Macettis) had been set on one essential belief: "Revolution begins at home."

The current publication wouldn't have happened without the generous support, motivation, and dedication of Giovanna Silva. Her enthusiasm and trust were the main forces pulling the pieces of this project together. The book, in fact, is part of a larger research project on "The Social Movements and the Architecture of the City." The research began and developed first at the International Institute of Social History in Amsterdam in 2016 and has been developing since then. I would like to thank Touraj Atabaki, who has been the endless source of inspiration and motivation for the research. Of course, none of these would have been possible without hours of interviews with Afsaneh Gidfar (Esfandiari), who simply believed in the project and shared with me her valuable memories, thoughts, and family archive. Finally, I would like to thank Samaneh Maddah for her vigorous effort translating these rather complex articles of *Bidari-e Ma*.

WAKE UP!

MARYAM FIROUZ

I feel the urge to express what I believe is truth, please forgive me if there is any false claim or inconsistency.

Over the past three years, when I was more closely in contact with people from different social classes, I have realized one major principle:
Today's Iranian society can be seen as a closed and darksome room, filled with cigarette and opium smoke. The inhabitants are so stoned and intoxicated that they can hardly move. Even if there is a ray of shining light and a piece of blue sky penetrating in, they seem so distant and unreachable that they cannot make the exhausted inhabitants take any step forward. "What's the point when we never get to fresh air and what we wish for, so why should we move?" they would say. As the smoke gets darker and denser, the people that have either never stepped in or had no guts to get themselves out of the room and to enjoy the blessing of a free world, an extended horizon, an open mind to open the doors every now and then and let the fresh breeze come in, they try to reason a way out and to show the path to salvation to the mute, to the weak, to the stoned.

This image sparks in my mind the more I read the newspapers, listen to people's conversations, and observe daily lives.

Among these men, who have always been privileged to read more and discuss more—those so-called elites—there is a group that is vapid and sluggish, so afraid of opening the window and taking the fresh air, they are waiting for someone to open the doors for them, or they would rather suffocate out of fear of taking the risk. They are not only drowning but putting their saviors down too. They are not aware that it is they who are the biggest threat to the people. There cannot be anything expected from others, when these gentlemen are seated mute, waiting for a miracle to descend from the sky.

What to do if the gentlemen are hit hard? This is the effect of their own conduct, and maybe just because of four pieces of carpet and three-month salaries or indolence, they compromise their social status and character.

But what about women? For years and centuries, the Iranian woman has been limited to a tiny, tedious space to live in with no opportunity whatsoever to flourish and to achieve intellectual autonomy and an independent character.

From the very first days, when she distinguishes right from left, she is forced to marry a man. Whether she is a poor girl or rich, this is the only path that society puts her on, that is to gamble her life blindfolded with a "yes," entering holy matrimony. And believe it or not, in this gambling, the woman is the loser in 100 percent of the cases.

The good or bad fortune of marriage is not my point. But the question is: In what space can the woman's character, talent, intellect, and intelligence best flourish? In what way would she benefit most, by listening to which valuable talk or reading which scientific article? All these gradually wane through boring, useless, and repetitive domestic labor such as childcare, without following the proper principles, emotional pressure by the husband, and poor hygiene. Soon her youth is blown away, and she turns into a narrow-minded woman spending her whole time thinking about "eggplant pickles and *Tebrizi* meatballs." God forbid I should consider such errands ill and untimely. But what should a woman do on top of these? And how can she get some learning? I am a woman, and I know how much time all this requires and how it exhausts the soul, the mind, and the body.

Over the past few years, all school doors have been opened to women, and women have been given freedom. Unfortunately, those mothers and housewives could not intermingle in that environment and satisfy their roles as women and mothers. And those who could benefit from this opportunity were girls whose families' fortune made it possible for them to do so. For such girls (of course, there are exceptions for whom everyone has high hopes), all sorts of boundless freedom are provided too, such as (cabaret) dance and gambling circles. Hence they had no time to study, comprehend, and learn. There were no guidelines for them to cultivate the joy of work and the passion to know. On the contrary, a still life where all is readily available for the fulfillment of any wish has brought them up to be languid, far from any act that requires endeavor and spirit. To be more free—as they imagine to be—they cling to the first man who comes their way and afterward let it be whatever it may. If they hear some words of value, with so much coquetry and vanity, they would say, "What have our men done that we as women are expected to do now?"

I am not sure if they understand their own words, I hope they don't, because otherwise they are not pardonable, they bring a bad name to women, and thus, with this hope, I address you by saying, "You, the women of Iran, the dear sisters, it is not your fault. You have been brought up as such from the very beginning. Be aware that you as mothers hold a heavy duty! You have to raise children. You have to raise men who are men of labor, men with guts. The good or evil of these people is partly in your hands. You have an impact on husbands, brothers, and fathers. And ask to have it. Don't be just the instructor of boys and the caretaker, but try to be their guide and mentor.

How much the truth uttered by a woman and a mother infiltrates a man's soul and heart, when she is all about sacrifice and devotion?

What are your goals? And what do you want from your men in fulfilling those?

Live life in such a manner that your soul and heart do not wilt by witnessing so much misery and hearing about so much whimpering.

Seek everyone's happiness and try as much as you can so that everyone has a share of bliss and comfort. Seek respect for every woman, don't belittle yourself with such words, strive for intellectual and financial independence, not just for yourself but for all! Now you would respond by saying that the Iranian woman has autonomy over her properties.

This is true for those of you who inherit properties, both material and intellectual. But for those who have nothing, for how long should they beg their husbands? Don't wish to be brought up as an idler. And, of course, those of you who one day will not be able anymore to bear life with a man you have chosen so inconsiderately and perfunctorily should give up this inheritance in return for your liberation. What will you do then? Beg? At whose door?

Wake up! Society won't turn into a paradise without your participation and effort. It is fundamental, and necessary too, to assess our aims, realize them, and live together in fulfilling our common goals.

A country, half of the population of which is idle and waiting for the other half to work, cannot progress, cannot develop further. Today they have every right to look at us as inferior. What have we done? What desire have we sacrificed? What trouble have we taken? Are we still expecting to be placed among those women of the world who have not only sacrificed their life and assets but also have relinquished their lives for the sake of their society's advancement and excellence? Read! There are plenty of books. Read useful papers and magazines. A noble man once mentioned in his article, "Do not refer much to idols such as Hafez, Sa'adi, Bergen, Plato and Khayyam"! What a shame! I am so sorry that

I have to admit that, except for a very few, we are not much familiar with these names and even less so with their words. If we had known them, a great step would have been taken forward, the minds would have been more ready and the path more open.

We are asleep, indeed. So unaware of the world inside and out! And that's why I would say, and I repeatedly say: Wake up!

It is true that it is not enough just to wake up. What's the use of having our eyes wide open to see the miserable life of almost everyone in this country, to see the social scars and blotches that have hardly left a healthy spot on this nation's body, to hear the moaning children and weeping mothers and get affected in our awakened and sensitive hearts by emotional pains, grief, desolation, and hunger, when we cannot think of a way out? When we are only an addition to the crying crowd and an extra burden? That day when, for the sake of this nation, its children and women I beseeched you to wake up were to ask you to strive to unite with one another sisterly, with utmost purity and contentment. The immensity and grandeur of the task is indescribable. This call should be reiterated everywhere, in any language and in any manner. Today is not a day when we can lead a life based on "May God will..." Nothing wrong with uttering these words, but let's launch efforts and spare no labor.

There is a famous French proverb that says: "Whatever a woman wants, that is God's want too."[1]

And it is true. Experience it and you yourselves will admit that a woman is known for her diligence, tolerance, intelligence, and plenteous feelings. This should be proved.

1 *Ce que femme veut, Dieu le veut.*

MARYAM FIROUZ

Perhaps everyone can express their goals in life. But it's so difficult to express the collective mission for a group of people.

Concerning the topic of the day, which is the mission of the Women's Association, the task has been made easy for me because not only the female members of the association, but also all Iranian women, have nothing at all of their own, so they cannot have diverse missions.

A woman has nothing in Iran, and in all voluminous lawbooks of the country, no mention has been made of women. If they make a slight reference to women, it's just to highlight their condemnation and nothingness. Please allow me to elaborate on the miserable social conditions of Iranian girls and women through examples that might be familiar to all ladies and gentlemen. In other words, I am going to narrate the story of some dead bodies pretending to be alive.

A while ago, when the government embarked on punishing ruffians, one of them was imprisoned and later sentenced to death.

The man married a fourteen-year-old girl, and when he was condemned, the young girl was pregnant. While grieving the death of her husband, sobbing and wailing, she gave birth to a boy. The newborn was as innocent as the young mother, unaware that, just before his birth, his father was taking his last steps toward death.

He was born ignorant and naive, like any other newborn. But those around him never forgot the fact that his father was a villain who was punished.

They forced the fourteen-year-old mother not to breastfeed the baby. No matter how desperately she was looking at her newborn, they tried to inculcate into her mind the thought "let him die because he will ultimately follow in his father's footsteps."

After two days of hunger, the baby perished, and maybe the relatives were right: how could the girl bring up a child? With what tools and resources?

This pure, innocent creature could only be brought up in the same opium-stricken environment with other ruffians, and since he was not accompanied by decent human beings, he could end up as a hanger-on.

[Second story:] A young woman, despite having a daughter, marries another man after the death of her husband. The man hates the daughter, so much that the mother has no alternative but to marry her eleven-year-old daughter off to a chauffeur. For a few months, the newlywed girl was doing fine until she got pregnant. All through her pregnancy, her husband reminded her that if she gave birth to a baby girl, he would divorce her. The girl went through days and nights in supplication and tears. But since at times prayers lead to curses, a baby girl was born, after all. Hearing the news, the father panicked, and although he was told time and again that a baby girl is a shower of blessings, he did not like this shower on his house. After months of negligence, he finally agreed to keep the mother and the baby at home. A while later, the young girl got pregnant a second time. Her husband threatened her, saying that the first time was a narrow escape but the second time would not be.

You can imagine the situation of the girl, this poor mother who had not chosen to be a mother, this child who had never tasted childhood and womanhood. She was begging magicians, fortune-tellers, and holy shrines day in, day out. There is a saying that goes "one who is dearer, suffers more." Maybe this girl was also a very dear one to God. I don't know. But anyway, the second child also turned out to be a girl.

This time, the husband didn't show up as long as his wife remained in bed, recovering. He stepped into the house only when he could throw the mother out, reasoning that she only gave birth to baby girls and was no good for him.

The sixteen-year-old mother left her two daughters at Omid Orphanage, left her home and belongings, and started wandering around the streets all alone with no support. Worse of all, she had no hope that something could be done or that some moves could be made. She had learned, in every cell of her body, far before this incident, that life was like this for her and those like her, thinking that there was surely a reason for her husband to abhor girls. This woman left home and chose the only path available to her fragile body and took refuge in one of the most miserable houses of this city, known as Shahr-e No,[2] among thousands like her. No one ever heard of her again. Her mother curses her every time she hears her name, and all her relatives have now come to the conclusion that, from the very first day, this girl was a misfit.

Third story: A middle-class family managed to bring up their daughter, up to the age of sixteen, but then they wished to marry her off so that she would have a guardian. The parents and the girl were all obsessed with this thought, consulting with each other on what sort of husband they should wish for. The girl asked their permission to go and work in an office, but how could they consent?

There are thousands of men in workplaces. How can a girl be left on her own in such places? Apart from that, just a handful of decent men would marry a girl who worked in an office. So for this and some other reasons, heated discussions took place between the parents and the girl. The parents wanted to choose a life for her, and maybe both sides were right.

Finally, one day a suitor of caliber showed up. Of course he was aged, but then could they hope that he would treat their daughter nicely? It's all right if he is not very young, if he is not handsome, at the end of the day, a man should be a breadwinner. He had three children from a previous marriage. That was also fine as long as he was well-to-do enough to feed everyone. Their daughter was young and could have children of her own. But the parents were cautious enough not to introduce the groom-to-be to their daughter immediately. And the poor daughter was so fed up with all the arguments and this boring life that she was ready to give herself up to anyone. Finally, she said yes to this marriage in just a second, which was enough to blow up a whole life. It is true that the world continued to be as it was, but the life of a girl who could be a good mother was wrecked.

The gentleman was well-off. But he could accumulate so much wealth because he didn't have the guts to spend any. He used to give her meager nourishment, and that was all. The girl had no life in a house where she lived with the older children of her husband. She lost all her youth and spirit and decided to get a divorce. However, the husband told her she had no chance for a divorce as long as she was alive. Her parents echoed the same thing. The girl continued struggling, and finally, one day, she committed suicide.

I have narrated three episodes that are repeated every day, and you have heard and seen thousands of them.

We are so used to such incidents that we can't grasp them as real miseries. You don't need to go far, just look at the horrendous, unimaginable life of thousands and thousands of women and girls in Iran. Let's look at South Tehran, where the neighborhoods resemble the Middle Ages, the area close to the brick kilns seems like a prehistoric spot. Spend two hours of your time in those ghettos and see hundreds of young women and girls, aged fourteen to sixteen,

2 The red light district of old Tehran.

living like rags. In these ghettos, their only shelter, their only amusement, their only hope that can take them away from their daily life even for a moment, is opium. Go and visit the houses in these ghettos, which are just there for people to smoke opium. Let's walk in this infamous neighborhood in the South and see the twelve-to-fourteen-year-old girls in utmost desolation struggling with the worst adversities. They will never reach the age of thirty, they will perish much earlier as a result of life's pressures and ailments. Look at these children who should just be happy and get ready for the future and who are now so pessimistic and miserable with all such illnesses.

It's like a flood that sweeps away whatever gets in its way, it's the flood of hunger and poverty, the flood of lawlessness, the flood of deprivation of rights that has pushed them down to a valley in South Tehran. They are disgusted and ignorant of the world around them as they gather all in one spot like lepers. Can you imagine that the children of these women will forever suffer pains and illnesses that the mothers are unable to cure? Who are these people? They are the girls and women of this land. They should bring up the future generations. So how come they are stuck in this whirlpool? Most of them were chosen for *sighe* (temporary marriage) to the village elder, the mullah, or a wealthy man just to serve the man as an entertainment tool, and later, when the period was over, they were left on their own.

Visit homes. Listen to the pains of women. Make friends with them. Talk to them as a sister. And you will see that most of them are struggling with difficulties. They all have common fears. They tolerate everything, every offence, every pressure.

Why? Only because if they leave their husbands, they have no means to earn a living, so they either have to put up with the situation or serve as maidens in this or that house.

Ask thousands of mothers who go through all sorts of pressures just not to get separated from their children. They bring up children with their very blood and flesh. The mothers who have indeed given life to these children now have no right over them. Under the name of the law, they have been deprived of their very natural right. If they want to stay with their children and not leave them with stepmothers or on the street, they have to bear whatever is happening at home. Are these women good mothers? Can these children be ready for life in a happy spirit and serve this country as proper warriors when they are witness to fights between their parents and the sorrow and tears of their mothers? It's absolutely impossible. One cannot forget the effects of the immediate environment. A girl brought up in such surroundings will believe that in the future she should shed tears, and from the very beginning prepares herself to bear whatever mishap may come. A boy brought up this way will see himself as a superior who can impose himself by force. But apart from that, both boys and girls will suffer as their mother suffers, and both are tearful because of her pain.

Women carry the heavy burden of economy. They are the most harmed as a result of financial pressures. They are in pain mentally and emotionally. And it's so ridiculous to find that society sees women as incomplete and weak. A woman bears the heaviest burden and does so with much vigor. And maybe to make her endure more, they have come up with such meaningless attributes.

Let's get away from the family and go to the whole country. Women are a major part of the workforce wherever one can find a piece of bread, wherever one can work, any factory—big or small. They work the same hours as men, but they're paid much less. Women have no rights here. Their voice is not heard anywhere, and since they have to think of their and their children's hunger, they agree to whatever meager wage they are offered, just to survive. In carpet-weaving factories, one sees little girls who should be playing instead. Their minds should be cultivated by useful knowledge, and yet they are in these factories, bent over and crooked, working ten to twelve hours a day just for a piece of bread. The carpet under our feet is woven and colored with the blood of several boys and girls. We have kept the carpet industry up and running on the lives of thousands of innocent children. And we still take pride in ourselves as Iranian industrialists.

It is a true statement, but we are not proud of that. If we know indeed that the carpets are woven by sacrificing the souls of our children, we can never be proud. We cannot be proud when we know that our current situation is bloodier than any damaging war could ever be.

We who have gathered here today will be upset if a thorn scratches our child's finger. Now come and have a look at six-to-seven-year-old children cleaning tragacanth as they sit around big trays, working with the plant with their delicate hands all through the day. As always, Iranian mothers have no alternative but to tolerate. The tragacanth is stained by children's blood. Blood is all over, from the elbow down to the fingers. But worse than the tragacanth thorn is the lawlessness of this society.

So that's why today the Women's Association seeks restoration of women's rights in every sense as its ideal. Every single one of us is ready to fight. We have woken up and would like to wake up our other sisters who are bending under the pressure of suppressive laws in this country.

Don't be weak. We want the Iranian woman, the Iranian girl, to be able to defend herself. We want the law to let her bring up a ruffian's child as a helpful, decent citizen. We want women to be able to live an independent life, instead of turning to prostitution, the day they realize they cannot continue living with their husbands. We want girls to be welcomed in families. We want a bright future for them. And we hope that every woman and girl has a chance to work so that she can survive financially and choose her husband herself, and, in case she cannot continue the life of matrimony, we hope that she is not forced to do so. We seek to rescue thousands of girls who are on the verge of *sighe*. We want laws. We strive to free Iranian girls, Iranian mothers, and the next generation in particular of this ailment, offering them a healthy, joyous life and not a life of smoke and opium.

We want mothers to know that they are not mere reproductive machines. The law should recognize that children belong to their mothers. The law should not allow the fruit of women's lives—a three-year-old boy or a seven-year-old girl—to be taken away from them. We want this barbarism to stop.

We wish for women to wake up and know their rights, to work and get paid in factories as men do. Because of the very fact that we are women and mothers, we want our girls to be freed from the tragacanth thorns and to save their delicate bodies from factories. The fact is that we want to bring up future women who will rescue Iran and will work alongside men for the progress of this country.

We are not fighting against men. On the contrary, we are reaching out to help them as sisters and mothers. Men should know that a woman is a big help. The world is a good example for them. Over the past years, whenever women got involved in an area or activity, they could save men from a whirlpool of miseries and failures.

We are fed up with such absurd and untrue expressions as "companion," "beloved," and "sweetheart." We look at life with open eyes and clear views. For years we have been imprisoned by fascinating expressions. Enough of that.

If, in your own words, women are mothers and it's the mothers who bring up good children, stop talking and get active. Be aware that a woman who is deemed incomplete, weak, and in pain can never bring up male lions for Iran.

Those who have passed the constitution have placed women—who could be their mothers, their sisters, and their daughters—with the insane and children in an article that is a cause of shame. What do you expect from children and the insane? Don't you think it's more of an insult to the followers of this law rather than just to women per se?

Iranian women have never refrained from fulfilling their duties so far. They have managed life with a strong will and have borne with social problems more than anyone else.

We are proud of being women. We have never verbally insulted our fathers, brothers, or sons. We are wise enough to know that insulting them is the same as insulting ourselves. We have always wished them advancement and excellence.

Today, as Iranian women, we want to join the civilized world where women have a place everywhere, a world that has not fully recovered from a devastating war but is breathing, a world that has sacrificed lives to free social slaves, a world that has realized that women should be involved in everything. The voice of the civilized nations that have been role models for us to date can be clearly heard: women are everywhere, even in politics. Relying on her stamina, intellect, and kind heart, a woman can have a say in the country's affairs as a woman and as a mother.

Today we would like to show these nations who have realized women's status that the Iranian woman is alive. We want to make the men of the world understand that the decent mothers, daughters, and sisters of this land consider themselves alive and civilized. They cannot be treated as insane and thickheaded.

OUR SISTERS AND DAUGHTERS!

MARYAM FIROUZ

In a book titled *Our Sisters and Daughters*, revered writer Mr. Ahmad Kasravi has informed all women and girls of his and a group of like-minded men's view of women.

Mr. Kasravi talks of hijab in the first chapter of the book. Relying on historical documents, he has made it clear to us that hijab is not a post-Islam phenomenon and that it existed in Iran prior to Islam. To prove this claim, he refers to the famous Greek historian Plutarch's narrative of the flight of a Greek commander to Iran:

> To send him off, his host thought of a plan as the Asians, Iranians in particular, greatly honor women and not only keep an eye on their wives, but carefully observe their bondmaids or their favorite women. They are so vigilant that they keep them at home all the time without letting them leave the house. On the road, women are accommodated in entirely closed tents carried on a palanquin. They provided the same tent and litter for Themistocles (the Athenian general) when he was on the road. The plan was to tell anyone who might stop them that they were carrying a young woman from... to be married off to an Iranian dignitary.

Now this excerpt of Plutarch's writing is of great value as we can comprehend a few points. Firstly, women's veiling and keeping hidden were traditions in ancient Iran. Plutarch was an honest writer, and his words are concrete. The word "chador," which is still used today and refers to the veil women wear, is another proof of his claim. Secondly, there was no tangible logic behind covering women. The practice was put in place because the powerful, the kings, didn't want anyone to see the faces of their women, and from what Plutarch writes, it is clear that this was a fashion among the wealthy and that later it was passed on to others.

Based on such reasoning, Mr. Kasravi is right in concluding that veiling is not an Islamic practice.

One common misunderstanding in Iran is to consider hijab an Islamic act. People believe that Islam has ordered women to hide themselves. This is not true. Muslim women at the time of Prophet Muhammad and even for some time afterward were not covering their faces. In all the available jurisprudential books, you can barely find a single one saying that women should cover their faces. Not only do these books not mention any such thing, but they also clearly reiterate that showing the face and the hands is allowed.

Sheikh Morteza Ansari, a well-known grand mujtahid of the century whose books and theses are studied by every seminary student, has written and reasoned on the topic. He notes that, at the time of Prophet Muhammad, women were not covering their faces. He refers to a narrative by the Prophet which says: "The Prophet was riding a camel. His cousin, Abbas, was a pillion rider. On the way, a female passerby stopped them to ask the Prophet a question. Muhammad stopped the camel and asked his young cousin at the back to look away, saying 'a young man close to a young woman and I was afraid evil emerges from between the two.'"

Sheikh Ansari says that some have resorted to this as a reason for women to cover their faces, whereas this narrative calls for the reverse, that is, if the woman's face was covered, why should Muhammad have said such a thing and made his cousin look away.

Then Mr. Kasravi concludes that the same way Arabs picked up so many things such as culture, courtesy, rules, and style through exposure to the Iranian civilization, they borrowed this habit of veiling women and promoted it since they deemed it a sign of grandeur and wealth.

Apart from these brief references, he has some other solid thoughts on the issue, mostly arguing that hijab was never there in Islam and that the clerics in Iran resorted to this tradition and supported it to their own advantage.

We are fortunate and thankful to Mr. Kasravi for providing such solid evidence to help us uproot such traditions favored by the clerics and to keep this shameful, nasty sack (the hijab) away forever.

It is on every woman and girl, wherever she is, to express gratitude to Mr. Kasravi and echo his words on this issue.

Under the pretext of hijab, women were separated from the public, under the pretext of the veil, they could not show up in associations and gatherings, they were totally cut off and unaware of the country's developments and public matters, they were completely ignorant of true knowledge. They were living in this country while having almost no sense of belonging to it, they could not have any.

And the same veiling and separation is taken as the reason women are so much into superstitions and know nothing but child-rearing and household chores.

With so much enthusiasm and optimism, I read the rest of the book, but the hope that glimmered through my reading of the first pages faded away quickly. Despite this well-written introduction, Mr. Kasravi concludes that women should take care of household chores and husbands.

They say the Iranian women should not follow the model of European women as women in Europe have no value, they are dragged into a miserable life by men who lead them to corrupt ways, they claim.

Here we notice that the reason behind a woman's misery is not the veil, because the European women—who, as described by Mr. Kasravi, are worthless—do not wear hijab. However, we do not consider men's lust as the only reason behind women's moral corruption in Europe or anywhere else. I assume that if we further explore the present societies, some more significant reasons will come to light.

We argue that women are worthless because they have turned into a cheap tool in the hands of the capitalist states, which take advantage of their work at home and their bodies outside. The same bourgeois states come up with a title [i.e. housewife] that hardly leaves a space for women to understand things and lift up their heads.

We say that if a woman is free, then she should be able to receive a proportionate salary to her work, should be able to provide for her own bread and butter. If society would provide some livelihood for women and would not take them as mere reproduction and pleasure machines, then women would not be forced into prostitution. This is the only path bourgeois societies provide for women. We say that sociopolitical awareness of women does not depend only on wearing / not wearing the veil. Rural women have never been covered, and yet they are kept uninformed. What we say is that the present social regulations treat women as ignorant puppets.

Does Mr. Kasravi believe that European women are miserable? How many men and youth have been seen there who have indulged in moral corruption, which happened just because they had no access to means for a decent life or because they suffered social pressures?

We argue that, in the modern world, one cannot define Europe under one single umbrella and rule it out as a model altogether.

The Soviet states are closer to us in such matters. We know that they involve women in all affairs, support their financial well-being, and protect them in matrimony through laws, and thus no single woman is found there who is subject to men's lust.

On page 16, Mr. Kasravi talks of ballrooms and dancing, of elegant dresses and heavy makeup. Who is he talking to? We should not forget the fact that we live in Iran, the land of misery, desolation, and hunger. Out of every 1,000 women, 999 of them struggle with such difficulties. They have no idea of a ballroom or a dance party. So this means that the addressees are a few wealthy women and girls of the country, and this is not right.

Page 18 states that virtuous women are ours the same way wicked ones are. Women are not a group of lepers who could be labeled as virtuous or wicked. Women are given birth by us, and we give birth to women.

It is true that you and we, we belong to one another, but the law of nature should not be ignored: if someone embarks on restoring her rights, she will succeed. So what's there to be expected from brothers, fathers, and husbands?

Till now we have been under the impression that we should expect them to do something for us, but whatever law is out there has been passed by these very sons and brothers. The only purpose of these laws was bringing about abuse, shame, and violation of rights of women.

Today we have grown up enough to say out loud that "rights are to be claimed and not granted." We should launch efforts in this direction. We don't want a son or a brother to pass a loose law out of mercy for us.

Unfortunately, Mr. Kasravi only mentions that much of women's rights, of which he can make fun and let thoughtless machos rebel against us.

I would like to count women's rights one by one: the same rights the gentlemen admit that we should have but that we are deprived of in this society.

Women's rights are tantamount to right to life, which means the right to education, the right to freely choose a husband, to become a mother and consider the child yours, the right to divorce, the right to employment, the right to use your innate talents, the right to be chosen, the right to choose, and finally, the right to be appointed a minister.

The book categorically notes that if a woman is to marry a man, that should be as per her parents' wish so that later she can have their support. We agree that the family should be in favor, but there should be laws so that a woman is not left with her parents as her sole potential defenders. Let's say the parents are dead or the husband does not listen to them. What should a woman do with all these suppressive laws in Iran?

We want to hold onto our own children. We have brought them up with so much pain, sacrificing our blood and flesh. We don't want to be a mere nurse and caregiver, giving birth to a child for somebody else. We can't let our emotions be governed by someone else. We want to have the right to separate from a husband the day we see that we can't take it anymore, when the husband insults us and considers us a mere tool to provide him with food and clothing. How can one expect unity between a man and a woman if there is no mutual respect out there? How can a woman have some dignity in her house when any time the husband wants, he can throw her out with no objection? Can one believe that such a woman can run her and her husband's life confidently? From among ourselves, sayings and proverbs emerge such as "Don't allow your husband to have a second shirt (don't allow him to accumulate so much wealth), because then he will think of a second woman." As long as men can be polygamous, divorce as they wish, and take away the children, there is no chance for harmony and benevolence to prevail in a family.

To date, others have decided about our good or evil. From now on, we want to decide ourselves. I think we no longer need a guardian like an immature child does. We'd rather shoulder responsibility for our own lives and decide what is good or bad for us.

As long as we have no authority to ratify laws, we have no chance of any accomplishment.

On page 19 Mr. Kasravi notes that God has created the female breed for certain tasks and the male breed for some others. Women are tasked with nest-making and child-rearing, sewing, cooking, and the like.

This is not very gentle of Mr. Kasravi. He is repeating the same thing as the clerics and the mullahs but in a sweet fashion. According to the mullahs, God created women to help men in realizing their pursuits, and that's the only way women come into the picture vis-à-vis men. If that's the case, it would be good to know on which hand God has placed the cooking recipes, on which hand the sewing methods? Between which facial wrinkles has God written about household chores for girls? Don't you think that the same pressure that kept women at home for years, asking them to just do such chores, is now making you assume such tasks as part of her nature—tasks that are of no worth compared to all industrial advancements today?

Elsewhere, he says that a woman can be a doctor, a nurse, a midwife, a dentist, a microbiologist... But don't you think that just because such institutes have opened their gates to women in recent years so that they can display their talents and capabilities, you are now in a position to write these lines admitting that women can do more than household chores and cooking?

But I ask you again if God has written somewhere on a woman's body that she cannot be an astronaut or anything similar, for that matter. Women living abroad do get involved in such areas, and they have been successful.

You call women touchy. Which women? Those women who have been only brought up to coquet and who get irked with anything? Or women who for years resisted any mishap and pressure? Regarding the first group, be assured that they themselves will not distance themselves from such a future when a man shows up who will buy coquetry, as they age, they will be left alone with all their problems and fragility. But about the other women, I reiterate that those with a good upbringing around us have proved that they can do anything and turn it into a success.

On page 12, the author describes how European women have managed to assist men in the war and do something for their nation in whatever discipline they could. If they had been brought up just to rear children, cook, and knit sweaters, today they would have just knelt down in a church, begging the priests—who are worse than our mullahs—for help or would have hurried to a fortune-teller or a magician, asking for a spell to save their child.

On page 13, you praise Ghareh Fatimah Kurdistani, a brave woman who could expel the foreigners from her land. You admire her, and yet on page 28 you keep saying that men need foodstuff to satisfy hunger, clothes to avoid nakedness, a comfortable home to rest, and so on and so forth. If you allow me to say so, you'd better say we need maidens who will just give us babies and make us feel comfortable. If that's the case, why do you admire courageous and noble women? If all they thought about was cooking and sewing, they couldn't have supported men on the battlefront. They couldn't separate rice, needle, and firewood from women's fate to give rise to thousands and thousands of *Ghareh Fatimahs* who are nailed down by the kitchen smoke.

You just want destitute women to go after work so that these women work and the fruits are harvested by those who are just into coquetry. We say work is for everyone, for every woman. We say a woman should not be brought up as inferior, always awaiting some benefit from the hard work of somebody else.

On page 21, you say that in wartime a woman should be aware of what's going on around her, that is, a woman is a tool to rear a child who will be the future soldier, and then who knows when a capitalist will wish for a destructive war to secure his own interests? That child, the only fruit of that woman's life, is now sent to war as a bullet shield.

We believe that, till the very end, a woman should have a say in the destiny of her offspring. She should have the power of discernment and should be granted the right to express her view. She should be able to oppose such pointless wars, which are nothing but a tool for exploitation in the hands of a few who take advantage of humanity, the children of these women. A woman should not allow her son or daughter to turn into flesh in front of a cannon, as the French say.

We say over and over again that she has to take part in all social affairs.

You are reprimanding girls and women who rush to buses on the street at eight in the morning and claim that nothing but lust drives them to work in an office (page 29) and then, quite furiously, you ask them if there is nothing for them to do at home or in the kitchen, so that they are now wandering around in the streets. It's a surprise that you have not researched the current circumstances of our country at all.

Be aware, Mr. Kasravi, that a lustful girl prefers to stay in bed at eight in the morning rather than run around on the streets, as you put it. Know that long hours of work take away her beauty, and such girls lose the only capital you consider worthy for a woman in contact with those you call lustful men and those we define as men and youth with no proper social upbringing.

Mr. Kasravi, there is work at home, but there is no bread there. Cooking is a necessity, but that needs rice and oil. Sweaters should be knitted, but the yarn must be bought. A girl with only a high-school diploma should rush to an office at eight in the morning just to earn a living, and there she is insulted. And in your book, you describe her hunger and no veil as lust. A single woman, a woman who has to provide for her children in the absence of a husband, or a woman who has to aid her husband, is humiliated by you. But be it in the cold or in the heat, she has to move because this humiliation will not bring bread to her table and coal to her fireplace. That's why we want today's men to stop passing laws for us. We should decide what is good or bad for us.

We praise the rural woman's help to her husband. Let me elaborate on the issue.

Her aid is not something new. For years the village woman has suffered, doing the heaviest tasks. When the village men are busy with their pipes, she is sweating hard. There is no end to her work. All through the year, day and night, she is industrious. She does all that because she needs the bread and because her work is not appreciated at all. She has no wage. And that's why giving birth time after time, with no hygiene, along with so much struggle, makes her old and frail, till she finally passes away. In your own words, you are enjoying your life, but we are suffering. The village woman has no rights whatsoever, and although she is from your community, you have never known her.

You look down at dowry. We also admit that women are not there for a deal. Those two people who have chosen one another should be willing to live together, but this union can be considered lasting and concrete only if the law does not hand over all available rights to just one party. I believe you are too optimistic, assuming that society is like a utopian paradise for the bride and the groom. But we see reality. We know that we cannot merely rely on the good mood and sacrifice of the partners. Having high hopes for the girl's parents' support is nothing more than a fantasy and, according to Mr. Kasravi himself, one cannot live on fantasies.

O, Iranian men! Enough of chained women who just cook. Enough of nurse women. Enough of slave women. This is the outcome of years of slavery of your sisters and daughters: this chaotic, filthy society. All these mullah traditions are the fruit of such a mentality and upbringing.

As one elite once said: "Don't shackle a woman by tiring and pointless chains of cooking and household chores. Don't tie down a woman under the name of freedom, which leads to nothing but destruction of her mind and body. The well-being of her child is the responsibility of the society." We echo the same. We cannot agree that the highest purpose of a woman is just cooking tasty dishes and knitting sweaters. For centuries this has been the case. For centuries she has done so. And what has been the outcome? What wage or benefit has she gained? She has put her best effort into this endeavor, and yet what's been the gain? And still as put by Mr. Kasravi, Reza Khan says that only in bread distribution do they utter the name of a woman.

Our loftiest ideal is not to call a woman's body an asset. We consider her talents and understanding as her biggest assets. We are the sisters and daughters of those men who make every effort in the path of freedom and restoration of our rights. We cannot be slaves and maidens deceived by these mesmerizing words.

HOUSE, HOUSEHOLD, AND THEIR CONSTRAINTS IN CONTEMPORARY TIME

FARROKH-LAQA ALAVI

A glance at the history of humanity makes us realize that, at the outset of human civilization, the boundaries of households and families were limited and all human needs were fulfilled within the household, which shouldered all social duties.

Later, given women's natural attention to childcare [they were withdrawn from some social tasks, consequently], the field of activities expanded [for men], and thus women were limited in their social advantages and authority. At the same time, social and political customs led to women's subjugation so extensively that, up until recently, men did not consider any essential role for women except that which pertained to matrimonial, affective labor, and care. They did not attach much importance and value to women.

Now, in a spirit of emancipation, women seek a character of their own and through a movement try to rid themselves of chains of slavery.

Since the proponents of timeworn old teachings and the bigots are opposed to any change or movement in social life, any evolution and social progress, whenever one talks to them about women, society, and gender equality, they say, "A woman's place is at home, a good woman should be interested in house chores and cater only to the needs of children and the man of the house." They are ignorant of the fact that, in modern times, the concept of house and household is different from the old days. Today, as a result of the evolution of civilization, domestic labor has been limited, and most of women's traditional responsibilities and tasks now are to be assumed by the society at large.

Today, limiting women's domestic labor is not in tune with world developments, and in fact, this is something in dire contrast to society's well-being.

Women's creativity and hidden talents have bloomed and have been clearly manifested as they entered into society, so much so that today they manage to take part in all affairs that used to be men's business. In today's world, it has been proven that women have succeeded very well in handling affairs entrusted to them.

Hence, it is far from fair to not ask anything of women except household chores and child-rearing despite all the evidence and experiences in the world. Moreover, if we explore the issue scientifically, it is crystal clear that once women can grow fully and have access to all conducive factors available to men, this gentle gender will also be competent enough in solving scientific matters.

Anyway, the meaning of family and household is completely different today from what it used to be centuries ago.

Certainly any society seeking advancement and progress should welcome women's cooperation, giving an opportunity to half of the country's population.

Similarly, the freedom-seeking and intellectual men of our country should also know that following the same old manner of limiting women to the walls of the house is tantamount to promoting backwardness in the country, knowingly. This will cause colossal damage to the economy, subsequently the path to perfection and civilization will be hindered, and life in general will lose its material and spiritual value in the eyes of the nation.

MARYAM FIROUZ

In response to Dr. [Freydoun] Keshavarz, the Tudeh Party representative, presenting a bill [in support of women's equal rights and right to vote] to the National Parliament,[3] Ms. Yaqkian published a comment on Iranian newspapers. The comment is directly quoted in *Ayandeh Magazine* vol. 1–2. The dame believes that this is a premature law for Iranian women, 99.9 percent of whom are illiterate, famished, and poor.

Does she think that the 99.9 percent of Iranian men who are entitled to vote are literate, well-fed, and wealthy? It's no secret to anyone that most Iranians—men and women—are illiterate, and almost 99 percent of them are underprivileged. Is this a reason to deprive men of their right and appoint a guardian for them instead? And is it to the benefit of the guardian if this illiteracy and ignorance continue? Is the mere knowledge of the alphabet sufficient for a person to protect his rights? That person can better reclaim a violated right that is indeed impartial. And if Iranian men and women cannot enjoy their basic and legitimate rights, they are not to be blamed. Instead we should hold accountable those who try to sell themselves as intellectuals while keeping the nation as starved and poor as they can, for the sake of their own lordship and material interests. These very people claim that the masses are not capable of having a say in their own affairs. We should hold these people responsible for the desolation of the Iranian nation—people who have made a monster of politics and try their best to portray this monster in as scary a way as possible. The nation's fear of this scarecrow gives them ample opportunities to loot further.

The lady reminds us of women's freedom under Reza Shah and some use and misuse of that freedom. I admit that some women misused this superficial freedom, but their horrid behavior should not be generalized. They come from a social class in which their sons, brothers, and fathers prefer to maintain the status quo for their own personal interests. On the material level, they are well-to-do enough to entertain these women through money. But leave this minority aside and consider the multitude of pious Iranian women and girls who have taken advantage of this tiny outlet and are now serving the nation alongside men. Not only Ms. Yaqkian but many Iranians believe that women didn't show any competence and that under Reza Shah they failed to benefit from their freedom the way they should have. It's very unfortunate that such a notion is out there. Just because Iranian women were allowed in schools here and there and the veils were taken off, they were assumed to be free. A woman is free when she has access to social rights, a woman is free when rotten old laws do not chain her down, a woman is free when she can benefit from her knowledge. A woman is not free if the law allows her husband to ban her from working if he wishes to, a woman is not free when she is doomed by laws that are just passed by antifreedom diehards, laws which, like a chain, keep her pressured and miserable. The same laws, ratified by reactionaries, keep the entire nation in famine and poverty while giving them a superficial freedom.

On another note, Ms. Yaqkian wonders why there is so much insistence on Iranian women's overtaking the French women, and she further adds: "I cannot understand this persistence in following France as a role model."

Many are of the opinion that this hastiness is pointless and that we need to move forward step-by-step, as if we were on a ladder. Can we request all to stop referring to such analogies and examples, which are out of place, for a while?

3 Iran National Parliament's minutes. Session 53, 15 August 1944.

Moreover, what we see is that the Iranians have been already intimidated by the long stairway, before taking the first step, they are numb and stoned beside the opium brazier. Today, in the time of spacecraft, do we still need to climb up a ladder to progress? So much effort has been launched by the advanced and civilized nations of the world, and now we should put all these advanced tools aside and stick to the same old wooden stairs? This is merely a way to promote outdated, foul views of people like Mr. Zia-o-ddin, who just talks about filigree, kohl, and henna. Why should the Iranian women go that far? All they need is to keep their eyes and ears open, see and hear that the path they are recommended to tread in a hundred years has been covered by other women overnight. One great leader used to say: "Involve a woman and a woman and a woman in all affairs. Open the doors of every institute and association to her and benefit from this colossal power which has remained dormant and wasted." And some people did! Do you think Russians were ahead of us? No. If not more famished and backward, at least they were the same as us. But they granted the right to vote to these same illiterate and starved women and today, thanks to the amazing activities of Russian women, the entire world is fascinated by this nation. Not only do Russian women fight on the battlefield and fly high in the sky, but they also manage the internal affairs of factories and businesses.

Experience proves that women can. Why shouldn't Iranian women take advantage of the experiences of other women of the world, instead of tasting the bitter experience of France? Today there are people in this country who present an article to the Parliament to restore women's rights. The one proposing is not just a formality, he is the representative of thousands of people. He proposes on behalf of himself, his party, and his nation. Every Iranian woman will be proud of the respect she has earned.

There is a famous saying that reads: "Only the one in pain knows the pain." And I am not just addressing the writer, but I am speaking to all Iranian women, to all women and mothers! Can anyone except ourselves restore our rights? Who else has tasted the bitter flavor of such laws other than a mother separated from her child, a homeless woman, a girl with no right whatsoever? And is there anyone except us who can break down these laws?

O, Iranian women, arise and be happy! Noblemen are out there who would support you. Wherever you are, in a city or a village, whether young or old, be with these grandees with all your spirit. Nurture their ideas to save yourselves and your daughters. The day will come when the chains of bigotry will break free of this foul desire of the enemies, and that's when, alongside men of the Parliament, we can regain our rights in our own home. Then we will be honored. Then we will overcome suppression and tyranny. Then we will be true women and mothers. Enough of servitude and slavery! Success is governed by the rock-hard determination of you, Iranian women!

THE LIFE OF WOMEN WORKERS. HOW DO WOMEN IN FRANCE PROGRESS? ESTABLISHMENT OF A LAUNDRY IN IVRY, SUBURBS OF PARIS, TO HELP THE FEMALE WORKERS

HOMAYOUN ESKANDARI

On Sunday, March 31, in the Ivry Municipality, representatives of central unions and Madame Marie Couette—as the representative of the unions in the Paris area—participated in the inauguration of a laundry center. The center was established for the welfare of women workers, to help them in household tasks. Fernand Leriche, the editor-in-chief of *La Vie Ouvrière*, attended the ceremony in person.

To address the problems that women workers must face on a daily basis, the Ladies Commission of the mixed unions seriously investigated the issue and finally, through some practical steps, managed to help women by establishing a laundry and mending center.

The Ladies Commission shared the proposed plan with the central council, which, noting the urgency and the significance of the matter, immediately studied it. The venue—which includes three nonresidential rooms at the corner of Bourgeois Street—was cleaned, painted, and furnished by the workers themselves. These united brave workers cleaned and prepared the place as soon as they were finished with their work in the factories. This is the result of cooperation and sacrifice. They scarred their hands with thorns of labor but managed to harvest beautiful flowers at the end.

La Vie Ouvrière published an article written by Marie Couette, the secretary of the Paris area unions. The title reads: "Let's Help Women Workers." Given the importance of this article in showing social activities and progress, we provide its translation here so that Iranian women can get familiar with this sort of cooperation and activities of women in other parts of the world:

> The Public Labor Union was established by our comrades in the Union Committee in September 1945 and clearly elaborated on the ways to develop production through women's labor.
>
> In order to let the woman worker also take care of her duties as a housewife and a mother, certain social measures should be taken. The establishment of child care centers in local unions makes it possible for mothers to work without constantly worrying about their children. One should bear in mind that, on top of the office work, a woman has a full-time job back home including cooking, sewing, washing, and the like. Taking such needs into account, to defend the rights of women workers, the Union Committee embarked on assisting women through setting up joint organizations (sewing and mending, laundry, cooking vegetables...).

We can highlight some of the actions that have already been taken in view of the urgency of the issue. Later, we can adjust them in practice to our own circumstances in Iran. But in order for our comrades to be able to establish similar entities here, we need to share a few points:

- the workrooms may be established in bigger institutes under the leadership of the Committee and with the participation of the employers,
- women working in factories can be expert or simple workers who know about mending and sewing... Expert women must be paid according to the union rates,
- the organizations that assist women workers should be established as per agreement of volunteers and run under the supervision of the syndicate and the leadership of the comrades in charge of women's affairs in the Committee,

– in order to help those who work in small factories where the establishment of an aid institute is not feasible, the representatives of unions can set up a clothing repair and laundry center that supports several small units. Employers will be involved, and the center will operate under the supervision of a committee comprised of representatives from all these many units.

There are challenges in this endeavor. But our gifted comrades overcome problems through some initiatives. In case an employer refrains from cooperating, he will be considered as ill-intentioned. Such people are usually deemed not very good patriots.

Different unions in Paris can start such workrooms based on local rules so that all women workers who work in small factories, or are far from home, can benefit. One should also seek assistance from municipalities and freedom-seeking unions (such as the Young Girls Organizations) that are pursuing the same objective of helping women workers. These institutes should be of use to men workers, too. One should bear in mind that such assistance can prove useful not only to women but also to married men.

The price of the product, whatever it is, should be fair. And since these institutes are all run under the supervision of the union, purchasing goods with a union card entails some discount.

Through such entities, we aid women workers. They will know the union better and get further interested in it. In a factory, an office, or an institute, women can keep doing their duty, which is nothing but production with utmost vivacity.

LUSTFUL DOLLS
A LIFE OF LETHARGY, BALONEY, AND FUTILITY

EDITORIAL TEAM, *BIDARI-E MA*

Our so-called "modern" women can be described in two words: lustful dolls. They are as worthy in the eyes of men as dolls are in the eyes of children. These living dolls indulge in makeup to turn into a better amusement tool and more exciting toys. These so-called modern women have accepted their fate as dolls, and they themselves contribute to such a destiny. What sort of behavior does such a doll display? A series of loose gestures and childish lewdness. At times one feels pity for such made-up women who copy movie stars through their fake looks. Is this the only purpose behind the creation of a human being? Wasting her time to turn herself into something for which there could be a demand? And to show up here and there with some artificial comportment, meaningless conversations, and facetious smiles? How embarrassing it is that although they care so much about their superficial look and beauty, they are devoid of any intellectual and spiritual beauty! Their spirit is banal, superficial, and bereft of any subtlety. What do they talk about? The boring repetition of some words about the look of this woman and the personal life of another one—jealous of this one and repulsed by the other one, empty compliments here and out-of-place coquetry there.

These so-called modern women have been dramatically corrupted as a result of the infiltration of a Hollywood culture. They have lost the sense of any serious human faculty of thought. Whatever they know of modernity and civilization is summed up in a blind imitation of fashion and makeup. Their understanding of a global culture is limited to some inharmonious dance, murmuring songs of Tino Rossi and Bing Crosby, paging through *True Romance* or other cinema magazines, and knowing a few Hollywood stars' names by heart. The list is completed by card games, a poor copy of a European lifestyle, and recently the American tradition of constantly chewing gum. In a country where miseries are everywhere and the majority are imprisoned by poverty and deprivation, these so-called modern women do not care in the least. They shed tears if they cannot buy this fabric or that piece of jewelry, but the tragedy of a nation's death does not touch them at all. Not only do they not think about the emergence of social movements, but they also ridicule such movements. How hollow and insignificant is life to them? How much are they into themselves, governed by their own selfishness?

What have schools taught them? Nothing. What happened to what they learned? Sent to oblivion. As long as beauty and cosmetics reign, there is no room for any other commodity. Even their understanding of day-to-day affairs is of no use. The family is ruined by their lack of concern and selfish attitude. In such a family, no one sacrifices anything to bring up a new generation, a new life. The lady of the house wanders around. Long nights, which make her lie in bed till noon, then some time in front of the mirror, and then another night... Husband's indifference, acceptance of a sort of loose conduct under the title of modernity, feeling ashamed of being a mother, a lady of the house, a parent... Proud in vulgarity, proud of living the life of a parasite. This is the true nature of our modern women! What can flourish in the inept hands of such a woman? She fills up her life with absurdity and irresponsibility, turning life into an empty, colorful, and transient bubble that leaves no impact behind. This happens when every single human being should leave a trace of his endeavors in this world and serve the society where he lives. Our society is in need of service more than anyone can even imagine. This country is dominated by death and scarcity. Continuous pain has desensitized people toward suffering, but still the piteousness of life is beyond words. The wind of American colonization and tyranny has wilted every plant. The self-indulgence and lustfulness of Hollywood stars in a capitalist wealthy country—where people do not struggle to earn a living—is understandable, but it is not comprehensible if it is imitated in Iran, the land of the hungry. Do these so-called modern women know that what appears on the movie screen is not the true reflection of the reality of life in the United States? It's just a means to deceive the people of the world. Do they know that, more than Hollywood stars, there are women in the States who work hard for their society?

The very narrow-mindedness and absurdity—the lack of national conscience and of human intellect—have made our female population passive in the face of any backward imposition, as if they were fast asleep. They act as if all the pains inflicted on them had nothing to do with them! With such lassitude and carelessness, no one can ever reach equality with men. To claim every single right, one has to sacrifice to some extent. There are no good people out there who will readily grant us rights if we only beseech them.

What makes us blatantly write about such a bitter truth? The urgent need for women to wake up. This waking up can materialize only through harsh criticisms and constant lashes of rebuke and warning. One should seriously fight against this doll-like, lustful, meaningless, and selfish life of the majority of so-called modern women. In the course of this fight, decent women will come to their senses and prevent the fall of our young women into a languid, worthless, and hollow life.

THE SIMPLER, THE PRETTIER

EDITORIAL TEAM, *BIDARI-E MA*

If a woman seeks to be beautiful, she has to care about her health more than anything else. She has to care for her skin to keep it acne free, shining and soft. To prevent girls and young women from putting a new cream or another powder on their skins and spoiling their faces, we provide some tips here below:

1 Every morning, before breakfast, drink some warm water without sugar. If you could add a few drops of lemon [juice], it would be even better.

2 If you have oily skin, for a month wash it with water flavored with a few drops of lemon [juice].

3 To cleanse your facial skin thoroughly, do the following at least two times a week: Boil some water in a pot. Add a few drops of benzoin tincture, which can be readily purchased in any drugstore. Then keep your face above the pot and cover your head with a big towel. Stay in that position for a few minutes. Keep wiping off your sweat.

4 After the steam facial, mix two teaspoons of soft hair-wash mud and one whipped egg white. Cover your face and neck with the mixture and lie down for twenty minutes. Then wash your face with warm water.

5 Now that your face is clean, massage one fingertip unit of cream all over your face and complement it with some powder. Avoid too much powder. It doesn't look nice on the face. Try to wear lipsticks in colors similar to the natural color of the lips. Don't wear purple or orange lipsticks. Be aware that the secret to beauty is simplicity, naturalness, and cleanliness. Don't forget to cleanse your face with a "cream" every night.

We will provide the recipe for this cream in the next issue.

Outfit: It is indeed very fortunate that long dresses became fashionable. I remember seeing women on the streets—some of them pretty chubby—who were in dresses above the knees with socks under the knee. I remember seeing women on the bus who were ignorant about the fact that they were not in their bedrooms. They were in tight skirts and suits and sat on small benches in an awkward manner. Not to mention the summertime! Showing naked legs above the knees. Believe me, it was not beautiful at all. It was somehow gross, I would say. Fortunately, long dresses are trendy now. We also present two models to our readers: two simple and pretty outfits.

Both of these outfits can be made with plain or floral-print cotton. One outfit includes a jacket and a skirt, good for spring and summer. It can be with sleeves or sleeveless. What we recommend is that you consider the color of your shoes and bag before you purchase the fabric, so that they match. More importantly, don't fall for any color that you see. Choose the color that suits your character. If you pay some attention and think well, you can always be stylish and beautiful without spending much.

حامد خسروی

بیدارشوید!

گزیده‌ای از مقالات بیداری ما

NARRATIVES – RELAZIONI N.7

MOUSSE
PUBLISHING

Publishing Editor
Ilaria Bombelli

Editorial Coordination
Matteo Canetta

Publication Design
Massimiliano Pace (Mousse)

Texts by
Hamed Khosravi © 2019
Bidari e-Ma © 1944-48
Maryam Firouz ©
Farrokh-Laqa Alavi ©
Homayoun Eskandari ©

Edited by
Hamed Khosravi

Translations
Samaneh Maddah

Proofreading
Erica Olsen

First edition: 2019

Printed in Italy by
Ediprima, Piacenza

ISBN: 978-88-6749-392-0
22 EUR / 25 USD

Published and distributed by
Mousse Publishing
Contrappunto s.r.l.
Corso di Porta Romana 63
20122, Milan–Italy

Available through:

Mousse Publishing, Milan
moussepublishing.com
DAP | Distributed Art Publishers, New York
artbook.com
Vice Versa Distribution, Berlin
viceversaartbooks.com
Les presses du réel, Dijon
lespressesdureel.com
Antenne Books, London
antennebooks.com

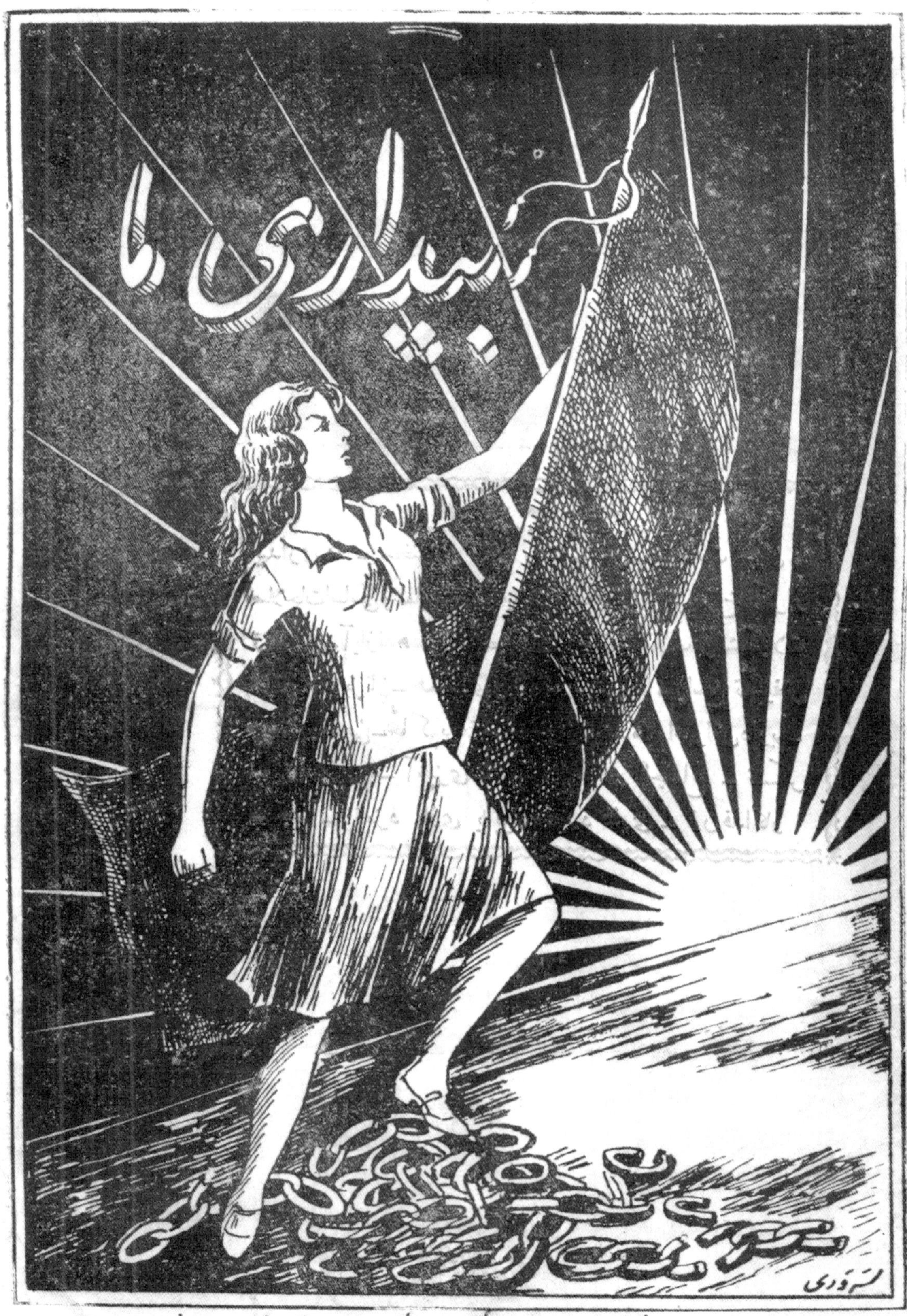

شماره ۲ سال اول ۱۳۲۳ مرداد

سخنرانی خانم دکتر کیامبخش

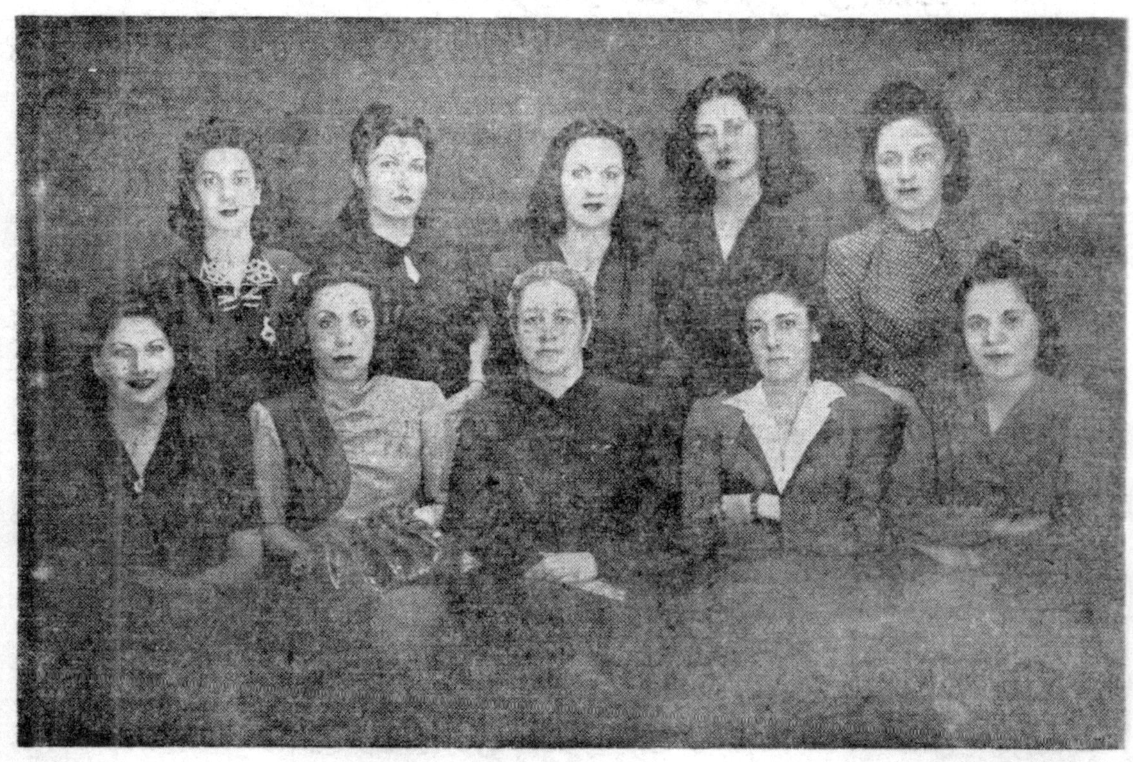

ردیف نشسته از راست به‌چپ

۱ـ بانو دکتر افتخار مقدم ۲ـ بانو دکتر هائده مالك ۳ـ بانو دکتر اختر کامبخش (کیانوری) ٤ـ بانو دکتر نصرت‌الملوك کاشانچی

۵ـ بانو دکتر حشمت عظیما

ردیف ایستاده ازراست به‌چپ

۱ـ بانودکتر ربابه کیانوری ۲ـ بانو دکتر اشرف‌الملوك مصاحب ۳ـ بانو دکتر شمس‌الملوك میرسپاسی ٤ـ بانو دکتر حشمت پزشك

۵ـ بانو دکتر کچکینه کاظمی

روحیکه در دست جهل و بی‌سوادی محبوس و مقید است چه زندانی مخوف‌تر و سهمناك‌تر از این !!!

روزیکه جامعهٔ ایرانی از دست جهل و بی سوادی آسوده شود و بعکس امروز عموم افراد آن تحصیل کرده و قادر به‌درك وظیفه‌نسبت بخود و اجتماع و میهن بشوند ملت بسعادت حقیقی خود رسیده است

زهرا ـ بیات

بیدار شوید !

ناچارم هرآنچه حس میکنم و به‌نظرخودم حقیقت است شرح‌دهم اگر خبط و اشتباه است امیدوارم مرا عفو فرمایند .

در ظرف این سه سال اخیر که‌تماس با مردم ـ مجامع مختلف طبقات‌متفاوت بیشتر شد یك اصل کلی به دستم آمده !

جامعهٔ‌ایرانی‌را میتوان‌تشبیه به اطاق بسته نیمه‌تاریکی پراز دود سیگار و تریاك کرد جمعی که در آن هستند بحدی‌خمار وتحت‌تاثیر این سم‌واقع‌شده‌اند که قادر بحرکت نیستند و اگر هم از لابه‌لای پنجره و پرده آفتاب درخشان و آسمان صاف را می بینند وبحدی فاصله اطاق تابیرون به نظرشان طولانی و پر از مانع است که پیش از حرکت خسته شده‌و میگویند چه فایده ما که به هوای آزاد و آنچه که آرزو داریم نمیرسیم پس چرا جای خود را عوض کنیم و مامورین دود دادن هم با سرعت مشغول هستند مردم هم که از اول تو نیامده یا همت نداشته اند خود را به بیرون رسانده از نعمت دنیای آزاد ـ مغز خالی از دود ـ فکر باز افق وسیع بهره ور شوند با اصرار درها را گاه گاه بازکرده نسیم بیرون را داخل میکنند و با دلیل و برهان به خاموش شده ها ـ ضعفاء داخل اطاق راه فرار ونجات را نشان میدهند

از خواندن روزنامه ها شنیدن صحبتها و گفتگوها سیر در وضعیت روزانه بیشتر این تشبیه در نظرم جلوه میکند .

مرد ها که همیشه توانسته اند بخوانند ، بحث کنند و بخصوص آن دسته مردمی که چشم چراغ این مردم حساب میشوند یا بعبارت دیگر روشنفکران ، در آنها جمعی دیده میشوند که با همین کسالت و خماری دم پنجره نشسته واز استنشاق هوای آزاد اباء دارند و منتظر هستند که سایرین برایشان درهارا باز کنند یا از ترس جریان هوا حاضرند خفه بشوند . اینها مانند غریقی هستند که به پر و پای منجی خود پیچیده و او را نیز به ته دریا میکشانند . اینها غافل هستند که بزرگترین خیانت و بالا ترین صدمه را به این مردم میزنند زیرا که انتظاری از سایرین نمیتوان داشت وقتی که آقایان خموش نشسته منتظرند که لقمه از آسمان بیفتد .

اگر به آقایان بر میخورد چه میتوان کرد تأثیری است که خود بارفتار شان ایجاد کرده اند وشاید بخاطر چهار تکه قالی و مواجب سه ماه و یا تنبلی موفقیت اجتماعی و شخصیت خودرا پایمال میکنند .

اما زنها ، قرنها و سالها است که زن ایرانی یك محیط کوچك یکنواخت داشته ودر آن زندگی کرده وکوچکترین موقعیتی نداشته که بتواند خودرا بسازد واستقلال فکری وشخصیت برجسته حاصل کند .

از روز اول که دست راست را از دست چپ می شناسد او را به شوهر میدهند . چه غنی و چه فقیر تنها راه زندگی و یگانه حرفه که جامعه برای او تهیه کرده همین است حیات خود را با یك بله قمار کرده و توکلت علی الله داخل زندگی میشود ، باور کنید که این قمار عموما صد در صد با باخت زن توأم است .

کار به سفید بختی و سیاه بختی نداریم از موضوع ما خارج است اما شخصیت او ، فکر او ، هوش او ، استعداد او در چه محیطی میتواند پرورش کند ؟ از شنیدن و خواندن کدام مبحث علمی یا سخنرانی سودمند ؟ تمام اینها به مرور ایام با کار های خسته کننده و بی ثمر و مکرر خانه- بچه داری بدون اصول صحیح - فشار روحی از طرف شوهر - بهداشت خراب از بین میرود و خیلی زود جوانی را از دست داده و یك زنی با فکر بسته میشود که تمام وقتش صرف ترشی بادمجان و نا راحتیش خراب شدن کوفته تبریزی است . نه اینکه خدای نکرده این قبیل کار ها را بدوبی

موقع بدانم آیا غیر از این زن چه میکند و چه راهی برای تحصیل و آموختن دارد ؟ من زن هستم و میدانم که این کار ها چقدر وقت میخواهد و چقدر جسم و روح را خسته میکند .

در این چند سال اخیر در تمام مدارس روی زنهارا باز کردند و بآنها آزادی دادند متأسفانه آن مادر ها در آن محیط نمیتوانستند بر بخورند که وظیفه زن و مادر چیست جمعی هم که میتوانستند استفاده کنند دخترانی بودند که وضعیت مادی و اقتصادی خانواده ایشان اجازه میداد برای این قبیل دختر ها (البته استثناء را کارنداریم ودلخوشی و امیدواری همه بآنها است) مجالس رقص و قمار هم آماده بود و آزادی بی سر و ته بی معنی داشتند . آنها دیگر وقت درس خواندن ، فهمیدن ، عبرت گرفتن نداشتند . رهبر و راهنمائی هم نبوده که لذت کار و ذوق آموختن را در آنها پرورش دهد بلکه بر عکس زندگی خاموش و حاضر بودن تمام وسائل برای انجام هر هوس آنها را لخت بار آورده و از فعالیتی کـه شهامت و همت لازم دارد بری کرده است . اینها برای بدست آوردن بخیال خودشان - آزادی کامل تری خود را به دامان اولین مرد میاندازند و برای بعد هم خدا بزرك است و اگر هم حرف حسابی را بشنوند با یك دنیا غمزه و افاده میگویند (مرد ها مان چه کردند که ما زنها بکنیم) ؟

نمیدانم آیا میفهمند چه میگویند یا نه امیدوارم که نفهمیده باشند چون در غیر این صورت قابل عفو نیستند و اسم زنرا بد نام میکنند باین امید و آرزو رو بشما کرده میگویم ای زنهای ایرانی ای خواهران عزیز شما مقصر نیستید از اول اینطور تربیت شده اید . فکر کنید شمامادرها وظیفه سنگینی دارید باید اولاد تربیت کنید باید **شما مردانی تربیت کنید که مردکار باشند و عرضه داشته باشند** یك قسمت بد و خوب اینمردم در دست شما است شما در شوهران ، برادران ، پدران تأثیر دارید و بخواهید که موثر باشید نه تنها مربی اطفال مرد وفروزنده اجاق او باشید بلکه بخواهید هادی و راهنمای هم بشوید .

چقدر حقیقتی که ازدهان مادر وزن، کسی که سرا پاش فداکاری وازخود گذشتگی است ، بیشتر بدل وجان مرد تـأثیر می کند!

میخواهید چه بکنید و مردانتان چه بکنند ؟

زندگی داشته باشید روح ودلتان ز دیدن این همه بدبختی وشنیدن این همه زاری کسل وپژمرده نشود

بخواهید که همه خوش باشند و تا درقدرتتان هست سعی کنید که همه بهره از سعادت و راحت ببرند ، بخواهید که هر زنی محترم باشد با گفتن این نوع کلمات خودرا کوچك نکنید ، بخواهید که استقلال فکری و مادی داشته باشید نه تنها برای همه . آلان جواب خواهید داد زن ایرانی در مایملك خود مختار است .

راست است برای شما که ارث میبرید اما آن دسته مردمی که هیچ ندارند چقدر باید چشمان بدست شوهر باشد. **خواهید گدا صفت بار بیائید** تازه خود شما روزی که نتوانستید بامردی که سرسری وبدون فکر انتخاب کرده اید زندگی کنیدباید همین ارث را ببخشید و ورقه آزادی را بگیرید بعد چه میکنید ؟ گدائی ! سر سفره کدام شخص ؟

بیدار شوید ! بیائید جامعه باین سرعت گلستان نخواهد شد اما همت و همکاری شما برای رساندن آن باین مقصود لازم است ما هم بسنجیم بفهمیم و زندگی داشته باشیم .

یك مملکت که نصف جمعیتش بی کار و منتظر کار نصف دیگراست نمیتواند ترقی کند نمیتواند آباد شود . امروز اگر به ما با نظر تحقیر نگاه کنند حق دارند چه کرده‌ایم ؟ از کدام هوس گذشته ایم ؟ چه زحمت بخود روا داشته ایم ؟ باز هم انتظار داریم که ما را در ردیف زنهای عالم که نه تنها از مال و زندگی صرف نظر کرده اند بلکه جان خود را نثار راه ترقی و تعالی ملتشان گردانیده اند حساب کنند ؟ بخوانید کتاب فراوان است روز نامه و مجله سودمند بخوانید یکی از استادان در مقاله خود اشاره کرده بود که از حافظ و سعدی ، برگن و خیام حکمت افلاطون صحبت نکنید چقدر جای تأسف و تأثر است و چه اندازه شرمنده هستم که باید اذعان کنم که به‌استثنای عده معدودی کمتر باین اسمها آشنا و خیلی کمتر از گفته ها شان اطلاع داریم اگر آنها را میشناختیم قدم بزرگی بر داشته شده بود و فکر ها خیلی آماده تر و راه خیلی باز تر بود

حقیقتاً خوابیم و از دنیای داخل و خارج بی خبرا اینست که میگویم و باز هم تکرار میکنم **بیدار شوید!**

راست است بیدار شدن کافی نیست اگرچشممانرا باز نموده و زندگی پر از زجر و شکنجه و تقریبا تمام مردم این مملکت را به بینیم ، اگرزخمها ودملهای اجتماعی که از پیکر فرسوده این ملت کمتر نقطه سالمی باقی گذاشته

مشاهده کنیم و صدای نالهٔ بچه ها و زاری مادر ها را بشنویم و درد های روحی ـ عزا ـ بد بختی ـ گرسنگی در دل حساس و بیدار شده‌ما ، تأثیر کند ، چه فایده دارد اگر راه چاره فکر نکنیم و بر جمع گریان افزوده سر بار و مزاحم هم بشویم . آنروزی که به نام این ملت و اطفال این مملکت و زنهای ایرانی تمنا کردم که بیدار شوید برای این بود که همت کنید تا خواهر وار و با کمال خلوص و رضایت دست اتحاد و اتفاق به یکدیگر بدهیم به اندازهٔ کار زیاد و وظیفه ما سنگین است که حد ندارد و این ندا در هر گوشه در هر جا به هرزبان و به‌هر نحو باید تکرار شود امروز روزی نیست که بخواهیم تنها با کلمه انشاء الله و امید خدا زندگی کنیم این کلمات را بگوئیم ولی کمر همت بسته و از کار وزحمت نیز دریغ نداشته باشیم .

مثل معروف فرانسوی **هر آنچه‌زن میخواهد خدا میخواهد** و مطمئنا حقیقت است تجربه کنید و خود به شخصه معترف خواهید شد زن به پشت کار ، تحمل ، تیز هوشی و حس سرشار معروف است باید ثابت کرد

مریم فیروز

بانو مریم فیروز

مقصود ما

شاید هرکس درزندگی خود بتواندمقصد وآرزوی خودش رابیان کندولی مقصد وآرزوی جمعی را بیان کردن کار بس دشواری است .

در موضوع امروزی ما که مقصود و آرزوی تشکیلات زنان است کار برمن سهل شده چه نه تنها زنان تشکیلات بلکه تمام زنان ایران چیزی دردست ندارند که مقصد آنها هم متفاوت باشد .

زن درایران فاقدهرچیزاست هیچ نوع حقی ندارد ودر سراسر کتابهای قانون بسیار عریض وطویل مملکت قانونی برای او وضع نشده ، اگرهم درجائی اسم آن او بمیان آمده است برای این است که محکومیت وبی حقی اورا تشدید کند واجازه میخواهم که وضع مذلت بار اجتماعی زنان ودختران ایران راباذکر چندمثال که شاید کم وبیش همه خانمها وآقایان باامثال آنها آشنائی دارند شرح وبعبارت دیگر سرگذشت رقت بار چند مرده زنده نما را نقل کنیم .

در چندی پیش که دولت تصمیم گرفت چاقو کشهارا مجازات کندیکی ازاینها رامحبوس وبعداً محکوم باعدام کرد .

این مرد بادختر چهارده ساله‌ای ازدواج کرد بود واین بچه درموقع محکومیت شوهرش آبستن بود وروزهائی که به عزای شوهرش نشسته بودو گریه وزاری میکرد پسری بدنیاآورد واین بچه یك روزه هم مثل مادر چهارده ساله‌اش بی گناه وخودش هم بی اطلاع بود که پیش از جنایت پیش از چاقو کشی قدم اوپدر اورا بطرف مرك سوق داده

مثل همه نوزادان غافل و بیخبر بدنیا آمد ولی اطرافیان او فراموش نکرده بودند که پدر او چاقو کش بوده ومجازات شده .

مادر چهارده ساله وبی خبر اورا وادار کردند که آن بچه راشیر ندهد وهر آنچه این بچه بحال نوزاد خود متاثر بود فایده نکرد وبه او اینطور فهماندند بگذار بمیرد چون :

عاقبت گرگ زاده گرگ شود

بعد از دوروز گرسنگی بچه از بین رفت وشاید هم حق با اطرافیان دختر بود چه این مادر چهارده ساله باکدام وسیله و کدام تربیت میتوانست بچه اش را بار بیاورد .

این موجود سالم وبیگناه هم در همان محیط افیونی وچاقو کشی بزرك شده وچون باآدمی بارنمی آمدگرگی شده بالاخره طفیلی خطرناك برای جامعه میشد .

...

زن جوانی با داشتن یك دختر بعد از اینکه شوهرش رااز دست میدهدشوهردیگراختیارمیکند .

این مرد ازبچه زنش بی حد بدش میآمد بطوری که مادر مجبور میشود دختر یازده ساله خود را بشوهری شوهر دهد تاچند ماهی زندگی

دختر کم وبیش به نمیگذشت تابالاخره بچه حامله شد در موقع حملش دائما شوهرش باو گوشزد میکرد که اگر دختر بیاورد او را طلاق خواهد داد بایك دنیا ترس شب‌وروز دختر دردعا وزاری میگذشت ولی ازآنجائی که دعاها گاه نفرین میشود تمام زاری تاثیر بعکس کرد و دختر دختری آورد بعدازشنیدن این خبر که برای او وحشتناك بود با تمام اینکه باو خوانده بودند که دختر باران رحمت است بر خانه خراب خود این باران را نپسندید وبعداز ماه ها بی اعتنائی قبول کرد که دو دختر را در خانه اش نگاه دارد چیزی نگذشت که بچه برای دفعه دوم حامله شد شوهرش باهمین کلمات باو گفت بدان یك دفعه جستی ملخك ولی برای دفعه دوم نخواهی جست .

خود شما ، مجسم کنید که در ظرف این چند ماه این مادر بیچاره این دختری که برخلاف اراده خودش مادر میشد ، این بچه که از حال زن بودن ودختر بودن خود هیچ چیزی ندیده بود چه زندگی داشته تمام شب جمعه ها تمام روزها پهلوی دعانویس ها ودست بدامن امامزاده های مختلف شد ، مثلی است معروف میگویند آن بنده که عزیز تراست بیشتر صدمه می بیند شاید این دختر هم در جزوبر گزیدگان الهی است نمیدانم ولی بار دوم هم دختر آورد .

این مرتبه شوهرش تااو دربستر بود بهانهٔ نیامد و روزی در خانه پا گذاشت که آن دختر رااز دربیرون کرد ومیگفت این زن دختر زاست وبه درد من نمیخورد باید برود .

این مادر شانزده ساله دوبچه اش را گذاشت خانه امید ، زندگی ونان روزانه خودرا به اجبار ترك کرد وبدون هیچ سرپرست وحامی در کوچه افتاد وبدتر از همه امید اینرا هم نداشت که ممکن است دست وپائی نمود ممکن است سعی کرد نه ، اوقبل ازخودش درخون وگوشت او آمیخته شده بود که زندگی برای او و امثال او همین است و الا بیخود شوهرش از دختر بیزار نبود . این زن رفت و تنها راهی که برای تن فرسوده و خسته ، برای جسم حیف او در دسترس بود انتخاب کرد و در یکی از پست‌ترین خانه های این شهر در میان هزاران نفر مثل خودش از بین رفت ودیگر اسمی هم از او نیست چون مادرش از شنیدن اسم او او را نفرین میکند تنها معلوم است که زنده است واطرافیان او همه حالا این تشخیص را میدهند که از اول این دختر ناجنس بدنیا آمده بود .

موضوع سوم — خانواده متوسطی که توانسته بود دختر زیبای خود را تا سن شانزده ساله تربیت کنند ولی دیگر حالا آرزو داشتند که او را شوهر دهند برای اینکه سرپرست داشته باشد . پدر و مادر و دختر روز ها در این فکر بودند تمام اوقات تنهائی خود را در مشورت میگذراندند که چه باید کرد وچه نوع شوهری باید برای او انتخاب کرد . دختر از آنها میخواست که برود و در بنگاهی کار کند آیا ممکن است باو همچو اجازه ای را داد .

هزاران حرف و هزاران مرد در این موسسات هست : مگر میشود دختری را دراین قبیل جا ها رها کرد و گذشته از این کمتر مرد جا افتاده حاضر خواهد شد که دختری را که باداره میرود بگیرد و بهزاران دلیل دیگر

میان پدر و مادر دختر مشاجرات بر پا شد . دختر میخواست زندگی خودش را انتخاب بکند پدر و مادر میخواستند زندگی او را آنها انتخاب کنند شاید هر دو طرف حق داشتند . بالاخره روزی خواستگاری موافق میل آنهاپیدا شد البته اگر جا افتاده بود در عوض امید این هست که با دختر شان مهربان باشد ؛ اگر خیلی زیبا نیست ؛ جوان نیست چه عیب دارد مرد نان آور باشد اگر سه بچه دارد از زن دیگر این که عیب مرد نمیشود داشته باشد نان همه را بدهد دختر آنها هم جوان است میتواند بچه داشته باشد ولی این احتیاط را کردند که داماد را به دختر نشان ندهند و آن قدر بچه بیچاره از زندگی یکنواخت و مشاجرات دائم خسته شده بود که حاضر بود برای رهائی خود را تسلیم هر کسی بکند و بالاخره « بله » بی مروت که یك عمر را در یك لحظه بباد میدهد از او گرفتند . راست است دنیا به هم نخورد ؛ زمین به آسمان نرفت ولی زندگی یك دختر که باید مادر خوبی بشود به هم خورد .

آن حاجی آقا متمول بود برای اینکه خرج نمیکرد و تنها نان بخور ونمیری به او بیشتر نمیداد و . در آن محیط خانه بچه شوهرهای بزرگتراز خودش زندگی را براو حرام کردند، تمام آمال وآرزو تمام جوانی خود را باخته واز دست رفته دید سعی کرد که طلاق بگیرد شوهرش به او گفت مگر موهایت مثل دندانهایت سفید بشود ، پدر ومادرش باو گفتند بالباست رفتی با کفنت باید بیائی او هم سعی میکرد همینطور خود را خلاص کند وروزی پدر ومادر دختر جوان خود را برای همیشه دردل خاك جای دادند وخود بکنار رفتند .

سه قصه یا زندگی که هرروز تکرار میشود وهزاران مثل آنها را دیده وشنیده ایم عرض کردم .

اینها بحدی عادی وهر روزی بحدی گوش وچشم ما به آنها عادت کردهٔ که نمیتوانیم آن راجز وبدبختیها حقیقتا بدانیم بخصوص اگرزندگ وحشتناك وغیر قابل تصورهزاران زن وهزا دختر این مملکت را در نظر بگیریم ، دوراحتیاج نیست برویم بیائید درپائین شهر درمحله هائی که حال و وضع آنهااز قرون وسطی حکایت مینمایددر نزدیك کوره پزخانه آن محیطی که از ماقبل تاریخ نمونه است دو ساعت وقت خود راتلف کنید ودرآن زاغه ها ، صدها زن جوان صدها دختران چهارده وشانزده ساله ، ژنده و وپاره به بینید تنها منزل وماوای اینها آن زاغه ها، تنها تفریح ،تنها دلخوشی وتنها امیدی که آنها رااز شرزندگی روزانه برای دقایقی خلاص میکند شیره است در شیره خانهائی که در همان زاغه ها ترتیب داده شده بیائید در محله معروف جنوب شهر قدم رنجه فرمائید ونگاهی بکنید اینجا گروه گروه دختران ۱۲ ساله ۱۴ ساله بافجیع ترین وضعی میبینید در گرداب مخوف بدبختی مذلت ومرض افتاده اند، اینهاهیچکدام به سن سی نمیرسند زود تر از این امراض وفشار زندگی آنها رااز پادرمیآورد ببینید که چگونه بچه هائی که تازه باید اول خوشی آنها باشد، باید تربیت برای آتیه شوند چه جور مرض آنهارا بیچاره وبد بین کرده

عیناً مثل سیلی که هرچه سر راه خود می بیند و بالاخره به دره میبرد سیل گرسنگی و برهنگی ، سیل بیقانونی و بی حقی آنها را هم بدره جنوب شهر رسانده و امروز مثل جذامی ها در یك جا جمع شده واز دنیا واز زندگی بیزار و بی خبرند آیامیشود تصور کرد که اجسام جوان بلکه بچه این دختران از درد، از امراض که هیچوقت آنها نخواهند توانست معالجه کنند برای همیشه رنجورشده اینها که هاهستند ؟ اینهاهمین دختران همین زنان ایرانند، اینها میبایستی نسل آتیه ما رابه مابدهند،ازچه راه باین گرداب افتادند؟ اغلب آنها دراول صیغه بودند چند روزی برای کدخدا آخوند یاصاحب ثروتی وسیله خوشی بودند بعد دیگرنه درامان خدا بلکه در سایه مرگبار جامعه بی قانونی افتادند و این است وضع فعلی آنها .

قدری سربخانه‌هابزنید ازدرددل زنان ایران آگاه شوید،دوستی کنیدخواهر وارصحبت نمائید می‌بینید اغلب آنها با بدبختی دست بگریبان هستندهمه اینهایك وحشت دارند، باهر چیزمیسازند تحمل هر نکبت، هر فشار

چرا ؟ تنها برای اینکه اگر از خانه شوهر بیرون بیایند وسیله زندگی دردسترس آنهانیست آنها باید درخانه این وآن تن بذلت کلفتی دهند یا همان‌راه‌هارادرپیش بگیرند.

بپرسید از هزاران مادر که تحمل هرفشار را میکنند برای اینکه ازبچه خوددست برندارند چه این زنان که باگوشت وخون خود اولاد خود راپرورش می دهند! این‌مادران که در حقیقت‌خالق این موجودات هستند هیچ‌نوع حقی به‌اولاد خود ندارند باسم قانون آنها رااز حق طبیعی خود محروم کرده‌اند، آنها اگر میخواهند اولاد خود راداشته باشند وآنها را زیر دست زن پدر یادر کوچه‌نگذارند باید بنشینند وبقول خودمازنان بسوزند وبسازند آیا این‌زنان مادران خوبی هستند ؟ آیا این اولادان وقتی شاهد مشاجرات پدر ومادر وقتی شریك غصه وغم مادر ، وقتی شاهد اشك اوباشند میتوانند قوی با روح شاد آماده زندگی ونبرد بار بیایند آیا میتوانند مبارزین حسابی برای مملکت شوند ؟ غیر ممکن است ، تاثیرات محیط تربیت اولیه‌را در هرفردی نباید فراموش کرد دختردر این محیط تربیت میشود برای اینکه در آتیه اشك بریزد و از گهواره خود را برای تحمل آفریده میبیند وپسر برای اینکه اوهم درآتیه زور بگوید وسروری کند اما قبل از آنکه باینجا برسند دل هردوشان از زجر مادر در زجر است واشك هر دو سرازیر

زن بار گران اقتصادیات را میکشد اوست که بیش ازهرکس صدمه وفشارمادیات را دارد، فکراً وروحاً هم در عذاب است ومسخره در این است که‌در این اجتماع زن‌راضعیفه وناقص مینامند سنگین ترین بار بردوش اوست واو باکمال‌قوت وقدرت این باررا تحمل کرده شاید برای همین است برای اینکه بیشتر ازپیش تحمل کند این اسامی بی مسمی را بر او گذشته اند

ازمحیط خانواده دور شویم ، بیائید در سراسر ایران آنجا که کار است آنجا که میشود لقمه نانی تهیه کرد درهر کار خانه چه بزرك و چه کوچك یکقسمت بزرك از کار گران زن هستند ساعت کار آنها بامرد برابر ولی مزد آنها خیلی کمتر است، چرا خیلی خوب روشن است ، چه زن در اینجا حقی ندارد صدایش قانوناً بهیچ

جانمیرسد و گرسنگی هم تعارف بر نمیدارد این است که خودش و بچه اش بامزد ناچیزی حاضرند جان بکنند تا از گرسنگی نمیرند در کار خانه های قالی بافی دختران کوچک را ببینید اینهائی که باید امروز در پی گردش و تفریح خود باشند اینها که باید مغز تازه و فکر بچه های آنها را با دانستنیهای مفید پرورش داد، پای کار گاهها خمیده و کج افتاده و برای روزی لقمه نان خالی ده الی دوازده ساعت گرد پشم را چون خورش با آن نان می خورند و تا یکبارچه قالی زیر پای ما میافتد با خون چند پسر و چند دختر رنگین و گل گون می شود و بهای جان هزارها بچه بی گناه صنعت قالی نگاه میداریم وافتخار میکنیم که ایرانی صنعتگر است.

راست است ولی افتخار نخواهیم کرد اگر حقیقة بدانیم که رشته های قالی باجان بچه ها مان بافته است، سربلند نخواهیم بود وقتی بدانیم که وضعیت فعلی ما از هرجنگ قهارتر و خونریزتر است.

ما که امروز اینجا جمعیم از رفتن یک خار به دست بچه‌مان نالانیم اما بیائید ببینید آنجائیکه کتیرا هست این بچه های شش هفت ساله کنار مجمعه‌ها روی زمین نشسته و با دستان ظریف خود این نبات را پاک میکنند، تمام روز کار میکنند مثل همیشه مادران ایرانی اینجا هم مجبور بتحمل هستند چه کتیرا با خون بچه‌ها آغشته است از پنبه تا آرنج خونین است از خار کتیرا بالاتر، از بی قانونی این اجتماع.

این است که امروز تشکیلات زنان مقصد و آرزوی خودرا حقوق زن از هر حیث قرارداده است، ما زنان فرد فرد آماده هر گونه مبارزه هستیم ما امروز بیدار شده و میخواهیم خواهران هم زنجیر خودرا که زیر زنجیر قوانین پست و ظالمانه این اجتماع کمر خم کرده‌اند بیدار کنیم

ضعیف نباشیم ما می‌خواهیم زن ایرانی دختر ایرانی بتواند از خود دفاع کند، ما میخواهیم قانون باو حق بدهد چاقو کش را بچه صالح و مفید بار بیاورد، ما میخواهیم آن روز که زن در خانه شوهر در فشار بود بتواند زندگی خود را اداره کند و تن بتن فروشی ندهد، ما میخواهیم که مقدم دختر در خانواده عزیز و محترم باشد و آتیه او روشن، ما آرزو داریم که راه کار کردن بر هر زن و هر دختری باز باشد و تکلیف وجدانی و مقدس او کار شود و از این راه وضع اقتصادی او تامین شود شوهرش را خودش انتخاب کند و اگر با شوهر نتوانست زندگی کند بتواند از خانه او بیرون بیاید، ما میخواهیم دست هزاران دختر که در پرتگاه صیغه شدن می افتد بگیریم و قانون داشته باشیم، ما آرزو داریم که دختران ایران، مادران ایران و بالاخص نسل آتیه خودرا از مرض خلاص کنیم و خوشی و زندگی سلامت بآنها بدهیم نه دود شیره و تریاک.

ما میخواهیم مادران بدانند که حقیقت ما در هستند نه ماشین بچه درست کنی، قانون بچه آنها را از آن آنها بشناسد، قانون نگذارد که ثمره زندگی او را پسر سه ساله و دختر هفت ساله از او بگیرند ما نمیخواهیم این وحشیگری ادامه پیدا کند.

ما آرزومندیم که زنان ما بیدار شده و واقف

بحقوق خود شوند وآنرا بگیرند ومطابق مردان درکارخانجات ودرهرجا مزد دریافت کنند ، ما زنان وما دران چون مادر وزن هستیم میخواهیم پنجه‌های کوچك دخترانمان رااز خار کتیراخلاص کنیم ، جسم کوچك آنها رااز سایه کار گاه ها نجات دهیم ، ما بالاخره زنان را میخواهیم تربیت کنیم که ایران راجات دهند وهمدوش وهمفکر مردان برای پیشرفت این محیط کار کنند .

ما مبارزه بر علیه مردان نمیکنیم برعکس مادست کمك وخواهری وبه‌آنها دراز کرده‌ایم ومردان بدانند که زن کمکی است بسیار مؤثر دنیا برای آنها نمونه است دراین چند سال اخیر درهرجا ودرهر رشته زنان بمردان کمك کردند و آنها را از غرقاب بدبختی وشکست نجات دادند .

ماز شنیدن کلمات دروغ وبی سروته دلبر ودلارام ویارخسته شده‌ایم مازندگی راباچشم باز وروشن می بینیم ، قرنها ماراباین کلمات دلفریب زندانی کرده اند ، بس است اگر بنابه قول خود شما ، زنان مادران هستند ومادرانند که فرزند خوب تربیت میکنند ازحرف بعمل وارد شوید و بدانید که زن بنده ، زن ناقص ، زن ضعیفه و رنجبر شیر نر برای ایران تربیت نخواهد کرد .

آنانکه قانون اساسی راوضع کرده اند زن یعنی مادر آنها ، خواهر آنها و دختر آنها رادو آنماده ننگین که لکی است در قوانین ما را درردیف مجانین وبچه ها قرار داده اند از دیوانه وبچه چه انتظار دارید ؟ آیا این تحقیر به‌پیروان این قانون بیشتر وارد است یابر زن ؟

زنان ایران تابه امروز از تکالیف خود سرنپیچیدند و درهر مورد ودرهر جا بااراده‌قوی چرخ دشوار زندگی را گردانده وبیش از هر کس ناملایمات اجتماعی را تحمل کرده اند .

ما افتخار میکنیم که زن هستیم وبه پسران پدران وبرادران خود هیچ توهین لفظی هم بسر آنها روانداشته ونداریم چه آنقدر فکر داریم که توهین آنها توهین بخود ما است وآنها راهمیشه در راه تعالی وترقی خواسته ایم .

امروز ما زنان ایران میخواهیم به دنیای متمدن ، بدنیائی که زن را در هرجا راه داده ، بدنیائی که هنوز از زیر چنگ قهار جنگ خلاص نشده ولی دارد نفس میکشد به دنیائی که برای آزادی بندگان وبردگان اجتماعی خون خودرا ریخته وهمین دنیا که فهمیده باید زن را درهر کاری شرکت داد ، بپیوندیم صدای ممالك متمدن که تابه امروز سرمشق ما بودند بلند است ، در هر جا زن ، در سیاست زن ، چه‌اوبافکر سلیم وقلب پر محبت ، بازوی توانا باکلمه دیگر مادر وار و زن وار میتواند رای خود را در امور مملکتی بدهد .

ماميخواهيم امروز به‌این دنیا به ممالك که مقام زن‌را درك کرده اند نشان دهیم که زن ایرانی نمرده است ، ماميخواهيم بمردان دنیا بفهمانیم که مادران وخواهران و دختران یك مملکت زنده که خود را متمدن میشمارند نمیتوانند مجنون ویا ناقص العقل باشند .

مریم فیروز

خواهران و دختران ما!

مورخ محترم آقای احمد کسروی در کتابی که بنام «خواهران و دختران ما» نوشته اندهر زن وهر دختری را متوجه کردند باین که بدانند عقیده ایشان و گروهی از مردان راجع به این موضوع چیست .

آقای کسروی قسمت حجاب رادر فصل اول مطرح کرده و از مدارك تاریخی استعانت جسته و برای ما روشن کرده اند که حجاب از اسلام نیست بلکه قبل از اسلام هم در ایران بوده است و برای اثبات این موضوع از کتاب پلو تارخ مورخ نامی یونان قصه فرار یکی از سرداران یونانی را بایران بشرح ذیل نقل میکنند ،

(برای روانه ساختن او میزبانش تدبیری بدینسان اندیشید که چون مردم آسیا بویژه ایرانیان غیرت زنانرا سخت نگاه میدارند نه تنها همسران خود بلکه کنیزان زر خرید یا بر گزیدگان را نیز سخت می پایند و چنان نگاهشان میدارند که بایدهمیشه درون خانه باشندو از در بیرون نیایند و هر گاه که سفر کنند آنان را در چادر های در بسته که از هر سوی آنانرا فرا میگیردجاداده برروی گردونه هامینشانند برای تمیستو کلیس (سردار یونانی) نیزیك چنان چادرو گردونه ای آماده کردند که روانه سفر گرددو چنین نهادند که اگر کسی در نیمه راه بایشان برخورده پرسش نماید بگویند دختر جوانی را از ایونا برای یکی از بزرگان ایران که بزنی گرفته میبرند) .

اکنون این نوشته پلوتارخ تکه اوجداری است و ما از آن چند چیز میفهمیم نخست آنکه رو گرفتن زنان یا نهانداشتن آنان خود را در ایران ازباستان زمان بوده زیراگذشته از آنکه پلوتارخ یك نویسنده راستگو بوده و سخنانش استوار است و اژه چادر و چادره که تا امروز در میان ما مانده است و به پوشاك آنچنانی زنها گفته میشود دلیل دیگر براستی گفته او میباشد دوم این نهانداشتن زنان بنیادی خرد مندانه نداشته واز آنجا بر خواسته که پادشاهان وزور مندان و پولداران نمی خواسته اند نگاه کس بروی زنان ایشان بیفتد و از سخن پلوتارخ هم پیداست که این شیوه نخست ویژهٔ پولداران می بودهو سپس ازآنان بدیگران رسیده)ص ۵ کتاب

آقای کسروی در تعقیب همین استدلالات متین میگویند که **روگیری از اسلام نیست.**

(یکی از دانسته های غلط در ایران آن است که روگیری زنان را از اسلام میشمارند . چنین میپندارند که اسلام دستور داده زنها رو گیرند در حالی که چنین نیست زنان مسلمان در زمان خود پیغمبر و تا دیر گاهی پس از آن زمان رو گشاده می بودند شما از همه کتابهای فقهی یکی را پیدا نخواهید کرد که نوشته باشد زنها رو گیرنددر کتابهای فقهی نه تنهارو گرفتن رانننوشته اند آشکاره نوشته اند که بازبودن رو و دستهای زن جائز است .

شیخ مرتضی انصاری که یکی از مجتهدان

بنام و بزرك قرن گذشته بود و کتابهای رسائل و مکاسب اورا همه طلبه ها درس میخوانند رساله ای در این باب نوشته و در آنجا دلیلها یاد کرده که در زمان پیغمبر اسلام زنها روگشاده می بودند از جمله مینویسد روایتی هست که پیغمبر بشتری سوار شده و یکی از پسران عمویش عباسی را بترك خود سوار کرده و از راهی میگذشت یکی از زنان عرب بسر راه آمده خواست چیز هائی را از پیغمبر بپرسد • پیغمبر شتر را نگاهداشت و آن جوان که بترکش بوده رویء اورا بسوی دیگر برگردانیده چنین فرمود یك زن جوان با یك مرد جوان ترسیدم شیطان بمیانشان در آید •

شیخ انصاری میگوید کسانی این را دلیل گرفته اند که زنها باید روگیرند در حالیکه این روایت وارونه آنرا میرساند زیرا از این روایت پیداست که آن زن رویش بازمیبود وگرنه رفتار پیغمبر شوندی پیدا نمیکرده باین معنی اگر آنزن رویش باز نمیبود جهت نداشت پیغمبر روی پسر عباس را برگرداند وآن سخن را فرماید (ص ٦)

آقای کسروی بعد از این نتیجه میگیرند که همانطور که اعراب با تماس تمدن ایران هزاران چیز را ازفضل، فرهنك، آداب تجمل از ایران اقتباس کردند این عادت را هم یعنی در پرده نگاهداشتن زنان که جزو بزرگی و ثروت بوده از آنها گرفته و در میان خود رواج دادند •

غیرازاین مختصری که نقل شد چند دلیل متین و استوار دیگر هم میآورند که ابدادر اسلام حجاب وجود نداشته بلکه این عادت قدیم ایران را آخوندها وملا ها برای پیشرفت و نفوذ خود دستاویز قرارداده و از آن حمایت میکنند •

ما خوشوقتیم واز آقای کسروی متشکریم که با دردسترس گذاشتن دلائلی چنان محکم و مدارکی چنان صحیح به ما کمك میکنند تا شاید ریشه این خرافات ملاپسند را از جا بر کنیم و این کیسه ننگین وشرم آور را برای همیشه از خود دور کنیم •

برهرزن وهردختری لازم است که از آقای کسروی تشکر نموده گفته های ایشان رادر این موضوع در نزد دیگران تکرار کنند •

(به دستاویز همان رو گرفتن و خود را پوشانیدن زنان از توده بیرون افتاده بوده اند به دستاویز همان رو گرفتن بانجمنها نمی آمدند از پیش آمدهای کشور و توده بیکبار ناآگاه می ماندند از دانستنی ها پاك بیبهره بودند در این کشور می زیستند و کمترین دلبستگی بآن نمی داشتند و نمی توانستند داشت)(ص ١١)

و همین رو گرفتن و دوری ازاجتماعات رادلیل میدانند که زن پا بند خرافات شده وهیچ چیز را غیر از محیط خانه وبچه داری نمیشناسد و نمی داند •

با یکدنیا اشتیاق بقیه کتابرا خواندم ولی متاسفانه در امیدی که صفحه های اول کتاب بروی ما باز کرده بود خیلی زود بسته شد چون آقای کسروی با وجود این مقدمه متین اینطور نتیجه میگیرند که زن باید بامور خانه و شوهر داری به پردازد •

میگویند (زنان ایران نباید از اروپائیها تقلید کنند چه زن در اروپاارزش ندارد وآنهارا دسته‌دسته مردان بد بخت کرده در راه های ننگین میکشانند •

اینجا باین موضوع بر میخوریم که وسیله بدبختی زن چادر نیست چه زنان اروپا که بی حجابند بنا به گفته خودآقای کسروی ارزش ندارند ولی ما تنهاو یگانه دلیل انحطاط اخلاقی زن را در اروپا یا تمام دنیا هوس ومیل مرد نمی دانیم گمان میکنم اگر در اوضاع و احوال اجتماعات فعلی مختصری دقت شود دلایل بزرگتر برای آن پیدا خواهیم کرد .

ما میگوئیم که زن از این لحاظ بی ارزش است که یکی از وسائل استفاده بدون خرج حکومت های سرمایه داری است از کار او که در خانواده انجام میدهد و از جسم او استفاده کرده بنام همین ممالك بورژوازی کلمه ننگینی را انتخاب کرده که باو فرصت سر بلند کردن و فهمیدن ندهند ما میگوئیم اگرزن آزاد بود یعنی میتوانست فرا ...و کارخودحقوق دریافت کندنان ولباس خودراتهیه کنداگر جامعه‌ای بود که وسیله تهیه معاش باو میداد واورا فقط وسیله تفریح و ماشین بچه درست کنی نمیشناخت زن مجبور به تن فروشی نمیشد این راه تنها راهی است که اجتماعات بورژوازی وبرای زن تهیه کرده ما میگوئیم کافی نیست که حجاب از بین برود که زن از دنیا و زندگی آگاه شود چه زن روستائی هیچوقت در پرده نبوده واز هرموجودی بی خبرتر است اینکار گران آن نداشتن کوچکترین حق او را از فهمیدن و آگاه شدن باز میدارد ما میگوئیم که این قوانین اجتماعی فعلی ماچه زن در پرده باشد چه نباشد اورا دست نشانده و محکوم خواهد کرد .

آیا آقای کسروی خیال میکنند که دردنیای اروپائیها زن بدبخت است ؟ آنقدر که دیده و مطالعه شده چقدرجوانان وچقدر مردان که به پست ترین درجات اخلاقی افتاده اند! تنها دراثر فشار اجتماع ونبودن وسائل برای پیشرفت ورسیدن به مقصود وزندگی آبرومند !

ما میگوئیم دردنیای فعلی نمیشود اروپارا دریك کلمه جمع کرده وخط بطلان را روی آن کشید .

ممالك شوروی بما نزدیکتر هستند ما میدانیم که در این محیط زن رادرهرکاری شرکت داده اند وضعیت اقتصادی او را تامین کرده اند درروابط زناشوئی ازاوبا قوانین پشتیبانی میکنند ودیگر نه تنها گروه گروه بلکه یکی یکی هم پیدا نمیشوند آن زنانی که دستخوش میل وهوس مردشده باشند .

درصفحه ۱۶ ازمجالس مهمانی بال رقص صحبت میشود وازلباس شیك وآرایش زیاد، روی صحبت باکیست ؟ ما نباید فراموش کنیم که در ایران درسرزمین زجروفلاکت درمیدان گرسنگی و برهنگی زندگی میکنیم نهصد و نود و نه نفر درهزار اززنان ایران با این مذلتهادست بگریبان هستند آنها نه بال میفهمندچیست ونه رقص را می شناسند ودرغیراین صورت میتوان گفت که روی سخن با خواهران و دختران معدود متمولین ایران است ونباید اینطور باشد.

درصفحه ۱۸ نوشته شده(زنان اگر نیکنداز مایند و اگر بدند ازمایند . زنان دسته جدامی نیستند تا سخن از نیکی یا بدیشان رود . زنان از مازاده اند وما اززنان زاده‌ایم)

راست است که ما وشما از همدیگر هستیم ولی قانون طبیعی را فراموش نباید کرد که اگر کسی درمقام دفاع وگرفتن حق خود برآمدخواهد توانست به آرزوی خود برسد و الا از دیگری چه برادر چه پدر و چه شوهرنباید انتظارداشت

ما تا به امروز اینطور فکر میکردیم ولی هر آنچه قانون در باره ما وضع شده به دست همین برادران و پسران بوده و تنها مقصد این قوانین توهین و سرشکستگی و پایمال کردن زن است

ما امروز آنقدر بیدار شده ایم که این کلمه بزرك را شعار خود قرار داده و بگوئیم **حق گرفتنی است نه دادنی** و باید خود در راه آن بکوشیم و نمیخواهیم که از روی رحم و شفقت پسری یا برادری نیمه قانونی برای رفاهیت حال ما وضع کند

متاسفانه آقای کسروی از حقوق زن آنچیزی را نقل میکند که بتوانند مسخره کنند و همان مردان خرافاتی و بی فکر را بر علیه ما بشورانند .

حقوق زن را اجازه میخواهم که یك یك بگویم ، آن حقوقی که بنابه گفته خود آقایان ما باید از آن برخوردار باشیم و امروز در این اجتماع بکلی محرومیم

حقوق زن حق حیات است یعنی حق فرا گرفتن تعلیم و ترتیب حق شوهر انتخاب کردن حق مادر بودن و بچه را از آن خود دانستن ، حق طلاق گرفتن ، حق انتخاب کار ، حق استعداد ذاتی خود را بکار انداختن ، حق انتخاب شدن ، حق انتخاب کردن و بالاخره حق وزیر شدن.

در این کتاب صریحا نوشته شده که زن اگر شوهر کند باید بمیل پدر و مادر باشد که روزی از او پشتیبانی کنند ص ۳۵ ما میگوئیم باید خانواده او راضی باشند ، راست است ، ولی باید قوانین وضع شود که او تنها دلخوشیش پشتیبانی پدر مادر نباشد فرض کنیم آنها مردند یا فرض کنیم شوهر اهمیتی به این حمایت نداد با قوانین ظالمی که در ایران است چه کنند؟

ما میخواهیم که بچه ما از آن ما باشد . با جان و گوشت و پوست خود او را پرورانده ایم ما نمیخواهیم که ما تنها پرستار و دایه باشیم و بچه برای دیگری بزائیم و تمام حس مادستخوش میل دیگری باشد ما میخواهیم روزی که دیدیم نمیتوانیم زندگی کنیم روزی که درفشار بودیم ، روزی که شوهر ما بما توهین کرد ، زندگی ما را فقط آلت راحتی ، وسیله تهیه غذا و لباس خود دانست از او جدا شویم و حق آنرا داشته باشیم . چطور ممکن است که یگانگی و محبت در میان زن و مرد باقی بماند اگر هر دوی آنها طرف احترام همدیگر نباشند ؟ چطور ممکن است زنی در خانواده شخصیت داشته باشد وقتی که شوهر او خود را چه عرفا و چه شرعا ذیحق میداند که او را هر دقیقه و هر آن که اراده کند از خانه اش بیرون کند و هیچ جا هیچکس باو ایرادی نگیرد آیا میشود قبول کرد که این زن بتواند با اطمینان خاطر زندگی خود و شوهر را اداره کند . از میان مردم و از آداب و رسوم خود ما امثالی بر میخیزد مثلی است معروف میان زنان (نگذار پیراهن شوهرت دوتا شود و الا فکر زن دیگر خواهد کرد)؟ تا مرد میتواند زن های متعدد بگیرد و تا میتواند بدلخواه خود زن را طلاق دهد و اولاد او را از او بگیرد غیر ممکن است محبت و یگانگی در خانواده حکمفرما باشد.

تا به امروز بد و خوب ما از مردم بوده ما امروز میخواهیم بد و خوب ما از خودمان باشد و دیگر فکر میکنم چون بچه صغیر احتیاج به قیم نداریم و بهتر است که مسئول تدزگیمان خودمان باشیم و نیك و بد ما از خودمان باشد.

تا خود اختیار نداشته باشیم که قانون وضع کنم باین حقوق نخواهیم رسید و هر زن روشنفکر ایرانی از آن مردانی که متاسفانه بقول آقای کسروی (ترانه بیجای نمایندگی بانوان را بمیان می آورند) پشتیبانی و طرفداری خواهد کرد .

درصفحه ۱۹ آقای کسروی میگویند (خدازنان رابرای کارهائی آفریده ومردانرابرای کارهائی) زنان‌رابرای خانه آراستن و بچه پروری ودوختن وپختن واینگونه کارها

آقای کسروی دراین مورد کم لطفی می فرمایند بابیان شیرین خود همان گفتار ملاها وآخوند ها را تکرار کرده اند آخوندهاهم میگویندخدا زن را برای تمتع مردآفریده اگرتنها وتنها برای این قبیل کارها مردان از آن استفاده خواهند کرد وموضوع دیگرچه خوب بوداگر خود مامیفهمیدیم که‌خداونددستور آشپزی‌را درکدام دست‌ودوختن رادر

کدام‌دست‌دختریاخانه‌داری‌را درکدام چین‌صورت نوشته ؟ آیا فکر نمیکنید همان فشار ظالمانه که اورا قرنها در خانه نگاهداشته‌وازاوهمین کارهارا خواسته شمارا هم واداز میکند که‌این‌قبیل‌اشتغالات را که با ترقی روز افزون صنعت کمتر وبی ارزش تر است جزو نوامیس طبیعی او بدانید ؟

درجای‌دیگر میفرمایند زن میتواند دکتر پرستار، قابله ، جراح دندانساز میکرب شناس ووو ... هم بشود آیا فکر نمیکنید که چون‌در این چند سال اخیر راه این قبیل موسسات را به روی او باز کردند و او توانست‌قابلیت و شخصیت خودرا در هریك از این رشته ها نشان بدهد شمارا براین داشته که حاضر شوید بنویسید که زن غیر از خانه‌داری و آشپزی کار دیگر هم می تواند بکند .

ولی بازمیپرسم آیا خداونددر یکی‌ازاعضای بدن زن نوشته که زن نمیتواند مهندس هوانورد یا چیز دیگر شود، به‌ببینید در دنیای خارج ازما در اینقسمت هازن شرکت میکند و موفق هم شده است .

شما زن ها را زود رنج میدانید . کدام زن هارا ؟ آن دسته زنانی که تنها تربیت یافته اند برای اینکه ناز بفروشند و از حرفی برنجند یا زنانی که تمام عمر با هزاران نا ملایم و فشار روبروشده‌وایستادگی‌میکنند ؟ آن‌دسته اولی مطمئن باشید خودشان هم از آینده‌شان دور نخواهندشد و تا روزی که مردان نازخر بیینند که دیگر با ناز باید هزاران‌چین و چروك موی‌سفید هم بخرند خودشان اورا در میان همان‌گرفتاری هاکه‌پیری و شکستگی است تنها سرگردان میگذارند ومیروند اما زنان دیگر باز میگوئیم آن هائی که‌تربیت شده اند در نزدیکی خودمان بما ثابت کرده‌اند که‌میتوانند دست بهرکاری بزنند و موفق‌شوند.

درصفحه ۱۲ شرح‌میدهید که چطور زنان اروپا توانستند در این رستاخیز جنك بكمك مردها بشتابند و در هر رشته برای نجات ملت خویش کار کنند اگر آن ها برای آشپزی بچه داری و ژاکت بافی تربیت شده بودند که‌امروز یا در کلیسا زانو زده از کشیشهای بدترازملاهای ما کمك میخواستند یا پهلوی فالگیر وجادو گر شتافته و نجات اولاد خود را از ورد و طلسم آن‌ها میخواستند .

در صفحه ۱۳ از قره‌فاطمه کردستانی تعریف میکنید،زن‌شجاعی که نتوانست اجنبی را مالك وطن خود بیبند و اورا میستائید و از طرفی در صفحه ۲۸ میگوئید که مردان احتیاج بخواربار دارند که‌گرسنه‌نباشند پارچه میخواهند که برهنه نباشند خانه راحت میخواهند که استراحت کنند و خیلی چیزهای دیگر،ببخشید خوب بود یکباره

یفرمودید ما کنیزانی می‌خواهیم که تنها رای ما بچه درست کنند و ما را راحت نگاه دارند پس چرا زنان شجاع وازخود گذشته را میستائید ؟ اگر تمام فکر لباس دوختن و غذا پختن بودند امروز نمیتوانستند از مردان خودحتی ر جبهه بشتیبانی کنند . هیمه و برنج‌وسوزن را ز سرنوشت زن دور کنند تا هزاران ره فاطمه‌ای که‌اردو د آشپز خانه منك شده اند سربلند کنند .

شما کار و پیشه را تنها برای زنان بیچیز یخواهید که این گروه‌زنان‌کار کنند و نتیجه اش ا زنان ناز دار و حسن فروش‌ببرند ما میگوئیم کار برای همه برای هر زن، ما میگوئیم زن باید پست بار بیاید و همیشه چشم و دلش دربی ست و ثمره رنج کس دیگر باشد .

ما درجائی میگوئید (صفحه ۲۱)جنك است زن ید از وضع دنیا آگاه باشد زن وسیله ایست که بچه اش را تربیت کند یعنی سرباز آتیه پرورانند تا کدام وقت دو سرمایه دار هوس کنند جنك عالمسوزی را برای نفع شخصی خود بپا کنند و آن بچه تنها نتیجه عمر زن را بدم اوله بفرستند .

ما میگوئیم تا آخرین دقیقه زن در سر نوشت اولاد خودش باید نظر داشته باشد اوهم باید تشخیص‌دهدوحتی‌حق اینرا داشته باشد که رای و عقیده خود را اظهار کند و باید بتواند . این جنکهای بیهودهٔ جلوگیری کند جنکهائی که تنها و تنها وسیله استثمار و استفاده معدودی ست از توده بشریت توده‌ای که اولاد اوست او باید اجازه دهد که پسر ودخترش‌بقول فرانسوی ها(گوشت دم‌توپ)شوند .

ما میگوئیم و باز هم میگوئیم او باید در تمام شئون اجتماعی شرکت کند .

شما دختران یا زنانی را که امروز ساعت۸ صبح در خیابانها و اتوبوسها بعجله میروند طرف سرزنش قرار داده و میگوئید هیچ چیز غیر از هوس آن‌هارا به‌رفتن اداره‌وکاروانمیدارد (صفحه ۲۹)و از آن‌ها با کمال تندی میپرسید مگر در خانه کار نبود آشپزی و خیاطی نبود که امروز در کوچه ها افتادید جای بسی شکفت است که شما در اوضاع کنونی کشور ما هیچ تحقیق نفرمود د .

بدانید آقای کسروی دختر هوس بازبیشتر میل دارد که ساعت ۸ صبح در رختخواب باشد تا بقول شما در خیابانها بدود بدانید که‌کار چند ساعت پی‌در پی زیبائی اورا از بین‌می‌بردو با تماس با مردان هوسباز این جامعه بقول‌شما، به قول ما مردان و جوانانی که تربیت اجتماعی ندارند ممکن است تنهاسرمایه که شما برای زن قائلید از دست بدهند .

آقای کسروی **کاردر خانه‌است اما نان نیست** آشپزی باید کرد ولی‌اول باید برنج و روغنش‌را تهیه کرد ژاکت باید بافته شود اما کانوایش‌رابایدخریدیك‌دختر تنهابایك دیپلم برای نان خوردن باید ساعت ۸ صبح بدود خودرا باداره برساند و درآن جا توهین شود ودر کتاب شما هم حس گرسنگی و برهنگی اوهوس نامیده شود . زنهائی با داشتن بچه برای کمك بشوهر یا پروراندن بچهای بی‌پدر خود ازطرف‌شماتحقیر میشوندولی در سرما وگرما باید دویدچون تحقیر نه نان در سفره او میگذارد و نه ذغال‌درکرسیش این است که ما میخواهیم‌مردان امروز برای ما آئین وضع نکنند بدوخوب ما ازخودماباید‌باشداز

کمك زن روستائی به شوهرش تعریف میکنیم اجازه میخواهم زندگی او را تشریح کنم

کمك او از امروز شروع نشده سالهاست که زن دهاتی مشقت میکشد و سنگین ترین کارهای ده را انجام میدهد در موقعی که مردان ده مشغول چپق کشیدن هستند اوجان میکند کار او تمامی ندارد تمام سال روز و شب زحمت دارد و این کارها رامیکنند چون باید نان بخورد و زحمت او هیچ جا حساب نیست و مزد نمیگیرد و این است که با زائیدن متوالی و نداشتن بهداشت و زحمت طاقت فرسا خیلی زود شکسته میشود و از بین میرود شما بنا بگفته خودتان ازاین زندگی حظ کردید ولی ما رنج میبریم چون زن دهاتی هیچ حق ندارد و با اینکه از شما بودند شما آنها را نمیشناسید !

شما مهر و جهیز را میگوئید بد است ما هم تصدیق میکنیم که زن خرید و فروش نباید بشود آن دو که یکدیگر را انتخاب کردند باید همدیگر را بخواهند وزندگی کنند امادرصورتی میتوان این ازدواج را محکم و پایدار دانست که قانون تمام حق را به یکی ندهد گمان میکنم قدری خوش بین باشید وجامعهٔ در خواب وخیال برای عروس و داماد خود فرض میکنید ما حقیقت را می بینیم ما میدانیم که نمیتوانیم تنها به خوش خلقی و گذشت طرفین تکیه کرده وامیدواری به تأثیر و پشتیبانی پدر و مادر دختر قدری شعر است و بنا بعقیده خود آقای کسروی باشعر نمیشود زندگی کرد

مردان ایران ! زن کنیز و آشپز بس است ، زن دایه بس است ، زن برده بس است ، این است نتیجه سالها بردگی خواهران ودختران شما ، این اجتماع کثیف وبهم خورده ، این ملابازیها همه ازاین نوع فکر و تربیت زائیده است .

بقول یکی ازپیشوایان (زن را آنقدر بازنجیر های خسته کننده وبی نتیجه آشپزی و خانه داری نبندید زن را باسم آزدی دراین بندها که غیر ازاینکه فکراو جسم اورا ازبین میبرد نتیجه دیگر ندارد نه بندید سلامتی بچه او بر عهده جامعه است . ازهردر وهرراه قانون باید باو کمك کنید شخصیت او را نگاه دارید) این است عقیده ما هم — ما نمیتوانیم قبول کنیم که بالاترین مقصد زن تهیه غذای لذیذ وژاکت بافی باشد قرنها این رویه را داشت قرن ها بهمین کار ها پرداخت چه نتیجه گرفت ؟ چه اجر و مزدی برای او قائل شدند ؟ بهترین قوا واستعداد خودرا دراین راه مصرف کرد چه حاصلی بدست آورد غیر ازاینکه بقول خود آقای کسروی رضاخان بگوید تنها در موقع نان قسمت کردن اسم زن ها را هم میاورند؟

مابالاتر وبزرگتر ازهرچیز نمیخواهیم بجسم زن اسم سرمایه گذاشته شود . سرمایه اورا ما فهم او استعداد او شخصیت او میدانیم ما خواهران و دختران آن مردانی هستیم که در راه آزادی وگرفتن حق ما می کوشند مانمی توانیم درلفافه این کلمات دلفریب کنیز و برده باشیم

✦✦✦✦✦✦✦✦✦✦✦✦✦✦✦✦

دختر جون تختخواب من مال بچهٔ تو من که نگاه این دو نفر را نتوانستم به بینم اما دل آرام ساکت و فداکاری پهلوی من تکرار میکرد این بچه واجب‌تر ازمن است.

ازآن روز من و پیره زن رفیق بودیم مرا نگاه داشته و روز بروز هم در اطاق بی در و پیکرش رنجور و به‌مرگ نزدیکتر میشد تنها مونسش من بودم اگر بدانید چقدر لذت داشت وقتی که انگشتان گره خورده لرزانش مرا لمس میکرد اما حال چند روزی است .....

بچه یتیم کنار کوچه در خواب خودّ را برسفره غذائی دیداز شادمانی درخواب خنده کرد ولکه ابری ازگوشه آسمان صاف پیدا شد و چنین گویند قصه دان ها وافسانه سرا ها که اگر چشمك ستارگان شروع شود وآن یتیم واو دقیقه دلخوشی پیدا کند اشیاء بصورت اول برمی گردند.

این بود که سکوت بی انتهائی دنیا را فرا گرفت تنها و دورا دور زوزه سگی با مهتاب بلند بود.

زن و خانواده

فرخ اقا علوی

خانه وخانواده

وحدود آن درعصر کنونی

اندك توجهی بتاریخ حیات بشر و اعصار گذشته ما رابدین امرواقف‌می سازد که درابتدای تمدن‌بشرحدودخانه و خانواده محدودوکلیه‌مایحتاج بشری بدست خانواده‌تهیه شده و تکالیف اجتماعی بگردن آنها بوده است.

پس‌ازاین دوره بعلت حس اطاعت و توجهی که زنان بپرستاری‌اطفال‌داشتند میدان فعالیت بیشترباز شد وبالطبیعه اختیارات‌وامتیازات‌از زنان سلب‌گردید ازطرفی عم تعلیم تربیت‌وجود زن‌را برای مرد پرورش میدادبطوریکه تا این اواخر هم مردان جزوظائف‌زناشوئی وپرستاری تکلیف دیگری را برای زن لازم نشمرده‌واهمیت وارزش خاصی برای زن قائل نبود.

ورح آزادی طلبی واستقلال نفس زنان را وادار باین‌امر نبوده که برای خود شخصیتی‌قائل شده و بوسیله نهضت طوق اسارت را از گردن خویش بردارند.

از آنجائیکه طرفداران اصول فرسوده وقدیمی ومرتجعین با هرنهضت وتغییری که برای پیشرفت جامعه در حیات اجتماعی پدیدار شود مخالف ودشمن هر نوع ترقی و تکامل اجتماعیند هنگامیکه‌نزدآنهااززن‌واجتماع وتساوی حقوق‌بین زن‌ومردگفتگو میشود میگویند جای زن درخانه است زن خوب باید علاقمند بخانه بباشد و فقط به پرستاری‌ومواظبت اطفال و رفع حوائج مرددر خانه بکوشد غافل از اینکه درعصرکنونی مفهوم خانه وخانواده با مفهوم آن درازمنه سالفه تغییر کرده و امروزه سیر تکامل تمدن تکالیف زن‌را درخانه کمتر کرده وکارهای‌خانه‌را که دراجتماعات اولیه بیشتر بعهده زنان خانواده ها بوده بگردن اجتماع انداخته است

امروز محدود کردن زنان بانجام امورخانه متناسب بااوضاع فعلی‌جهان نیست ودرحقیقت‌کاملا بضرر اجتماع است.

زیرا قوای خلاقه و استعداد نهائی زن در نتیجه ورود باجتماع بطور قابل ملاحظه رشد و تظاهر کرده است چنانکه امروزه توانسته است در کلیه اموریکه مردان در آن وارد میشدند شرکت کرده و بطوریکه بر دنیای امروزی ثابت شده است از عهده انجام وظائف مرجوعه بخود بخوبی برآمده اند .

بنا بر این شرط انصاف نیست که ما بر خلاف مشهودات وتجربیات همه دنیا از زنان جز تربیت اطفال وخانه داری چیزی نخواهیم بعلاوه اگر از نظر علمی بتحقیق و تحلیل این مسئله برآئیم بخوبی مبرهن است که در صورت رشد کامل وتهیه عواملی که برای مردان موجود است این جنس لطیف نیز از حل مسائل علمی عاجز نیست

بهر صورت مفهوم خانه وخانواده در دنیای متمدن امروزی باقرون واعصار گذشته بکلی متفاوت است .

بدیهی است که هر جامعه که خواهان ترقی و پیشرفت خویش است باید همکاری زنان را استقبال کند ومیدان را برای ایندسته که نیمی از سکنه کشور را تشکیل میدهند باز بگذارد .

با این ترتیب مردان آزادیخواه وروشنفکر کشور ماهم باید بدانند که اگر رویه سابق یعنی محدودیت زنان در چهار دیوار خانه و خانواده دنبال شود مملکت ما دچار عقب افتادگی عمدی خواهد شد واز این لحاظ لطمهٔ بزرگی نیز باقتصادیات کشور وارد خواهد آمد وبالنتیجه از سیر مدارج کمال وتمدن باز خواهد ماند وزندگانی عمومی از نظر اجتماع ارزش مادی ومعنوی خودرا از دست خواهد داد

نقل از نامه رهبر

فتوای تحفه فلسطین

راجع بچادر سیاه

بقرار اطلاع صحیحی که بما رسیده چند تن اززنان بی بضاعت که از شهرداری کمك میگرفته اند اخیراً که برای دریافت ماهیانه مراجعه کرده اند ازطرف مامورین شهرداری بآنها اخطار شده که آقا فرموده اند **تا چادرسیاه نپوشید بشما کمك نخواهد شد**

این یك دلیل قاطعی است براین که ادارات ودستگاه حاکمه ما بمنظور حفظ مصالح ملی و اکثریت این مملکت نیست زیرا همچنانکه همین ادارات در عصر دیکتاتوری **باشاره دیکتاتور** چادر ها را بزور سرنیزه از سر پیره زنان در ملاءعام میکشیدند امروز هم **باشاره دلال همان دیکتاتوری** با این نیرنك ها زنان ما را مجبور بپوشیدن چادرسیاه میکنند و میخواهند یك دوره ارتجاعی سیاهی برای ما پیش آورند از اداره ای که بدستور اشخاص با عائله هزار و پانصد نفر کارگر تیره بخت بازی میکنند جز این انتظاری نیست **که دستور آقا** را کورکورانه برخلاف شئون اجتماعی ما اجرا کنند.

تشکیلات زنان

کلاسهای اکابر با بیسوادی زنها مبارزه می کنند

بادست خودش دو تا استکان درست کرد یکی به جعفر داد یکی به زنیکه هر دو زهر مار کردند حالا جعفر میگه چشم ندیدزنیکه را دارم ومیگه اشرف من‌رو ببخش من اصلا لشم خودم میدونم اما درست لش هم نیستم!

خوانندگان! این داستان را خواندید

وباور کنید این فداکاریهای اشرف صورت حقیقت دارد و اشرفی هم وجود دارد با این همه از خودگذشتگی وفداکاری!!!

مریم فیروز

زنان ایران باید در انتخاب شرکت کنند

به مناسبت تقدیم ماده واحده از طرف آقای دکتر کشاورز نماینده حزب توده به مجلس شورای ملی خانم یقکیان شرحی در روزنامه ایران کنونی نوشته بودند که مجله آینده شماره ۱ ـ ۲ عیناً آنرا نقل کرده است خانم نامبرده معتقدند که برای زنان ایرانی که ۹۹٫۹ در صد آن بی سواد پا برهنه و گرسنه هستند گذراندن چنین قانونی زود است.

آیا خانم نویسنده خیال میکنند که صددرصد مردان ایرانی که حق انتخاب کردن و انتخاب شدن دارند با سواد، سیر و پوشیده هستند؟ بر هیچکس پوشیده نیست که اکثر ملت ایران چه زن و مرد بی سواد و تقریبا ۹۹ در صد آنها لخت هستند آیا این دلیل کافی است که حق را از مردها هم بگیرند و فعلا برای آنها قیم تعیین کنند؛ و چقدر آنوقت به نفع قیم است که این بی سوادی و بی خبری ادامه پیدا کند. و آیا باشناختن الفباء کافی است که یك فرد بتواند از حقوق خود دفاع کند؛ آن کسی بهتر می تواند حق پایمال شده را ادعا کند که حقیقتاً بی حق باشد و اگر امروز در ایران مردان وزنان به گفته خانم نویسنده نمیتوانند از حقوق خود چه شرعی وچه عرفی استفاده کنند برآنها چندان ایرادی نیست آن افرادی مقصر هستند که در عین اینکه خودرا روشنفکر میدانند برای استفاده مادی و سیادت خود توده مملکت را در برهنگی و گرسنگی نگاهداشته وتشخیص هم میدهند که این توده نمیتواند در امور مربوط بخود شان صاحب رای باشند ما آن اشخاص را مسئول مذلت مردم ایران میدانیم که سیاست را به صورت لولو در آورده و با تمام قوا سعی میکنند این لولو را وحشتناکتر جلوه داده تا خود با آسودگی از پس این مترسك مشغول چپاول و غارت باشند.

آزادی زنان در دوره رضا خان و کمی استفاده و سوء استفاده از آن را خانم نویسنده گوشزد میکنند.

تصدیق میکنم که بعضی از زنها از این **آزادی ظاهری** سوء استفاده نموده اند ولی نمیتوان رفتار زننده آ نها را عمومیت داده آنها از طبقه هستند که پدران برادران و پسران آنها میل دارند که وضع فعلی ایران برای منافع شخصیشان به همین حال باقی بماند و آنقدر وسیله مادی داشتند که بتوانند این زنها را با تفریحاتی که تنها پول میسر میکند اغفال کرده و بازی دهند این عده خیلی قلیل را کنار گذاشته و متوجه فوج فوج زنان و دختران پاك ایرانی هستیم که از همین مختصر آزادی استفاده کرده و امروز همردیف مردانی مشغول کار و خدمت هستند نه تنها خانم نویسنده بلکه خیلی از مردم هم عقیده دارند که زنها بی عرضگی نشان داده و از آزادی دوره رضا خان آنطور که باید استفاده نکردند جای بسی تأثر است که این نظریه موجود هست . چون زن ایرانی را در چهار مدرسه راه دادند و چادر از سر او برداشتند او را آزاد فرض میکنند . زن موقعی آزاد است که حقوق اجتماعی داشته باشد زن موقعی آزاد است که قوانین پوسیده وهزار ساله او را زنجیر نکند ، زن موقعی آزاد است که بتواند از معلومات خود استفاده کند نه اینکه قانون به شوهر او اجازه دهد که مانع کار کردن او بشود و تمام عمر محکوم قوانینی باشد که تنها و تنها به دست مرتجعین آزادی کش وضع شده قوانینی که مثل زنجیر های سنگین اورا درمذلت وفشار نگاه میدارند همانطور که قوانینی به دست همان مرتجعین وضع شده که رنجبر و توده ملت ایران را با صورت ظاهر آزادی در بدبختی و وگرسنگی نگاه میدارند .

درجای دیگر نویسنده میگوید چه اصراری است که زنان ایرانی از زنان فرانسوی جلو بیفتند من نمیفهمم چه ابرامی است دراینکه حتما مافرانسه را دراین موضوع سرمشق خود قرار دهیم ؟

عقیده خیلی ها براین است که این شتابزدگی معنی ندارد وپله پله نردبان را باید بالا رفت آیا میشود درخواست کرد که برای مدتی از این تشبیهات واز این مثالهائی که چندان مورد ندارد صرفنظر شود ؟ وگذشته از این ما می بینیم که ملت ایران قبل از اینکه پاروی پله اول نردبان بگذارد از زیادی پله ها اورا ترسانده وپای منقل تریاك اورا میخکوب کرده اند .

آیا انصافا امروز دراین قرن طیاره نیز باید هنوز برای صعود ازنردبان بالا رفت ؟ آیانتیجه زحمت ملل متمدن ومترقی برای ما این است که ماوسائل بسیارعالی پیشرفت را که در دسترس داریم کنار گذاشته وهمان پله های چوبین هزارساله خود را بگیریم ؟ این نظریه تنها وتنها ترویج افکار پوسیده وشوم مستر ضیاالدین ها است که صحبت ازملیله وسرمه ووسمه میکنند

چرا زنان ایران راه دور بروند گوش و چشم باز کنند وببینند وبشنوند که زنان راهی را که به آنها توصیه میشود صد ساله بروند دریکشب طی کرده اند .

یکی ازپیشوایان بزرگ میگفت . (زن و زن زن را درتمام کارها دخالت دهید در هرموسسه وهر بنگاه را بروی او باز کنید و ازاین قدرت عظیم که خاموش وبی ثمر مانده استفاده کنید)

این کاررا هم کردند . آیا ملت روسیه وتوده مردم آن از ما جلوتر بودند ؟ نه اگر بگوئیم عقب مانده‌تر گرسنه تر میتوان گفت به صورت

فعلی ما به همین زنان گرسنه و بی سواد حق رأی دادن وانتخاب شدن دادند و امروز بافعالیت غریب وعجیب زنان خود دنیا را مات ومبهوت کردند . نه تنها درجبهه درصف اول میجنگند نه تنها در هوا پروازمیکنند بلکه اغلب کارهای داخلی کارخانجات بنگاه‌ها را امروز زن اداره میکنند

به تجربه ثابت شده است که زن میتواند .

چرا زنان ایرانی از نتیجهٔ تجارب دنیا استفاده نکنند که بروند ازنتیجه تلخ فرانسه بچشند ؟

امروزهم دراین مملکت مردمانی پیدامیشوند که این ماده واحده را تقدیم مجلس کنند و حق زن را بخواهند آن پیشنهاد کننده یك نفر وکیل نرمایشی نیست بلکه‌نماینده‌هزارهانفرازتوده ملت است او از طرف خود حزب خود و مردم ایران این پیشنهادرا میکند و هرزن ایرانی است که‌از این احترامی که باو شده مفتخرباشد

مثلی است معروف میگویند صاحب درداز درد خبر دارد و من تنها رویم به خانم نویسنده نیست بلکه خطابم به تمام زنان ایران است زنان ومادران ! آیا غیر از خود ماکسی میتواند حق‌ما را بگیرد آیا غیراز یك مادرازاولاد دور یك‌زن بی‌خانمان یك دختر بی‌حق کسی‌مزه تلخ این قوانین راچشیده است ؟ وآیا غیرا ز خود ما کس دیگر میتواند آنهارا درهم بشکنند ؟

زنان ایران برخیزید وخوشوقت‌باشید که رادمردانی ازشما حمایت میکنند . در هرکجا هستید در هر گوشه چه در شهر چه در ده چه پیر وچه جوان با جان ودل با این ها باشید و از فکر آنها تقویت کنید برای نجات خود شما و دختران شما است آنروز زنجیر های ارتجاع میل پست طمع ننگین دشمنان‌خودرا درهم‌خواهد شکست که دوش‌بدوش مردان درخانه ملت درخانه خودمان حق خود را بخواهیم آنوقت **سرفراز خواهیم بود آنوقت زور وظلم‌را مامغلوب کرده‌ایم آنوقت‌زن زن ومادر خواهیم بود بس است بردگی و بندگی و موفقیت بسته به همت خلل ناپذیر شما زنان ایران !**

تو که خونین جگر هرگز نبودی کی از خونین جگر ها با خبر بی

خداوندا مو بیزارم از این دل شوو روزان در آزارم از این دل

زنها روزهای یك‌شنبه ازچهار ساعت بعد از ظهردرتشکیلات زنان‌میدان بهارستان حاضر شوید سخنرانی های سودمند از طرف اعضاء تشکیلات زنان همه هفته میباشد شرکت نمائید

ترجمه بانو همایون اسکندری

زندگی زنان کارگر

زنان در فرانسه چگونه پیشرفت میکنند

ایجاد موسسه رخت شوئی و اتو کشی درایوری
(حومهٔ پاریس) برای کمك بزنان کارگر

در تاریخ یکشنبه ۳۱ مارس نمایندگان شهرداری ایوری و نمایندگان اتحادیه‌های مرکزی و بانوماری کوئت از طرف اتحادیه های ناحیه پاریس در افتتاح یك مرکز رخت شوئی و اتوکشی شرکت نمودند و موسسه مزبور برای رفاه حال زنان کارگر تخصیص داده شده تا در قسمتی از امور خانوادگی آنان تسهیل شود و از طرف روزنامه «لاوی اوریر» سر دبیر آن لریش شخصاً در انجام این مراسم عالی حضور یافت.

در مقابل مشکلاتی که روزانه برای زنانی که در خارج از منزل اشتغال دارند پیش می آید کمیسیون بانوان اتحادیه های مختلط جداً مشغول مطالعه موضوع گردیده و باطرح نقشه های عملی برای مساعدت بزنان بوسیله ایجاد مراکز مشترك رخت‌شوئی - اتوکشی - رفوگری و غیره ... موفق بحل قضیه گردید.

کمیسیون بانوان طرح مزبوررا بنظر شورای مرکزی رسانده که با درك اهمیت وفوریت موضوع بلافاصله مشغول اجرای آن گردید محل موسسه مزبور که عبارت از سه اطاق غیر مسکونی در کوشه کوچه بورژوا بلافاصله معین شده نظافت رنك کاری بخاری و مبله کردن و تهیه کلیه وسائل لازم بدست کارگران انجام شد این کارگران متحد و با شهامت بعد از اتمام ساعات کارشان در کارخانه بدون هیچ درنگی در زیبا کـردن، تمیز کردن و آمـاده نمودن منزل مزبـور شتافتند .

اینست نتیجه معاضدت و ازخود گذشتگی دست خود را بخار زحمت رنجاندند ولی عاقبت گل مطلوب را چیدند و بوئیدند ،

در روزنامه « لاوی اوریر » مقاله ای تحت عنوان « بزنان کارگر کمك کنیم » توسط ماری کوئت که منشی اتحادیه های ناحیه پـاریس است درج شده چون این مقاله از نظر نشان دادن پیشرفت و فعالیت اجتماعی جالب توجه است اینست که ترجمه آنرا ازلحاظ آشنائی زنان ایرانی بـه فعالیت وطـرز همکاری نسوان سایر ملل از نظـر خوانندگـــان می گذرانیم :

« اتحادیه عمومی کار بوسیله رفیق ما (بنوآزاکن) در کمیته اتحادیه که درماه سپتامبر ۱۹۴۵ تشکیل گردید بطور وضوح بیان نمود چگونه ممکن است تولید محصولات را بوسیله استفاده از کار زنـان توسعه داد .

ولی برای اینکه زن کارگر بتواند بانجام وظایف اجتماعی کدبانوئی

مادر خانواده موفق شود لازم است که تصمیمات اجتماعی جدیدی اتخاذ کند.

ایجاد موسسات پرورش و نگاهداری بچه‌ها در اتحادیه های محلی بمادر اجازه میدهد که بدون دغدغه خاطر همیشگی راجع بتأمین و حفظ بچه خویش بکارش ادامه دهد.

و بعلاوه باید در نظر گرفت که زن اضافه بر کار اداری مجبور است که بقدر یك روز کار هم بمحض ورود بخانه اش در آنجا انجام دهد از قبیل (طبخ - شست وشو - دوخت ودوز و غیره).

با درنظر گرفتن این حوائج کمیسیون اتحادیه ها برای مدافعه از دسترنج زن در برنامه خود نکات زیر را در نظر گرفته است مساعدت بزن بوسیله ایجد سازمانهای مشترك (رخت شوئی - دوخت و دوز - طبخ سبزیجات وغیره ..)

در این مورد جدید و از نظر فوریت انجام احتیاجات مزبور ما میتوانیم چند قسمتی را که عملی شده است یادداشت کنیم بعداً بوسیله تجربه و عمل خواهیم توانست تغییراتی در این مقدمات بدهیم ومابرای آنکه رفقای ما بتوانند چنین سازمانی را ایجاد نمایند از ذکر این چند نکته ناگزریم.

کارگاهها ممکن است درمؤسسات بزرك که تحت رهبری کمیته مؤسسه وباشرکت کار فرمایان تأسیس شود.

کارگران زن کارخانه ممکن است هم از کارگرن حرفهٔ باشند ویا ازکارگران خسته باشند که از خیاطی و رفوگری سر رشته داشته بطوریکه برای آنها تقبل اینکار بمراتب آسانتر ازکار درکارخانه باشد

وزنان متخصص اجباراً برطبق تعرفهٔ اتحادیه دستمزد دریافت میدارند.

تمام این سازمانهای کمکی برای کارگران زن باید با موافقت داوطلبان مؤسسه برقرار شود ودر تحت نظر سندیکا و رهبری رفقای مسئول کمسیون دسترنج زن اداره می‌شود.

برای کمك بکارگرانی که درکارخانه های کوچك کار می کنند و ایجاد یك مؤسسه برای هریك ازآنها ممکن نیست نمایندگان اتحادیه ها میتوانند یك مؤسسه رخت شوئی ورفوگری واطوکشی ازکارخانهای مختلف باشرکت کارفرمایان ودر تحت نظارت یك کمیته مرکب از نمایندگان اتحادیه های هرکارخانه ایجاد نمایند رد شرکت کارفرما را نباید بهانه انجام ندادن اینکار قرارداد البته در این صورت اشکالات زیادی‌موجوداست‌ولی‌رفقای‌ماباستعداد و ابتکارات زیادی بر مشکلات غلبه خواهند نمود ولی درصورت‌سرباززدن کارفرما از دادن کمك امر آسانی است که‌اورابفرمان‌کارگربسوء نیت‌معرفی نمود ومعمولاًاین قبیل‌اشخاص‌میهن‌پرست‌بدی‌هستند.

مراکزمختلفه اتحادیه‌ها درپاریس‌اتحادیه‌های‌ملی‌وایالتی‌می‌توانند این کارگاهها را برطبق اساس محلی تشکیل داده تا کلیه کارگران زن‌که مجزا درکارخانه های‌کوچك کار می‌کنند یا اینکه دور از منزل خودشان می باشند بتوانند استفاده‌کنند ودر این مورد باید ازمساعدت شهرداری وتشریك مساعی اتحادیه‌های‌آزادیخواه محل‌که دارای‌همین هدف مساعدت بزنان کارگر میباشند (از قبیل سازمان دختران جوان وغیره مساعدت طلبید.

این مؤسسات باید برای مردان کارگر هم مورد استفاده قرار گیرد زیرا نباید فراموش کرد که این کمك همانطور که بدرد زنان می خورد بمردان بازن هم که مایل باشند کمك میکند.

قیمت محصول باید هر چه ممکن است عادلانه تعیین شود و چون این سازمان های مختلف درتحت رهبری اتحادیه اداره می شود بنا باارائه کارت اتحادیه تخفیفی هم برقیمت معین شده می توان قائل گردید.

بوسیله این تشکیلات ما بزنان کار گر مساعدت خواهیم کرد و آنان بشناختن و دوست داشتن اتحادیه بیش از پیش ترغیب می شوند ودرکارخانه یا مؤسسه ویا اداره زن قادر است که درکمال بشاشت به انجام وظیفه خویش که عبارت از تکثیر محصولات است ادامه دهد.

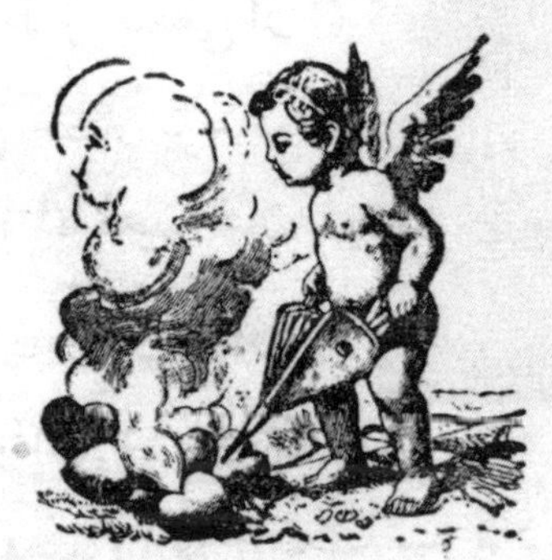

بیداری ما

ارگان مرکزی تشکیلات دموکراتیک زنان ایران

شماره ۳ اردیبهشت ماه ۱۳۲۷ سال چهارم

عروسك های هوسباز

زندگی تنبل ، مهمل و بی سر انجام

زنهای باصطلاح « متجدد» ما را میشود با دولفظ توصیف کرد : عروسك ، هوسباز . عروسك هستند یعنی همانطور درنظر مردان ارزش دارند که عروسکی در نزدکودکی ارزش دارد . این عروسکهای جاندار وبا شعور برای آنکه بهتروسیلهٔ سر گرمی باشند، بازیچهٔ دلپذیرتری درنظرجلوه کنند ، تنها مشغله ای که برای خودقائلند خود آرائی است . سرنوشت عروسك بودن خودرا زنهای باصطلاح متجدد پذیرفته‌اند و خود بآن‌سرنوشت کمك میکنند . خوی ومنش یك عروسك(اگراین عروسك بیاندیشد وزندگی کند) چه چیزمیتواند باشد ؟ مشتی اطوارسبك ومشتی هوسبازی کودکانه . گاه شخص ازدیدن این زنهای آراسته که با تقلیدحرکات ستارگان سینما ، قیافه‌ورفتار تصنعی بخود میگیرند واقعا رقت میکند . آیا یك انسان‌فقط برای همین درست شده؟ روزی چند ساعت وقت خود را بکشد تا خود را لایق ذوق خواستاران بیارایدوسپس با مقداری خندهٔ لوس‌وگفتگوی‌بی پایه‌ورفتاری‌ناهنجاروساختگی در همه‌جا ظهور کند؟ چقدرشرم‌آوراست که این زنان ودختران آراسته با همهٔ دقتی که درزیبا ساختن ظاهر خود بکاربرده اند ازهرگونه آراستگی فکری ومعنوی وزیبائی روحی وباطنی‌عاری

هستند. روح آنها مبتذل ، سطحی ، فاقد : باریك اندیشی وظرافت است. موضوع سخنانشان چیست ؟ تکرار خسته کننده سروضع آن زن وزندگی داخلی زن دیگر. غبطه باین و دشنام بآن - تعارف لوس دراینجا وعشوه نامناسبی درجای دیگر.

این گروه باصطلاح متجدد زنها بطور شگرفی بوسیلهٔ رخنهٔ تمدن هولیوود فاسد شده اند. هرگونه طرز تفکرجدی وبشری را ازدست داده اند. تجدد وتمدن آنها در تقلید کورکورانه مد وآرایش خلاصه شده. و آشنائی آنها با فرهنگ جهانی به چند رقص ناموزون وزمزمه تصنیف های بینگ کراسبی یا تینوروسی وخواندن مجلات « ترو رمنس » یا مجلات دیگرسینمائی واز بر دانستن اسم چندستارهٔ هولیوود محدود است. چند بازی باکارت ، یك تقلید ناقص ازترتیبات زندگی اروپائی واخیراً بخصوص امریکائی باضافه جویدن دائمی سقزمجموعهٔ دانش آنها را تکمیل میکنند. در کشوری که رنج ازدر ودیوار میبارد و اکثریت مطلق مردمش در پشت میله های زندان محرومیت و فقرجان می کنند این زنان باصطلاح متجدد درقید هیچ چیز نیستند. برای کوچکترین عقب ماندگی خود ازتقلید مد یا خرید فلان پارچهٔ یاتهیه فلان جواهرشدیداً اشك می ریزند ولی درام مرگ باوزندگی یك ملت برای آنها تاثرآور نیست. نه فقط درمقابل جوشش نهضت های اجتماعی بفکرفرو نمی روند بلکه آنرا مسخره می کنند. مفهوم زندگی درنزد آنها چه اندازه حقیر و بی معنی است ؟ تا چه حدبت وجود آنها مسحورشان کرده وچه خودپسندی غریبی برآنهاحکومت میکنند؟

مدارس باین ها چه آموخته ؟ هیچ - آنچه که فراگرفته اند چه شده ؟ بدست فراموشی سپرده شده. تا بساط رنگین جمال وآرایش باقی است به کالاهای دیگر نیاز نیست. حتی فهم عادی هم بدردشان نمی خورد - خانواده درزیرنگاه تحقیروعدم مواظبت آنهادستخوش پریشانی است درآنجا برای ایجادیك زندگی، یك نسل نوین کسی برخود رنجی هموار نمی کند. ساعت های خانم خانه بی مصرف می گذرد. شب زنده داری خسته کننده با خواب کسالت آور تاظهر، سپس وقت گذرانی درمقابل آینه آرایش وآنوقت تجدیدشب نشینی.... لاقیدی شوهر،قبول یك نوع جلافت اخلاقی بنام تجدد، شرم ازبانوی خانه بودن شرم ازمادر بودن ، شرم ازخانه داری وفرزند پروری ... افتخاربه ولنگاری ، افتخاربه طفیلی گری چنین است خطوط اصلی حیات روحیات بانوی باصطلاح متجدد ! چه چیزدرزیردستهای ناماهر این بانومیتواند رشد ونمو کند. او محیط خودرا با پوچی و سبکی انباشته می کند وزندگی را بحباب رنگین ، تهی و گذرنده ای بدل میسازد که اثری ازخود بجای نمی گذارد وحال آنکه هربشری باید بنای یادگاری از کوشش خود در کنار این معبر کهن سال انسانها باقی بگذارد. بجامعه ای که درآن زیست میکند خدمتی نماید این جامعهٔ ما ، بیش از اندازه تصورمحتاج خدمت است. دراین کشورفضای صرف ومحرومیت مطلق تسلط دارد. رواج ودوام مصائب حساسیت را زائل کرده ولی رقت آور بودن زندگی برون از حداست. باد سام استعمار و استبداد هر گیاهی را در این

خشکانده و پژمرانده . اگرخودآرائی‌وهوسبازی ستارگان هولیود دریك کشورسرمایه داری ثروتمند که درآنجا گذران عموم باجان کندن روزانه ملت ما در خورمقایسه نیست قابل فهم است ، تقلید این اطوارها درایران ما سرزمین گرسنه ها قابل فهم نیست . آیا این بانوان باصطلاح متجدد میدانند که زندگی پردهٔ سینما انعکاسی ازواقعیت زندگی امریکائی نیزنیست بلکه وسیلهٔ تخدیروفریب مردم دنیاست ویا می‌دانند که پیش از آنکه در امریکا ستارگانی باشند زنانی نیزهستند که برای جامعهٔ خودکارمی کنند ومی کوشند ؟

همین مهملی و کوته فکری و نداشتن کوچکترین قریحهٔ اجتماعی، وجدان‌ملی، شعورانسانی موجب شده است که درمقابل تحمیلات ارتجاعی جامعهٔ زنان ما مثل آنکه درخواب است . مثل آنکه حتی بلیاتی که براووارد میشود باو مربوط نیست . بمسئله تساوی با مرد نمی‌توان بایك چنین لاقیدی وسستی جامهٔ حقیقت پوشاند . باید برای بدست آوردن هرحقی رنجی بر خود هموار ساخت. خیرخواهانی وجود ندارند که حق‌را با تضرع تسلیم کنند .

چه چیز ما را وامیدارد که این حقایق تلخ را با صراحت بنویسیم ؟ نیازشدیدی که به بیداری زنان وجود دارد . این بیداری را باید با یك انتقاد سخت وشدیدی . با کوبیدن مدام ضربات تازیانهٔ توبیخ وشماتت عملی ساخت . لازم است برضد عروسك مآبی وهوس بازی ، برضدزندگی خودپسندانه ومهمل گروه وسیعی ازبانوان باصطلاح متجدد ما شدیداً وجداً مبارزه شود . در این مبارزه زنان شرافتمند متنبه خواهند شد و از سقوط زنان جوان ما دریك زندگی تنبل ، سست وبی سرانجام‌جلوگیری بعمل خواهد آمد .

ما از مرك نیرومندتریم ما به جامعه بشریت نوابغ و مشاهیر تقدیم داشته و مایه فخر ومباهات نسل آتیه بشر هستیم .

اگر بخواهید زیبا باشید هرچه ساده‌تر بهتر

برای اینکه زن زیبا باشد باید قبل از هرچیز سلامتی خود را حفظ نماید تا پوست صورتش لطیف شفاف بی جوش وسالم بماند ما برای اینکه دختران و زنان ندانند چه بکنند وهرروز کرم تازه ویا پودرجدیدی بصورت نمالند و از اینراه پوست صورت خود را ضایع وخراب نکنند دستوراتی چند مینویسیم

۱ـ هر روز صبح قبل از ناشتائی یك لیوان آب گرم بدون شکر بنوشید واگر آب یك لیموترش تازه درآن بریزید بهتر است

۲ـ اگرصورتتان خیلی چرب است مدت یکماه هر روز درآب شستشو قدری آب لیموی تازه بریزید

۳ـ برای اینکه پوست صورتتان حقیقتا تمیز شود هفته دو بار به طریق زیر عمل نمائید :

یك قابلمه آب را جوش آورده ودرآن چندقطره « تنتور بانژوان» که میشود به آسانی ازدواخانه ها تهیه کرد بریزید وبعد یك حوله بزرك روی سرخود وقابلمه بیاندازید وچند دقیقه صورت خودرا روی بخارآب نگاه دارید ومرتبا هم عرق صورت خودتان را پاك کنید .

٤ـ بعد از بخور دوقاشق مرباخوری گل سرشورنرم ویك سفیده تخم مرغ که قبلا زده شده داخل کنید واین خمیررا روی تمام صورت و گردن بمالید و۲۰ دقیقه‌دراز بکشید بعدازآن صورت راآرام‌آرام باآب نیمگرم بشوئید

۵ ـ وقتی که صورت شما تمیز شد به‌اندازهٔ یك‌پشت ناخن کرم به‌تمام صورت مالیده یك گرد پودر روی آن بزنید و حتی المقدور پودر زیاد نزنید که روی صورت تخته تخته شده و منظرهٔ بسیار بدی پیدا خواهد کرد سعی کنید که ماتیك لب شما رنك طبیعی داشته باشد و از رنگهای بنفش و پرتقالی دوری نمائید بدانید که سر زیبائی درساده‌بودن و تمیزبودن و طبیعی بودن است البته فراموش نکنید که هرشب قبل ازخواب صورت خودرا با « کرم» خوب تمیز کنید .

ما دستورالعمل ساختن این کرم‌را درشماره آتیه خواهیم داد .

لباس ـ حقیقتا جای خوشوقتی است که مد لباس بلند شده یادم می‌آید که درخیابانها زنهائی رامیدیدیم که ماشاءاله قدری‌هم چاق بودند لباس بالاتر از زانو میپوشیدند و جوراب خودرا پائین زانو گره میزدندوداتوبوس خانمهائی را میدیدیم که بدون اینکه توجه کنند دراطاق خودشان نیستند با دامن تنك و کوتاه که تایك‌وجب بالای زانو میجست روی نیمکتهای کوچك با طرز بسیار بدی مینشستند تابستانها که چه عرض کنم پاهای برهنه تا بالای زانو. باور کنید که هیچ زیبائی نداشت و حتی هم زننده بود خوشبختانه حالا دیگر لباس بلند شده است.

ما هم دومدل لباس‌را برای خوانندگان خود میکشیم.

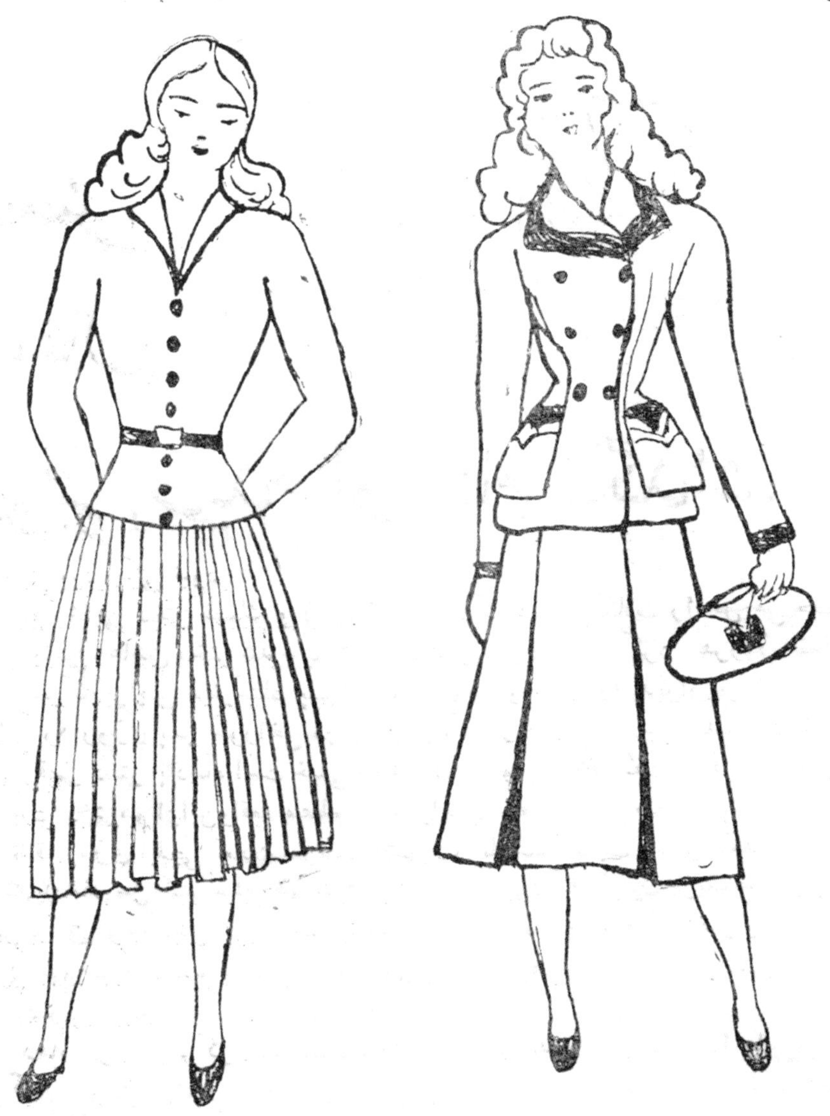

دو لباس ساده و قشنگ

هردوی این پیراهن‌ها را میشود باچیت‌ساده یاگلدار دوخت یکی ازآنها ژاکت و دامن است که‌هم به‌دردبهار وهم بدردتابستان میخورد ومیشود با آستین یابی‌آستین دوخت چیزی‌راکه ما توصیه میکنیم این است که قبل ازخرید پارچه یادتان باشد که کفش و کیفتان چه رنگ است و چه‌رنگ پارچه به آنها میخورد و بالاتر از همه شیفته هررنگی که دیدید نشوید بلکه فکر کنید که چه‌رنگ به‌پوست و موی شما میآید اگر قدری دقت وفکرداشته باشید حتما با خرج کم میتوانید همیشه باسلیقه وخوش‌لباس باشید

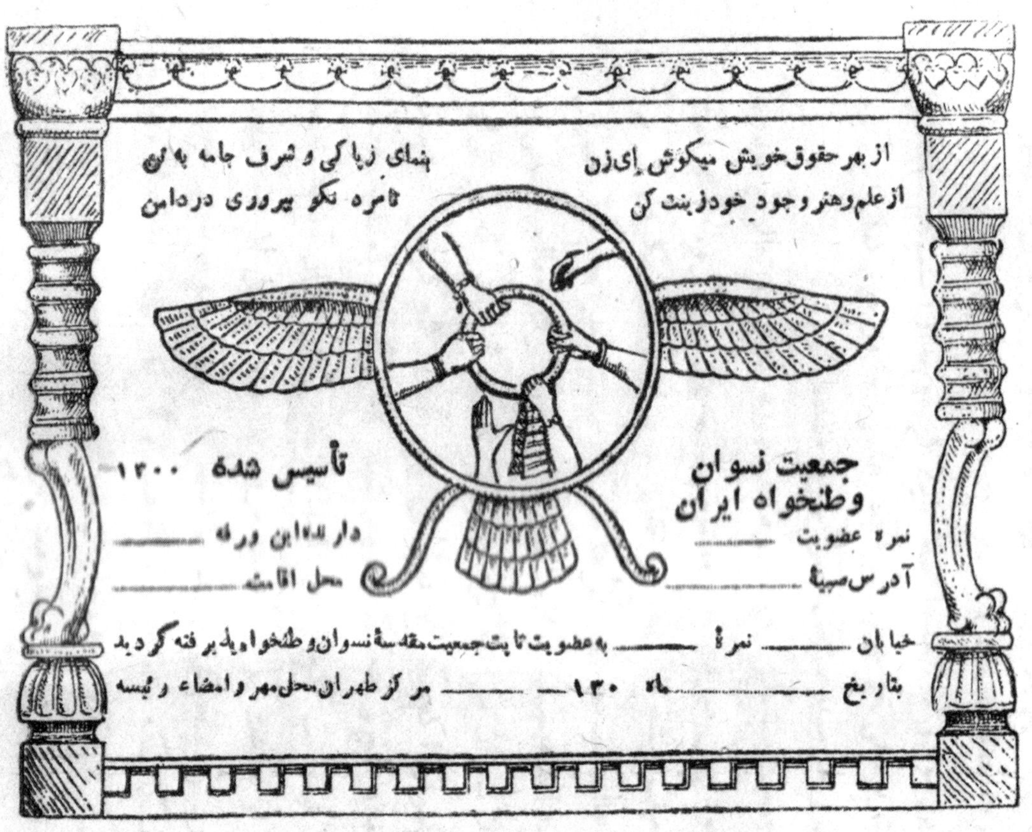

از بهر حقوق خویش میکوش ای زن — همای زپاکی و شرف جامه به تن

از علم و هنر وجود خود زینت کن — ثمره نکو پروری در دامن

جمعیت نسوان وطنخواه ایران — تأسیس شده ۱۳۰۰

نمرهٔ عضویت ______ — دارندهٔ این ورقه ______

آدرس صحیح ______ — محل اقامت ______

خیابان ______ نمرهٔ ______ به عضویت ثابت جمعیت مقدسهٔ نسوان وطنخواه پذیرفته گردید

بتاریخ ______ ماه ۱۳۰ ______ ______ مرکز طهران محل مهر و امضاء رئیسه

نمونه کارت عضویت جمعیت نسوان وطنخواه